D1239114

PITTSBURGH REPRINT SERIES

General Editor

Dikran Y. Hadidian

Corrigenda: *Magna Carta Latina* (2nd Ed., 1975)

Page

45, Sect. 41, line 6 alãs
48, Sect. 47a, line 11 egressum
52 no. 8 impossibile
62, line 7 (cf. section 41)
67, Sect. 66a, line 15 exemplum
89, Sect. 90a, line 1 vel Deum
170, line 31 Slavonic
192, Sect. 163, line 6 guages Portuguese

1

Magna Carta Latina

Magna Carta Latina

The Privilege of Singing, Articulating and Reading a Language and of Keeping It Alive

SECOND EDITION

BY

EUGEN ROSENSTOCK-HUESSY

Late Professor
Breslau University
and Darthmouth College

WITH

FORD LEWIS BATTLES

Professor of Church History
and History of Doctrine
Pittsburgh Theological Seminary

The Pickwick Press
Pittsburgh, Pennsylvania
1975

Library of Congress Cataloging in Publication Data

Rosenstock-Hussey, Eugen, 1888-1973.
    Magna carta Latina.

    (Pittsburgh reprint series ; no. 1)
    English or Latin.
    1. Latin language--Grammar--1870-
I. Battles, Ford Lewis, joint author. II. Title.
PA2087.R8 1975   478'.2   75-23378
ISBN 0-915138-07-7

T A B L E   O F   C O N T E N T S

Part One

Singing Latin: A Primer for Chorus Work

Part Two

Articulating Latin

c

d

Part Three

Reading Latin

Part Four

Keeping a Language Alive

Lesson XXVIII: Evolution of Language

Part Five

Texts

PREFACE

In our day excellent physicians attend
the deathbed of college and high school Latin.
The different cures which are prescribed to
galvanize the corpse of classical literature
are of astonishing variety and will, no doubt,
provide a respite to the patient. We, at least,
wish to begin our own textbook with an acknowledgement of the debt we owe to the efforts of
Beeson, Miss Waddell, Harrington, Nunn, Rand,
Scott, Rogers and M. W. Ward, Gaselee, Paul
Lehmann, Tourscher, and a very long list of
others.

For many particulars, we are simply walk-
ing in their footsteps. The general topic
of our task, however, is different. We no
longer care to minister like physicians to the
dignified old classical Latin. The wonders
of language that are one universal miracle
for speaking humanity all over the world, re-
flected in that special language which is the
source of much of English, French, German,
Italian and Spanish literature - these are the
theme of our book. Life is more than classics.
We have learned and know intellectually what
is meant by "the classics"; yet our own conscience and imagination and intellectual responsibility, stung by a painful experience of
classicism, have learned how the spiritual
and imaginative life of the race is injured
by the humanistic falsification of language
and literature. The life of the Word is more
than the classics. The grammar of mankind is
more than that of any one language.

We have learned and we know intellectually
what is meant by the classics. Yet, our own
conscience and imagination and intellectual

responsibility were not however aroused to come
to their rescue. They were afflicted with an
injury that affects the spiritual and creative
life of the race. And this injury was, and is,
committed in the name of the classics, or at
least of that falsification of language and
literature which is called humanism and which
enthroned the classics. With this book, we
are turning against our own cowardice, not in
defending the classics, but in passing on more
profound expressiveness of our own life.

When my son dropped Latin, I knew something
was bound to happen. College Board requirements
compelled him to do two hundred verses of Vergil
weekly. I had been "in Latin "-- reading, writing and speaking -- for forty years, almost without interruption. And now I found myself ask-
ing my son to give up Latin after only two and
a half years of study.

Something was wrong with our boy's Latin.
And so his teacher and his father sat down to
try to discover wherin they had failed the
younger generation. It was as it always is
when the older generation fails. We had not
been honest with our children. We had permitted at least three discrepancies between our
faith and the classroom requirements. We had
allowed (1) an accidental phase in the study
of language, (2) an obsolete, two-thousand-year-
old method of grammar, and (3) a prejudiced
selection of literature, to tyrannize the boy,
when both father and teacher themselves no
longer acknowledged these strictures.

Latin is taught after the Alexandrian
method, as though sounds make a word, and
words a sentence. Unfortunately, language is

something stronger than a house of cards. The
Latin texts we read were chosen originally because they seemed "pure," "golden," pre-Christian.
Unfortunately, these are no qualifications in
the eyes of mature people. Latin is treated
as a language separated from all our speech by
two thousand years. Unfortunately -- or fortun-
ately -- however, Latin is the matrix of much,
indeed most, of our thinking and speaking today.

Why do we love Latin?

Why is the Latin grammar an adequate frame
in which our minds can move?

Why are we glad to be able to read Latin?

Not because certain people in certain
days spoke a classical language, not because
Greek slaves teased Roman schoolboys with certain ideas and words about grammar, not because we want children to read two hundred verses
of Vergil as a College Board requirement.

Yet Latin is alive and will continue to
live. Law and religion, medicine and science
become clear to one who uses Latin. Two-thirds
of our English vocabulary is Latin. The most
precious documents of English constitutional
history -- including the Magna Charta, the
basic document of Anglo-Saxon liberties --
are in Latin. All Christian prayers were
minted in the Latin language; "secular" rhyme
and song came into the national languages from
Latin sources.

Tomorrow's Latin must be practical. It
must have to do with our own ideals and our
own way of life, and not merely be an interpretation of the civilization of Cicero. However, "practical" must not be understood in the

sense of superficial. It is superficial, we
believe, to scratch the surface of a remote
classical world; it is practical to go to
the roots of the tree of our own life by means
of the central Latin texts that any educated
member of our modern society should be able
to read -- texts so close to the center of
our civilization that all national literatures impress us as radii extending from this
center.

Our book purposes to teach Latin around
some fifty pages of such texts. It is
built around the Benedictine Service,
constitutional law, and the finest gems of
mediaeval epigraphy and poetry -- most of
them works that have undergone hundreds of
translations. These testify to their hold on
man's imagination. But unfortunately the
translations are valueless. There exist
about one hundred and fifty versions of the
Dies Irae, Dies Illa alone; Cicero cannot
boast of nearly so many. Perhaps it is a good
working hypothesis that texts translated most
often should come first, particularly as nearly
every translation is inadequate.

As already stated, we are fully aware
that unceasing efforts are made by teachers
to smooth out the path of the Latin student.
Latin "funnies," Latin crossword puzzles, Latin
clubs aid and do their part to amuse him. Furthermore, the common trend goes decidedly toward the addition of mediaeval texts. Mediaeval
grammars, dictionaries and texts are increasing.
However, even so charming a book as Miss Waddell's
apologizes and says: Be calm, a bit of unruly
mediaeval Latin will not spoil the classical
rules that you rammed down the students' throat
with so much effort. We quote from her Mediaeval

<u>Latin for Schools</u>: "It is hoped that the actual Latin will not be subversive of all good discipline, for the texts have been revised. In the Middle Ages one could quite happily say 'Dixit quod' or 'Dixit quia' for 'He said that' instead of the accusative and infinitive; and Miss Broughall has pointed out and corrected many other less heinous things which authors did freely in the Middle Ages, and which we are taught with great difficulty not to do now." This is an unpleasant situation.

Even the Reverend Mr. H. P. Nunn, in his excellent <u>Introduction to Ecclesiastical Latin</u> (2nd. ed., Cambridge 1927), thinks it his duty to support the prevailing cant. "We may heartily agree that the Latin of the Golden Age is supreme and unapproachable." Yet we read on the previous page: "Much of classical Latin is highly artificial, not to say unnatural; the authors wrote for a society of litterateurs who in most cases thought far more of style than of matter." We would be most insincere if we pretended to agree heartily that Ciceronian Latin is supreme and unapproachable. This and similar remarks though repeated ad nauseam for four hundred years seem to us rather silly. They betray an inhuman misunderstanding of the great sacraments of human speech.

A third specimen of desperate apology occurs when texts are published (we quote from a new book): "...with the usages which offend most against classical syntax removed." Our schoolboys, indeed, are paying a high price to the classical bias of the days of Henry VIII. At that time this inflation of Ciceronian style paid in cash because it gave the nation a good conscience for confiscating church property. What dividend does it pay today?

It is here that the modern parents'
fault becomes evident. What parents as members of the professional class that uses
Latin as a daily tool and who live with Latin
must make plain, is that they don't give a
damn for the purism of Erasmus of Rotterdam,
Laurenzo Valla, or Scaliger, and the Humanists'
myth of "golden Latinity." The teacher, it
must be proclaimed, shall no longer apologize
for his reforms. As long as he does, the
double standard of "classic" and "unclassic"
poisons everything -- Latin and the teacher,
the children and their parents. There is no
such thing as the "classics" for the future
generation; there is, and there will be, the
Latin language and literature.

Adults in every field -- architecture,
technical invention, poetry, philosophy,
law, linguistics, and medicine -- are hard at
work to create a mediaeval philology that
will be as colorful, as rich, and as varied
as classical philology. The anti-mediaeval
bias of the humanists, who had to build up
the myth of a golden Latinity so that they
might destroy Scholasticism and Papacy,
is meaningless in our days. In every field we
must replace, with biological insight and
evolutionary principles, the bookish principles
of the Renaissance Humanists.

When we root ourselves firmly in the period
A.D. 1000-1500 as the greatest period of Latin
literature, we make the task reasonably easy
for our youngsters. Grammatically and psycho-
logically, Mediaeval Latin is more open to
them than classical Latin. Mediaeval poetic
texts are easier and often more interesting
that Vergil, though the latter was a great
poet. Where else in the world does one deny
the facilities of richer plus easier beginnings
to students?

All this does not mean that classical
Latin should not come into their ken at all.
Quite the contrary, "golden Latin" will
seem relatively easy to them and relatively
interesting after an acquaintance with the
Magna Charta and the Vulgate. Golden Latinity,
then, should form the distant horizon, the
ultimate perspective, of two Latin milleniums.
And we have been peculiarly attentive to give
students an opportunity to understand that
Augustan Age. We have given here the complete
Res Gestae Divi Augusti. The old Romans were
soldiers and financiers and lawyers, and this
can be realized when one hears one of the
Caesars telling his acts in the lapidary language of an inscription. It is only through
such a source that the central features of
pagan Rome may be put in relief.

Our zeal for the great texts, however,
does not imply any contempt of grammar as a
weary or dry sequence of rules to be learned
by rote. "His Father's Latin" would not
be true to the father's faith if it treated
language as a mere tool or, as people are
impudent enough to style it, as a means to
an end. Language has equal rank with literature. A tree's leaves are no less admirable
than the tree. The whole beauty of the mind's
life is as much in its tiny cells as in the
most coherent creations. We would, then,
commit the sin of sins, the sin against vivifi-
cation, if we treated language as material,
as a mere vehicle for ideas. The lists of
declensions or conjugations or words themselves are sources of reverence, delight, sur-
prise, and discovery. The details of the
growth of articulated speech may well make
us catch our breath. We, at least, have nowhere

tried to repress our delight. Like physics
and chemistry and biology, grammar is full of
reality, and of the beauties and problems of
reality. Languages are the revelations of
mankind, and grammar is the key. In this sense,
any educated person needs grammar as an introduction. This key opens the door into philosophy, law, science, poetry, and religion, in the
accepted sense of these five words. For philosophy satisfies the eagerness for clarity;
religion the loyalty to overwhelming values;
law the power of responsible judgment; poetry
allows us to sing; and science stills our
curiosity about the speechless world. Language itself has been called the science of
the sciences. In the first part of our textbook, the unity of articulated speech permeates
all these diverse activities.

In the immense field of Latin grammar, so
many have tried their hand successfully that
any further effort may be expected to be
either not new or not useful. We have not
made innovations where excellent models ex-
isted. We have drawn from ancient, mediaeval,
and eighteenth century grammar books as often
as from the most modern. Wackernagel and
Vendryes were as inspiring as St. Augustine
or Matthieu de Vendôme. We feel, however,
that our conception of the universal character
of language introduces a scientific, that is
to say, general, interest, because in studying one pre-European grammar the students
visualize the matrices of human thought and
expression in general.

And now we venture the following recommenda-
tions to you, dear reader. Treat this book as
you treat any book. Read it first right through
in one stretch. Forget that it is, among other
things, a grammar. In reading from beginning

to end you will find what has moved us to enthusiasm. Then you may settle down to the process of learning and working out lesson after lesson. In your first reading, you may safely overlook any too complicated detail. The important point is that you should catch the complete rhythm of the book before you store away its individual lessons in your memory.

And now, after the author has enjoyed writing the book, one question is left: Who is the reader for whom we so fervently have spoken Latin in this book?

Let us divide this question into two questions: (1) Who should become our reader? (2) Who will become our reader?

The first question may be answered simply by pointing to the origin of our enterprise. Fathers and sons should have a common ground of studies and interests. The privilege of singing, articulating, reading, and keeping a language alive, is not bestowed on school children only or on adults only. A textbook and a book for every open-minded reader may be, in some cases at least, one and the same thing. In our case, the book may be compared to a mirror. We all, whether wearing flannels or silk, whether shaving or putting on rouge, use mirrors to check our looks. Anybody who speaks -- and who does not speak? -- has use for a reflecting instrument to see how speech looks from the outside. And in reflecting on Latin, the essentials are more easily grasped, "for distance lends enchantment to the view."

Thus, the first part of the question may be both asked and answered by the asker: You should be our reader.

And who is actually going to be the reader
of this our book? This second part of the question is disagreeable. Let our subscribers put
this question; let the public answer it.

                    Eugen Rosenstock-Huessy
                    Four Wells
                    Norwich, Vermont

Preface to the Present Edition

After <u>Magna Charta Latina</u> had passed from generation to generation of students at Dartmouth College, copied and recopied by them, sometimes with notes of the professor's comments incorporated in the text, a copy fell into my hands in 1953. Experimental use of the first few chapters with students of Latin at the Hartford Seminary Foundation brought **a uniformly favorable** response. As a consequence, in the summer of 1955, Dr. Rosenstock-Huessy and I revised the text of the first twenty-eight chapters, and a mimeographed edition was produced that went through a number of small printings. Continuing use in classroom gave rise to minor changes in approach and detail, but the basic plan remained unchanged.

We now for the first time offer the complete text of the <u>Magna Charta Latina</u>, both the grammar and the chrestomathy, in printed form. A few additions and changes have been made.

Much work has been done in the study of the Latin language since the first form of <u>Magna Charta Latina</u> appeared. It seemed appropriate, however, that the original preface, which states the genesis of the book as well as its formative principles, should stand unchanged.

Employment of <u>Magna Charta Latina</u> with generations of students, mainly college graduates coming to Latin for the first time as an elective subject, has demonstrated several things. First, it is absolutely right that Latinity be regarded as an organic whole -- from the earliest remains of the pre-classical language to the latest uses in the twentieth century. Secondly, with this book a mature

student can, in the course of a single semester,
attain some proficiency in Latin. Thirdly,
and most importantly, this introduction to
Latin becomes a liberating force in the student's
life; he is prompted to speak Latin for himself,
not merely to "break a code" and render it
passively and haltingly into a sort of half-
English. Henceforth he will move about his own
time and place a different, changed, person
because he has caught a glimpse of man's
sublimest possession, speech.

This is a great deal to expect of a
"textbook." Yet, if the miracle had not
happened repeatedly, the two questions raised
at the close of the original preface could
not be answered so forthrightly.

> Ford Lewis Battles
> Norwich, Vermont
> Pentecost 1966

Preface to the Second Edition

Obiit Eugenius ante diem iv Kal. Mart. A^oDⁱ MCMLXXIII.
Quid novi, hodie etiam vivus, adderet in Magnam Cartam
Latinam?

We have tried to answer this question by adding several
small readings in his style: two of his maxims in Latin
dress, lines from Cyprian, Augustine, Calvin and others; we
have amplified grammatical explanations in a few places;
finally, we have corrected such errors as have come to
light. Several references to *Speech and Reality* (Norwich,
Vermont: Argo Books, 1970) have been supplied for fuller
discussion of points here only lightly touched.

> *Per orationem vivit societas humana:*
> *sine oratione moritur.*

die cinerum, A^oDⁱ MCMLXXV.

> *Ford Lewis Battles*
> *Allison Park, Pa.*

Part One: Singing Latin
A Primer for Chorus Work

Musical, grammatical, literary, and
scientific Latin material all appeal to different facets of our nature. The child, the
adolescent, the man, the philosopher within
all of us, belong to the singing, studying,
reading and thinking community in which Latin
plays an essential part. Whether we think
of our reader as a High School student, or
a College junior, or a graduate student of
Law, Medicine, Philosophy, History or the
Ministry -- all may wish to join a choir in
which the great works of musical art are
studied and performed, and through which the
following Latin texts are perpetuated from
generation to generation. And men and women
in all walks of life may come to be interested
in Latin through their choir work.

We have tried here to furnish the necessary
material to conductors of choirs and to their
members for a simple understanding of the
underlying texts. For those who do not sing,
the same pieces offer an important supplement
to the collection of texts gathered at the
end of the book. This part of our texts,
Singing Latin, then, may serve either as the
door for those who sing and play, or as the
rounding off of the picture of Latin literature.

Explanatory note on the use of Part One:
This part may be used without any knowledge
of Latin or Latin grammar proper. Take it to
concerts or services whether you are singing
yourself or just listening to the music.

The texts made famous by great music may
be classified into two groups. One group is
taken from the Mass, the other from the Mass
for the Dead.

The names for the different pieces of
music, in both groups, are taken from their
first words. "Requiem" is the first of the
Mass for the dead; similarly, Gloria, Pater
noster, Ave Maria, Credo, Dies irae are names
derived from the first word of each text.

We have taken stock of the texts composed by Palestrina (1526-95), Pergolese
(1710-36), Bach (1685-1750), Hadyn (1732-
1807), Mozart (1756-91), Bruckner (1824-96),
and Allegri (1582-1652). The texts, of course,
are nearly identical, with the exception of
some variations in the "Dies irae."

* * * * * * * * * * * * * * *

Read the following texts as often as you
can, and compare the English words below. Don't
trouble yourself with learning by rote. And
get well-acquainted with the sentences by
reading or humming them aloud to yourself. You
may freely make mistakes in the pronunciation.
These won't do any harm. You may consult the
lessons on pronunciation [Lessons XXVI-XXVII],
if you wish. This, however, is not the main
point. The main point is that you see how
simple and how sublime the ideas expressed
are, and acquire a sense of the form of the
sentences in which they are expressed. Latin
is more economical than English. "Te Deum
laudamus," for example, is untranslatable
literally in three words.

Stanley Tagg of Pittsburgh, Pa., has pre-
pared (1974) a tape of some of the following
texts as set by various composers: Pater Noster
(Stravinsky); Kyrie (Bach, Poulenc); Agnus Dei
(Mozart); Gloria (Beethoven); Ave Maria (Verdi);
Credo (Bach); Requiem Aeternum (Durofle); Dies
Irae (Verdi).

a. Pater Noster (Mt 6:9-13)
(cf. Sect. 104, p. 105, below.)

Pater noster qui es   in   coelis,
Father our   who art in   heaven

sanctificetur   nomen   tuum;
hallowed be   name   thine

adveniat   regnum   tuum;
may come   kingdom   thine

fiat   voluntas   tua
be done will   thine

sicut   in   coelo   et   in   terra.
as   in   heaven also on earth

Panem   nostrum   cotidianum   da   nobis   hodie,
bread   ours   daily   give us   today

et   dimitte   nobis   debita   nostra,
and dismiss   us   debts   ours

sicut   et   nos   dimittimus   debitoribus   nostris,
as   also we   dismiss   debtors   ours

et   ne   nos   inducas   in   tentationem
and not us   lead   into temptation

sed   libera   nos   a   malo.   Amen.
but   free   us   from evil   Verily

b. Kyrie

The Kyrie is a Greek text preserved in the Western Church because Greek was the oldest language of the church at Rome. In Latin it is called *Miserere*. The most famous musical setting is that of Allegri.

Kyrie   eleison
Domine   miserere
O Lord, have mercy
Christe   eleison

Christe   miserere
O Christ, have mercy
Kyrie   eleison

Domine   miserere
O Lord   have mercy

c. Agnus Dei

Agnus Dei   qui   tollis   peccata   mundi,
Lamb of God   who   bearest away the sins   of the world

        parce   nobis,   Domine;
        spare   us,   O Lord

Agnus Dei   qui   tollis   peccata   mundi
Lamb of God   who   bearest away the sins   of the world

        exaudi   nos,   Domine.
        harken to   us,   O Lord

Agnus Dei   qui   tollis   peccata   mundi
Lamb of God   who   bearest away the sins   of the world

        miserere   nobis.
        pity   us

d. The Gloria in excelsis Deo

)(Also called the Great Doxology (the great glorification)

Gloria   in   excelsis   Deo
Glory   in   the heights   to God

Deus pater   omnipotens
God   Father   Omnipotent

Et   in   terra   pax   hominibus   bonae   voluntatis.
And   on   earth   peace   to men   of good   will

Domine,   (Fili   Unigenite   Jesu   Christe)
O Lord,   (Only-Begotten Son   Jesus   Christ)

Domine   Deus   Agnus   Dei,
O Lord   God   Lamb   of God,

Filius   Patris
Son   of the Father

Laudamus   te
We praise   thee.

Benedicimus   te
We bless   thee

Qui   tollis   peccata   mundi.
Who   bearest away the sins   of the world

Glorificamus   te
We glorify   thee

(suscipe   deprecationem   nostram)
(accept   humble prayer   our)

Adoramus   te
We adore   thee

Qui sedes ad   dexteram
Who sittest at   the right (hand)

(suscipe deprecationem   nostram)
(accept   humble prayer   our)

Propter magnam gloriam tuam
For   great   glory   thy

quoniam tu solus   sanctus
because   thou alone (art) holy

Domine   Deus,   rex coelestis
O Lord   God,   King of heaven

tu   solus Dominus
thou alone (art) Lord

Tu   solus altissimus
thou alone (art) the highest

Jesu   Christe
O Jesus Christ

Cum Sancto Spiritu
with the Holy Spirit

In gloria Dei Patris
In the glory of God the Father

e. Ambrosian Hymn

Te laudamus, Domine, omnipotens
Thee we praise, O Lord,   omnipotent,

Qui sedes super Cherubim et Seraphim,
Who sittest above   Cherubim and Seraphim

Quem benedicunt angeli,   archangeli;
Whom   bless   the angels, archangels;

Et laudant Prophetae et   Apostoli.
And praise Prophets   and   Apostles

Te laudamus, domine, orando,
Thee we praise, O Lord,   by praying,

Qui venisti peccata solvendo.
Thou who camest the sins to dissolve.

f. Ave Maria

Ave Maria, gratia plena
Hail! Mary, with grace filled

Dominus tecum
The Lord with thee

Benedicta tu in mulieribus
Blessed (art) thou among women   (Lk 1:42)

Et benedictus fructus ventris tui Jesus.
And blessed (is) the fruit of womb thy, Jesus
                                 (Lk 1:43)

Ora pro nobis peccatóribus,
Pray for us sinners,

Nunc et in hora mortis nostrae. Amen.
Now and in the hour of death our. Verily.

g. The Credo

Credo in Deum,
I believe in God

Patrem omnipotentem Creator coeli et terrae;
the Father omnipotent Creator of heaven and earth

Et in Jesum Christum, Filium eius
And in Jesus Christ, Son His

unicum Dominum nostrum,
unique Lord our

Qui conceptus est de Spiritu Sancto,
Who conceived was from the Spirit Holy

natus ex Maria virgine,
born out of Mary virgin

Passus sub Pontio Pilato,
Suffered under Pontius Pilate

Crucifixus, mortuus, et sepultus;
Crucified, dead, and buried

Descendit ad inferos,
He went down to the underworld

Tertia die resurrexit;
Third day He arose

Ascendit ad coelos;
Went up to the heavens

Sedet   ad   dexteram Dei
sits   at   the right hand of God

Patris   Omnipotentis
the Father   Omnipotent

Inde   venturus   est
Thence   coming   he is

judicare   vivos   et   mortuos.
to judge   the living and   the dead.

Credo   in   Spiritum   Sanctum,
I believe in   the Spirit   Holy,

sanctam   ecclesiam   catholicam,
the holy   Church   catholic,

sanctorum   Communionem,
of the saints   communion,

remissionem   peccatorum,
remission   of sins,

carnis   resurrectionem,
of the flesh resurrection,

vitam   aeternam.   Amen.
life   eternal.   Truly.

h. Ave Maris Stella

Ave   maris   stella
Hail   of the sea   the star

Dei   mater   alma
God's   mother   beneficial

atque   semper   virgo,
and   forever   virgin

felix   caeli   porta,
happy   of heaven gateway

sumens   illud   "Ave"
taking up   that   "Hail"

Gabrielis   ore;
from Gabriel's   mouth

funda   nos   in pace,
establish   us   in peace

mutans   nomen   Evae.
changing   the name   of Eve

Solve   vincli   reis;
Dissolve   the bonds   of the accused

Profer   lumen   caecis;
Bring   light   to the blind

mala   nostra   pelle;
evils   ours   dispel

bona   cuncta   posce;
goods   all   ask for

Monstra   esse   matrem;
show (thyself)   to be   (our) mother

sumat   per   te   precem!
may He accept   through   thee   the prayer

i. Office for the Dead

(Originally: Mass on the Second of November, All Souls)

Requiem   aeternam   dona   eis,   Domine,
Rest   eternal   give   them,   O Lord

et   lux   perpetua   luceat   eis.
and   light   everlasting   may (it)shine   to them

Te   decet   hymnus,   Deus   in   Sion,
Thee   befits   a hymn   God   in   Zion

et   tibi   reddetur   votum   in   Jerusalem.
and   to Thee   shall be rendered   the vow in   Jerusalem

Exaudi   orationem   meam,
harken to   prayer   my

ad   te   omnis   caro   veniet.
unto   Thee   all   flesh   shall come

Libera   me,   Domine,   de   morte   aeterna,
deliver   me   O Lord   from   death   eternal

die   illa   tremenda
on day   that   tremendous

quando   caeli   movendi   sunt   et   terra.
when   the skies   are to be moved   and   the earth

dum   veneris   judicare   saeculum
while   Thou shalt   come to judge   the age

per   ignem.
through   fire

Tremens   factus   sum   ego
trembling   became   I

et   timeo,   dum   discussio   venerit
and   I fear   when   the test   will come

atque   ventura   ira,
and   to come   (thy) wrath

dies   irae,   dies   illa,
day   of wrath   day   "the"

calamitatis   et   miseriae,   dies   magna,
of calamity   and   misery   the day   great

et   amara   valde.
and   bitter   most

Pie   Jesu,   Domine,   dona   eis   requiem.
pious   Jesus,   O Lord,   give   them   rest

Domine,   Domine,   Jesu   Christe,   Rex   gloriae,
Lord   O Lord   Jesus   Christ   King   of glory

Libera,   libera,   animas   omnium   fidelium
deliver   deliver   the souls   of all   the faithful

defunctorum
defunct (dead)

de   poenis   inferni   et   de   profundo   laco;
from   the punishments   of hell &   from the deep   lake

libera   eas   de   ore   leonis,
deliver   them   from the mouth of the lion

ne   absorbeat   eas   tartarus,
lest   absorb   them   the abyss

ne   cadant   in   obscurum.
lest   they fall into   the dark

Signifer   Sanctus   Michael
flagbearer   Saint   Michael

repraesentet   eas   in   lucem
shall   present   them   into   the light

quam   olim   Abrahae   promisisti
which   once   to Abraham   thou promisedst

et   semini   eius.
and   to the seed of him

Hostias   et   preces   tibi,   Domine
hosts   and   prayers   to Thee, O Lord

laudis   offerrimus.
of praise   we offer

Tu   suscipe   pro   animabus   illis
Thou   take (them)up in favor of souls   those

quarum   hodie   memoria   facimus.
of whom   today   (in) memory   we keep (do)

Fac   eas,   Domine,   de   morte
make   them   O Lord   from   death

transire   ad   vitam.
transit (cross over) into life

Agnus   Dei,   qui   tollis   peccata   mundi,
Lamb   of God   who bearest away the sins   of the world

dona   eis   requiem   aeternam.
give   them   rest   eternal

Benedictus   qui   venit
blessed   he who   comes

in   nomine   Domini,   Hosanna.
in   the name of the Lord Hosannah (*lit.*: help ye)

Pleni   sunt   caeli   et   terra   gloria   tua.
full   are   the skies and earth of glory   thy

*j. Sequence, sung in monastery & army
    in the tenth century (attributed to
    Notker of St Gall)*

Media   vita
in the midst of life

in   morte   sumus;
in   death   we are

quem   quaerimus   adiutorem,
whom   we do seek   a helper

nisi   te,   Domine,
but   thee   O Lord

qui   pro   peccatis   nostris
who   for   sins   our

iuste   irasceris?
righteously art angered?

Sancte   Deus,   Sancte   Fortis,
O holy   God   holy   Strong One

Sancte   et Misericors   Salvator,
O Holy   and Merciful   Savior

amarae   morti
to bitter death

ne   tradas   nos.
not mayest thou surrender us.

k. The Dies Irae

Dies   irae,   dies   illa,
Day   of wrath day   that (very)

solvet   saeclum   in favilla,
shall dissolve the age   into ashes

teste   David   cum   Sybilla.
witnessing David   with   the Sybil

Quantus   tremor   est   futurus
What   a tremor   is   to be

quando   judex   est   venturus,
when   the judge is   to come

cuncta   stricte   discussurus.
everything strictly   examining

Tuba   mirum   spargens   sonum
The trumpet marvellous spreading   the sound

per   sepulchra   regionum
through the graves   of (all) the regions

coget   omnes   ante   thronum.
shall force all   before   the throne

Mors   stupebit   et   natura
Death shall be stunned and   nature

cum   resurget   creatura
when   rerise   the creation

judicanti   responsura.
to the judging one   giving answer

Liber   scriptus   proferetur,
Book   written   will be brought forth

in   quo totum   continetur
in   which the whole   is contained

unde   mundus   judicetur.
whence   the world   is to be judged

Judex   ergo   cum   sedebit,
The Judge then   when He will take His seat

quicquid   latet,   apparebit;
whatsoever is hidden   will appear

nil   inultum   remanebit.
nothing unvindicated   will remain

Quid   sum   miser   tunc   dicturus?
What   am I   miserable then   going to say

quem   patronum   rogaturus
whom   as patron   going to invoke

cum   vix   justus   sit   securus?
since scarcely the righteous may be secure

Rex   tremendae   majestatis
O King   of tremendous   majesty.

qui   salvandos   salvas gratis,
who those who shall be saved saveth gratutiously

salva   me   fons   pietatis.
save   me   fountain of piety

Recordare   Jesu   pie
Recall   O Jesus pious

quod sum   causa   tuae   viae
that   I am   the cause of thy   way   (Calvary)

ne   me   perdas   illa   die.
so that not me   thou mayest let perish on "the" day

Quaerens   me   sedisti   lassus,
Seeking   me   thou wert sitting exhausted

redemisti   crucem passus,
thou hast redeemed (me) the cross suffering

tantus. labor   non   sit   cassus.
such a big labor   not   should be destroyed

Juste   judex   ultionis,
O righteous judge   of vengeance

dcnum   fac   remissionis.
the gift   make   of remission

ante   diem   rationis;
before the day   of accounts

Ingemisco   tanquam   reus
 I am groaning likewise   as a guilty one

culpa   rubet   vultus   meus,
from guilt reddens face   mine

supplicanti   *parce*   *Deus.*
him who kneels praying spare   O God

Qui   *Mariam*   *absolvisti*
Thou who Mary (Magdalene) didst forgive

et   *latronem*   *exaudisti*
and   to the thief   didst harken

mihi   *quoque*   *spem*   *dedisti.*
to myself also   hope   thou hast given

Preces   *meae*   *non*   *sunt*   *dignae*
prayers   my   not   are   worthy

sed   *tu*   *bonus*   *fac*   *benigne*
however thou, good,   act   kindly

ne   *perenni*   *cremer*   *igne.*
that not by everlasting I be burnt fire

Inter *oves*   *locum*   *praesta*
Among the sheep a place allow

et *ab* *hoedis*   *me*   *sequestra.*
and from the goats me   separate

Confutatis   *maledictis*
After confuting the maledicts (cursed ones)

flammis   *acribus*   *addictis*
to flames   biting   given over

voca *me*   *cum*   *benedictis*
call   me   with the benedicts (blessed ones)

oro   *supplex*   *et*   *acclinis*
I am praying on my knees and stretched out

cor   *contritus*   *quasi*   *cinis*
(my) heart contrite   like   ashes

gere   *curam* *mei* *finis.*
take   care   of my end

Lacrimosa   *dies*   *illa*
Rich with tears (will be) day   that

qua   *resurget*   *ex* *favilla*
on which shall resurrect from ashes

Judicandus   *homo*   *reus;*
To be judged is the man accused

Huic   *ergo*   *parce,*   *Deus!*
him   therefore spare   O God

Part Two: Articulating Latin*

1. <u>Articulated Speech</u>. When you yell
"iiiih" and your chum yells back "iiiih",
you are two little animals making inarticu-
lated noise. When you, however, say to
him: "Now listen, Johnnie," and he says,
"I listen, Billy," you are two people speaking together in articulated speech. What is
the difference between the two cases? In
articulated speech, the process of listening is clearly defined between another person and yourself. You summon him to act as
a listener. He picks up, in his answer, his
part as listener. The rôles are distributed
between you two, because one and the same
act first is suggested as an order on your
side; then, the same act is acknowledged as
a voluntary reaction on his side. You and
he enter in this specific relation. In an-
swering you, "I listen," he partly identifies himself with you since he admits that
he knows exactly what you mean. Furthermore
he preserves his personality by adding "I."
Speech is both identity with, and distinction between, people. It is like weaving a
pattern out of several fibres. For his "I
listen" is not the same sound as your "listen."

*For an expanded form of this essay, see Eugen Rosenstock-Huessy,
Speech and Reality, ch. 2 "Articulated Speech," pp. 45-66
(Norwich, Vermont, Argo Books, 1970).

It passed through his conscience and con-
sciousness and he had to reshape it before
he passed it back to you. Now the sentence
"I listen" carried back to you something
quite different from the noise "iiiih." It
was now a declaration of cooperation, of
acknowledgement of his having heard you.
A sentence is a personal relation between
answerable people. Articulated speech is
communication between responsible people

2. _Grammar_. When a man writes a patriotic
poem or a whole book, he tries to communi-
cate a responsible idea to responsible
people. His poem is one whole. His book is
a unity. You cannot break it up piecemeal
without destroying its meaning. Articulated
speech, then, may be as long as the _Bible_ and
still convey only one idea; in the case of
the _Bible_, that of the government of the living God. The whole _Bible_, then, is a unity
out of thousands of sentences and tens of
thousands of words. It is in the whole book.
A brick bridge and a heap of bricks do not
have the same meaning. We build bridges
by articulated speech, and the words are the
bricks. We cannot explain the bridge by explaining the bricks. Speech moves in sentences. The words inside any one sentence

are parts of the sentence. When we wish to
build bridges in a foreign language like
Latin, we must learn how to build sentences.
Bricks may serve for a bridge by being united
together with mortar or iron bars or by dove-
tailing. You learn Latin by learning the
mechanics of how in Latin words are knitted
together and dovetailed into each other for
articulating sentences, paragraphs, poems,
or books.

Grammar is the science of building bridges
between responsible people and the knittings
are called by a number of technical terms:
conjugation, declension, plural, singular,
tense, mood, etc.

3. _Inflection_. "Peter went to the big town"
is an English sentence in which every word
must keep its place lest the meaning be destroyed. We cannot say, "To Peter went town"
without corrupting the meaning. However,
English has certain words which can change
their places in the sentence with impunity.

    We may say, "Peter went to the big town
                quickly."
        or, "Peter went quickly to the
                big town."
        or, "Quickly Peter went to the
                big town."
        or, "Peter quickly went to the
                big town."

Why is it possible for quickly to fit in almost anywhere in the sentence? Quickly has an ending -ly by which it is clearly separated from quick and to quicken. The ending -ly in English makes a word into the concomitant of a verb, an action. There-fore, it is called an "ad-verb" in grammar. Endings, then, may free the language from a rigid word order.

4. Latin Inflection. Latin takes advantage of this device. Practically any word can take any place in a Latin sentence because endings explain nearly every single function within a sentence.

> "Peter went to the big town quickly"
> runs in Latin: Petrus ībat ad urbem
> magnam celeriter.

Peter is Petrus, the - us showing that Peter is the subject (i.e. stands in the Nominative). Ībat has three specific qualities: "ī" implies the action of going (the so-called root of the verb); "ba" implies that the time of the action is the past: this is called the grammatical tense; "t" describes the rela-tion of the person to the speaker and indi-cates how many persons are spoken of. In contrast to English where went may go along with you, I, or they equally as well as with

<u>Peter</u>, <u>Ībat</u> always refers to one person who
is neither the speaker nor a person directly
addressed by the speaker. <u>Ībat</u> always refers
to a third person in the singular.

Petrus Ībat ad urbem magnam celeriter.

<u>Ad</u>, to, comes nearest to English usage.
In most cases (not all) it will antecede the
place toward which the motion is directed.
On account of this rigid position it is singled out by a special means; it is a preposi-
tion, that is to say in a position which pre-
cedes the noun that it connects with the motion. Prepositions may have been gestures
of hand and body of the speaker, at first,
like nodding, pointing, shrugging the shoul-
ders, etc.

Petrus Ībat ad urbem magnam celeriter.

<u>Urbem</u>, too, has an ending like <u>Petrus</u>
but in this case the ending is-<u>m</u> which
makes it clear that the noun <u>urbs</u> plays a
dependent part in the sentence. While Petrus is a nominative, urbem is an accusative.
(The defendant in court is accused by the
plaintiff - "I accuse him": hence the "accused," here "him," is placed in the accusative. "Him" is the accusative of <u>he</u> and ends
in <u>m</u> like <u>urbem</u> from <u>urbs</u>.)

Petrus ibat ad urbem magnam celeriter.

Magic means amount of power. <u>Magnam</u> defines the <u>urbem</u> by adding a quality, <u>big</u>. In thus adding (in Latin ad-jecting) a quality, the adjective <u>magnam</u> conforms to the noun in all its peculiarities: number - one town, not more than one; gender - Romans speak of a town as an Englishman speaks of a ship, as "she"; and case - urbem is accusative. Therefore, <u>magnam</u> expresses bigness of a feminine singular accusative.

<u>Celeriter</u> is an adverb like quickly, the Latin ending being -<u>iter</u>, the stem <u>celeri</u>-,

5. <u>Grammatical Terms</u>. To sum up we may list all our grammatical terms.

<u>Nouns</u> -	Persons or things have to be put in a certain case, number, and gender.
<u>Verbs</u> -	Their main purpose is to specify an action or process that takes place; they must express tense and indicate the person concerned.
<u>Adjectives</u> -	These are the concomitants of nouns. They qualify nouns. They take endings which agree in gender, number, and case with the nouns they modify. Often these endings serve to clarify the gender, number and case of the noun.

Adverbs - These are the concomitants of
       verbs. They have no inflection
       because they qualify the pro-
       cess expressed in the verb;
       still they are usually recog-
       nizable by their peculiar ad-
       verbial endings.

Prepositions - These precede the nouns they
       govern, and explain their re-
       lations to the verbal action
       of a sentence. They replace
       gesticulation.

6. Stems: potentialities. Any process which
impresses us so that we try to express it in
language ordinarily lends itself to verbal,
substantival, adjectival or adverbial usage.
Most words therefore spread into verbs, nouns,
adjectives, and adverbs. In grammar the
nucleus from which the words accuse, accuser,
accusative, accusing, and accusingly, branch
off is called a stem. The stem, then, is not
a word in itself; it is the potentiality for
real words. Behind the grammatical divisions
into verbs, nouns, etc., there is meaning.
And quite as elusive as the logical meaning
is the linguistic stem. Nevertheless the
stem is operative in every moment of the life
of a language, and is spread out into the
different classes of words. This spreading
out we call articulation. Without this

spreading out the stem is a "mere lifeless block." In actual speech a mere stem is never met with. The stems are inarticulate potentialities of speech. Speech is the articulate realization of stems. And this is the secret of articulate language.

7. <u>Words</u>, <u>derivations</u> <u>of</u> <u>a</u> <u>stem</u>. In Latin the stem is the articulation of a word by adding endings and prefixes (gratulate, con-gratulat-ions). The shortest form usually appears in the Imperative which at the same time is the shortest complete sentence in language, and comes nearest to the inarticu-late (even animal) cries.

```
        ī........go!
      redī........return!
      exī........go out!
      īte........go! (plural)
   ī-tūrus........one who will go
praeteritum........(a thing) gone by
     iēns........going
     īmus........we go
       eō........I go
    euntō........they shall go
     ivī........I have gone
  ex-i-tus........exit, outgo, end
  initium........(initiation)beginning,
                            entrance
      īre........to go
    i-ter........way
itinerārium........itinerary
```

A Latin inflected word consists of two parts,
stem and ending. In this respect it may be
compared to a tree. Just as a tree has a
trunk and branches which do not change and
leaves which fall in Autumn and come again
in Spring, so the stem of a Latin word does
not change but the endings do. The stem is
the trunk and branches of the tree, the endings the leaves. One stem begets many words
as in the example above. Those words are
inflected in many ways.

8. Key Forms. But these fluttering leaves,
these changing endings, are regulated by a
few rules which make it easy to recognize
and to use them. For example, a word like
carta in the famous Magna Charta, has many
endings according to its use in a phrase or
sentence, but one single rule regulates the
formation of all those endings. When we know
one certain form of a word, carta, or necessitās, animal or sensus, we know all. The same
thing that is true of nouns like charter, wind
(ventus), day (diēs), is true of verbs like to
form, to hold, to send, to do, to hear. The
following list, then, gives the six key forms
of the objective (i.e. noun) use and the four

key forms of the verbal use of a stem.

Nouns are separated into general groups
called declensions, and verbs into conjugations which traditionally have been
given numbers in a certain way. We have
given them the proper declension or conjugation numbers here.

Objective Use
(Nouns)
Genitive Plural
Declension
1st cartā ⎫
2nd ventō ⎬   -rum
5th diē ⎭

3rd necessitāt ⎫
3rd animali   ⎬   -um
4th sensu   ⎭

Verbal Use
(Time-words, Zeitwort)
Third Person Plural
Conjugation
1st forma ⎫
2nd tene ⎬   -nt

3rd mitt ⎫
3rd faci ⎬   -unt
4th audi ⎭

LESSON I

9. First Declension

Singular

1. Nominative	magna carta	the great charter
2. Genitive	magnae cartae	of the great charter
3. Dative	magnae cartae	to the great charter
4. Accusative	magnam cartam	the great charter
5. Ablative	magnā cartā	by (with or from) the great charter

Plural

1. Nominative	multae cartae	(the) many charters
2. Genitive	multārum cartārum	of many charters
3. Dative	multīs cartīs	to many charters
4. Accusative	multās cartās	many charters
5. Ablative	multīs cartīs	by (with or from) many charters

10. First Conjugation *

gubernāre – to govern

Present Active

Singular		Plural	
3. gubernat	he governs	gubernant	they govern
2. gubernās	you govern	gubernātis	you govern
1. gubernō	I govern	gubernāmus	we govern

*The reasons why we have reordered the Alexandrian list of grammatical forms in presenting the Latin verb are detailed in Rosenstock-Huessy, *Speech and Reality*, ch. 4, "Grammar as Social Science," pp. 98-114.

11. Sentences
   1. Anima ŏrat. 2. Ancilla labŏrat.
   3. Ancillae labŏrant. 4. Rēgína regnat.
   5. Rēgínae regnant. 6. Nŏs labŏrāmus vŏs orātis.
   7. Ŏrāmus prŏ patriā. 8. Ŏrŏ et labŏrŏ.
   9. Nŏn gubernäs stellās. 10. Grātia regnat.

12. Dovetail
   Below are given some English sentences and
the Latin words necessary to translate sentences.
Dovetail the Latin words into sentences like the
English ones, using proper endings.
   1. The farmers improve the soil: agricola
      ēmendāre terra.
   2. Graciousness adorns a woman: grātia
      ornáre fēmina.
   3. You give thanks for your lives: dare
      grātia prŏ vīta.
   4. The poets walk through many lands:
      poeta ambulāre **per multus terra.**
   5. A Magna Charta does not delight a
      queen: magna carta rēgína ñon
      dēlectāre.
   6. The churches sing: ecclēsia cantāre.
   7. The water filters through the land:
      aqua percolāre terra.
   8. In many countries the farmers govern:
      in multa terra agricola gubernāre.
   9. Many girls work with the farmers:
      multa puella laborāre cum agricola.

13. Sentences
   1. Magna Carta est regína cartārum.
   2. Viam grātiae ambulāmus.
   3. Stellae sunt multae.
   4. Prŏ patriā et ecclēsiā ŏrātis.
   5. Cartäs poetārum ēmendŏ.
   6. Ancilla aquam percolat.
   7. Poeta cum fēminā et fīliīs magnā viā
      [on...] ambulat.

8. Vītam animae cantant poetae.
9. Rēgīna dōnat poetīs magnīs.
10. Per vitam labōrāmus et dēlectāmus,
    clāmāmus et cantāmus.

14. *Word List*

Britannia, -ae (f.) Britain
agricola, -ae (m.) farmer
ancilla, -ae (f.) handmaid,
 female slave
anima, -ae (f.) spirit, soul
aqua, -ae (f.) water
ecclēsia, -ae (f.) church
fēmina, -ae (f.) woman
poeta, -ae (m.) poet
rēgīna, -ae (f.) queen
stella, -ae (f.) star
terra, -ae (f.) land, earth
via, -ae (f.) road, way
vīta, -ae (f.) life
ambulāre, to walk
fīlia, -ae (f.) daughter
grātia, -ae (f), graciousness,
 favor, thanks, beauty
magna (adj.) large, great
multa (adj.) much
poenitentia, -ae (f.) repentance
puella, -ae (f.) girl

patria, -ae (f.) fatherland
gubernāre, to govern
labōrāre, to work
ōrāre, to pray
ornāre, to adorn, equip
percolāre, to sift, pass
 through, filter
regnāre, to rule
est, he (she, it) is
cantāre, to sing
clāmāre, to cry out, shout
dare, to give
dēlectāre, to delight, please
donāre, to give
ēmendāre, to mend
et (conj.) and
sunt, they are
in (prep.) in, on ⎫
prō (prep.) for ⎬ (with abl.)
cum (prep.) with ⎭
per (prep.) through (with accus.)
nōn (adv.) not

14a. Prayer which Calvin customarily used before his lectures.

Det nōbīs in caelestis suae sapientiae mystēriīs cum vērō
pietātis profectū versārī in glōriam suam et aedificātiōnem
nostram. Amen.
("May the Lord grant that we may contemplate the mysteries
of His heavenly wisdom with truly increasing devotion, to
His glory and to our edification. Amen.")

LESSON II

15. <u>Second Declension   Masculine</u>

Singular | Plural
Nom. bonus amīcus | servī fīdī
Gen. bonī amīcī | servōrum fīdōrum
Dat. bonō amīcō | servīs fīdīs
Acc. bonum amīcum | servōs fidōs
Abl. bonō amīcō | servīs fidīs

Nom. perītus magister
Gen. perītī magistrī
Dat. perītō magistrō
Acc. perītum magistrum
Abl. perītō magistrō

Plural
Nom. magistrī, agrī, masters, acres
Gen. magistrōrum, agrōrum, of the ...
Dat. magistrīs, agrīs, to the ...
Acc. magistrōs, agrōs, the masters ...
Abl. magistrīs, agrīs, by ..., with...

16. <u>First Conjugation</u>

Perfect Active
Singular
gubernāvit-he has governed
gubernāvistī-you have governed [1]
gubernāvī-I have governed

Plural
gubernāvērunt -they have governed [2]
gubernāvistis -you have governed [3]
gubernāvimus -we have governed

1. often abbreviated "gubernāstī."
2. often abbreviated "gubernārunt."
3. often abbreviated "gubernāstis."

17. <u>Sentences</u>
1. Deus est dominus. 2. Dominī est terra
3. Christus est fīlius Deī. 4. Nōs populī

Deī sumus. 5. Angelus nuntiāvit Mariae.
6. Stellae ēnarrant glōriam Deī. 7. Chorī
angelōrum laudant Dominum. 8. Ad Dominum
clamāvī. 9. Misericordiam Deī adōrāmus.
10. Iēsus populōs congregāvit. 11. Puer
Iēsus Ioseph et Mariae obtemperāvit. 12. Apostolī prō ecclēsia labōrāvērunt. 13. Apostolī
mundum superāvērunt. 14. Multī populī in
mundō magnō sunt. 15. Ō, Domine, salvāvistī
mundum. 15. Americānī cum multīs amīcīs in
Eurōpā superāvērunt Britanniam.

18. <u>Dovetail</u>
1. The boys obeyed the master: puer
   obtemperāre magister.
2. The master governed the choir of many
   boys: magister gubernāre chorus multus
   puer.
3. The expert maids have filtered the water:
   perītus ancilla percolāre aqua.
4. We are many sons and many daughters of
   God: sumus multus fīlius et fīlia deus.
5. In great countries the experts not the
   farmers have governed: in magna terra
   perītus nōn agricola gubernāre.
6. The farmers of the world have plowed the
   land for many years: agricola mundus arāre
   terra per multus annus.
7. The angels announced to the farmers the
   son of God: angelus nuntiāre agricola
   fīlius deus.
8. The people of Great Britain obeyed the
   good queen: populus Britannia obtemperāre bonus rēgīna.
9. We tell the glories of God to the boys
   and girls: ēnarrāre glōria deus puer
   et puella.

19. <u>Word List</u>

amīcus, -ī (m.) friend
angelus, -ī (m.), angel, messenger
annus, -ī (m.) year

chorus, -ĭ (m.) chorus, choir
Deus, -ī (m.) God
dominus, -ĭ (m.) lord
filius, -iĭ (m.) son
adōrāre   to worship, reverence, pray earnestly, be-
        seech, supplicate, implore, honor
glōria, -ae (f.) glory
magister, -trĭ (m.) master, teacher
mundus, -ĭ (m.) world
perĭtus, -a, -um   skilful, expert
populus, -ĭ (m.) people
puer, -ĭ (m.) boy,
servus, -ī (m.) slave
congrɛgāre   to assemble, congregate
bonus, -a, -um   good
ager, agrĭ (m.) field
sum   I am   sumus   we are
arāre   to plough
ёnarrāre   to narrate, tell
nuntiāre, to announce
superāre   to overcome
obtemperāre   to obey (with dative case; see 130d)

19a. Saint Augustine on the Word Deus.

Et tamen Deus, cum dē illō dignē dĭcĭ possit, ad-
mĭsit hūmānae vōcis obsequium, et verbĭs nostrĭs
in laude suā gaudēre nōs voluit. Nam inde est et
quod dĭcitur Deus. Non enim revera in strepitū
istārum duārum syllabārum ipse cognoscitur; sed
tamen omnёs latĭnae linguae sciōs, cum aurёs eōrum
sonus iste tetigerit, movet ad cōgitandam excel-
lentissimam quandam immortālemque nātūram.

Augustine, *De doctrina Christiana*, 1.6.6.

AUGUSTINE, DE TRINITATE

De Doctrina Christiana, 1.5.5

Unus Deus
  ex quō omnia
  per quem omnia
  in quō omnia.

Ita Pater et Filius et Spiritus Sanctus

  et singulus quisque hōrum Deus,
  et simul omnēs unus Deus;

  et singulus quisque hōrum plēnā substantiā,
  et simul omnēs unus Deus;

Pater nec Filius est nec Spiritus Sanctus,
  Filius nec Pater est nec Spiritus Sanctus,
  Spiritus Sanctus nec Pater est nec Filius.

Sed Pater tantum Pater,
  et Filius tantum Filius,
  et Spiritus Sanctus tantum Spiritus Sanctus.

Eadem tribus aeternitas,
  eadem incommutabilitas,
  eadem maiestās,
  eadem potestās.

In Patre unitās,
  in Filiō aequālitās,
  in Spiritū Sanctō unitātis aequālitātisque con-
                                        cordia.

Et tria haec unum omnia propter Patrem,
          aequālia omnia propter Filium,
          connēxa   omnia propter Spiritum Sanctum.

LESSON III

20. <u>Second Declension</u> <u>Neuter</u>

Nom.	lignum siccum	dry wood	ligna sicca
Gen.	lignī siccī		lignōrum siccōrum
Dat.	lignō siccō		lignīs siccīs
Acc.	lignum siccum		ligna sicca
Abl.	lignō siccō		lignīs siccīs

21. <u>esse</u> <u>to be</u>   Present Indicative

est	he is		sunt	they are
es	you are (thou art)		estis	you are (plur.)
sum	I am		sumus	we are

Imperfect Indicative

erat	he was	erant	they were
erās	you were	erātis	you were
eram	I was	erāmus	we were

22. <u>Sentences</u>
1. Deus in coelō et in terrā regnat
2. Coelī ēnarrant glōriam Deī.
3. Deus refugium et firmāmentum incolārum terrae est.
4. Angelī iubilant in coelō.
5. Christus regna mundī superāvit.
6. Peccātum regnum grātiae in animā vastat.
7. Stellās nōn adōrāmus.
8. Bellīs multīs terrās vastāvērunt populī.
9. Antīquīs ligna terrae **magnō** servitiō erant.
10. Magnārum et parvārum stellārum magnus numerus est in firmāmentō.
11. Ex antīquō Britannī gubernāvērunt Novam Angliam.
12. Pugnāre prō patriā peccātum nōn erat antīquīs.

23. <u>Dovetail</u>
1. We were many when we fought: multus est cum pugnāre.
2. Through many centuries the Romans governed the kingdom of Great Britain: per multus seculum Rōmānus gubernāre regnum magnus Britannia.

3. The arms of the girl were not big in comparison with the wood: bracchium puella
   nōn est magnus prō lignum.

4. The experts do not fight the stars:
   perītus nōn pugnāre stella.

5. Against the church and for the church many
   have fought: contrā ecclēsia et prō
   multus pugnāre.

6. For many years war lasted (was) for the
   Americans against the timber of the
   land: per multus annus bellum est
   Americānus contrā lignum terra.

24. <u>Word List</u>

   antīquus, -a, -um old, ancient
   auxilium, -ī (n.) aid, help
   cupidus, -a, -um desirous
   bellum, -ī (n.) war
   bracchium, -ī (n.) arm
   coelum, -ī (n.); plural: coelī, -ōrum (m) heaven
   firmamentum, -ī (n.) firmament, the heavens, foun-
                          dation
   incola, -ae (comm.) inhabitant
   iubilāre to rejoice
   lignum, -ī (n.) wood
   mūnificentia, -ae (f.) munificence, generosity
   numerus, -ī (m.) number
   palātium, -ī (n.) palace
   peccātum, -ī (n.) offense, sin
   parvus, -a, -um small, little
   regnum, -ī (n.) kingdom
   servitium, -ī (n.) service
   signum, -ī (n.) sign, standard
   habitāre to inhabit
   pugnāre to fight
   vastāre to lay waste
   contrā (with accusative case) against (often in hos-
          tile sense)
   cum (or quum), conjunction, when, since (&c.)

LESSON IV

25. <u>Vocative</u>. As the imperative is the verbal
    form nearest to an interjection, so the
    vocative is the interjection form of a
    noun, and is used in personal address. How-
    ever, it is not conspicuous except in the
    masculine (singular) of the Second Declen-
    sion which ends in "us."

    --us:e e.g., Domine, O, Lord!
    --ius:i e.g., mī fīlī, O, my Son!
                  ocelle,   O, "apple of my eye"!
    (oculus means eye; ocellus, little eye)

    Of nouns other than those of the Second
    Declension in "us" no particular vocative
    exists; the nominative is used.

26. <u>Recapitulation of the First and Second</u>
    <u>Declensions</u>. The adjectives ending in
    "-us" or "-er" reflect the declension of
    all the words that have "-ōrum" and "-ārum"
    (as servōrum, lignōrum, ancillārum) in the
    genitive plural. A great French linguist
    formulated the rules of gender in this
    terse way: a feminine is a noun the modify-
    ing adjective of which takes the feminine
    ending, i.e. magna carta. The same principle
    is true for the masculine: magnus vir; or
    neuter: magnum bellum. The "a" forms of
    the adjectives always express the feminine
    gender, the "us" forms, the masculine, the
    "um" the neuter. Thus, the adjective always
    will show the gender, the number and the case
    of the noun.

    > Hymnus clārus laudat dominum.
    > Hymnī sunt clārī
    > Puellārum pulchrārum nōn est magnus numerus.
    > Fēminās esse sānctās Germānī putāvērunt.
    > (That women are holy the Germans held)

Singular

Nom.	clārus*	clāra	clārum
Gen.	clārī	clārae	clārī
Dat.	clārō	clārae	clārō
Acc.	clārum	clāram	clārum
Abl.	clārŏ	clārā	clārŏ
	m	f	n

Plural

Nom.	clārī	clārae	clāra
Gen.	clārŏrum	clārārum	clārŏrum
Dat.	clārīs	clārīs	clārīs
Acc.	clārōs	clārās	clāra
Abl.	clārīs	clārīs	clārīs
	m	f	n

* Adjectives of the 2nd decl. in -er, e.g. pulcher (stem pulchr-) differ from adjectives in -us only in the nom. sing. masc.

27. Word List

bonus, -a, -um, good
certus, -a, -um, a certain
dexter, -tra, -trum, right hand position or
    direction
fecundus, -a, -um, fertile
futūrus, -a, -um, going to be
integer, -gra, -grum, whole, upright
īra, anger, ire, wrath
iustus, -a, -um, just, righteous
lūcidus, -a, -um lucid, clear, radiant
lucratīvus, -a, -um lucrative
noster, -tra, -trum our
persōna, -ae (f.) person
plēnus, -a, -um, full
pretiōsus, -a, -um, precious
rēctus, -a, -um, right, righteous
rubeus, -a, -um, red, ruddy
sacer, -cra, -crum, sacred, holy
sānctus, -a, -um, holy

solidus, -a, -um, solid
vānus, -a, -um, empty, void, vain
vērus, -a, -um, true
nunc, now
semper, always

28. Sentences
    1. Sānctus, sānctus, sānctus est Dominus
       Deus Sabaoth.   **(Isaiah 6:3)**
    2. Magna est misericordia Deī.
    3. Iustus es, Domine.
    4. Verba Deī vēra sunt.
    5. Templa Deī sāncta sunt.
    6. Pretiōsa est grātia Deī.
    7. Iusta sunt iūdicia Deī.
    8. Grātiā plēnā es, Maria.
    9. Servī fuistis, nunc dominī estis.
    10. Deus refugium nostrum est.
    11. Praeceptum Dominī lūcidum est.
    12. Iustitiae Dominī rēctae sunt.
    13. Vāna est glōria mundī.
    14. Magnum est gaudium bonae conscientiae.

29. Dovetail
    1. As persons of integrity we do not obey
       our wrath: persōna integer nōn obtem-
       perāre noster īra,'
    2. The old countries were full of timber,
       now they are fields and precious to the
       farmer: antīquus terra est plēnus
       lignum nunc esse ager atque pretiōsus
       agricola.
    3. Vain souls, you have not been true to
       the Lord!: vānus anima, nōn est vērus
       dominus.
    4. O just Lord, O clear sky, O holy life,
       always you are new and always of old
       you were: iustus dominus, lūcidus
       coelum, sanctus vīta, semper est novus
       et (atque) semper ab antīquus est.

5. Take the right way to the fertile fields;
   the left way was not the right way:
   via dexter in fecundus ager, sinister
   via est non rēctus via.
6. The heavens, the heavens are the Lord's,
   but the earth he gives to the righteous
   people: coelum coelum est dominus
   terra autem dare iustus populus.
7. The world has not always been radiant
   to the women: mundus nōn semper est
   lūcidus fēmina.
8. The slave does not rule his master:
   servus nōn gubernāre magister.

29a. Additional Sentences

1. Deus īrae et Deus misericordiae unus Deus,
   omnipotēns, Pater aeternus, totum mundum
   gubernat.
2. Pretiōsae Deō vītae sanctōrum.
3. Ad dextram Deī sedet (=sits) Christus Dominus noster.
4. In templō rubeō glōriam Dominī adōrāvērunt
   et cantāvērunt chorī virórum et puerōrum.
5. Bone Deus, per Iēsum Christum superās mundum et diabolum.
6. Integer vītae, plēnus iustitiā et misericordiā est magister magistrōrum.
7. Dōnāte nōs vītā pretiōsā rectāque. (Note
   construction with dōnāre. But cf. the
   liturgical text: Dōnā nōbīs pācem.)
8. Vāna īra non lucrātīva; vērā glōria semper
   pretiōsa.
9. Fēminae pulchrae grātia est donum Deī.
10. Per rectam viam ad templum Dominī ambulā-
    vimus.
11. Īra regīnārum regnum nōn rectē gubernat.

LESSON V

30. <u>Third Declension</u>. The key forms servōrum,
ancillārum, lignōrum show that the stems
of all the nouns hitherto considered ended
in "o" or "a." What about words ending
in the many others sounds? Latin built up
a mixed declension called the third for
all words ending in "i" or one of the consonants. Of course the innumerable words
ending in "i" and those ending in "s" or
"p" or any such sound, could not very well
produce the same forms all the way through.
The key forms which end either in "-um"
or "-ium" still betray the fundamental
dualism within this group.

In a preliminary way we shall first
consider two extreme forms, one pure I-stem,
and one pure consonant stem.

the ivory tower [Cant. 7:5]
Nom. turris eburnea
Gen. turris eburneae
Dat. turrī eburneae
Acc. turrim eburneam
Abl. turrī eburneā

the just governor
Nom. gubernātor iustus
Gen. gubernātōris iustī
Dat. gubernātōrī iustō
Acc. gubernātōrem iustum
Abl. gubernātōre iustō

Plural
Nom. turrēs   eburneae   gubernātōrēs iustī
Gen. turrium   eburneārum gubernātōrum iustōrum
Dat. turribus   eburneīs   gubernātōribus iustīs
Acc. turrēs   eburneās   gubernātōrēs iustōs
Abl. turribus   eburneīs   gubernātōribus iustīs

31. <u>Word List</u>
    a. *Vocabulary for I-stems*
       puppis acūta, puppis acutae (f.) the pointed
         stern (of a ship)
       vīs, vīs (f.) force/ virēs, virium (f.) forces, power
    b. *Vocabulary for consonant-stems*
       arbor alta, arboris altae a high tree
       Cerēs, Cereris Goddess of Cereal grains
       tellūs, tellūris (f.) earth
       lēx, lēgis (f.) law
       cinis, cineris (m.) ashes[1]
       salvātor, -tōris (m.) savior
       timor, -mōris (m.) fear
       sermō, sermōnis (m.) speech, discourse
       Caesar, -aris (m.) emperor
       homo, hominis (m.) man (i.e., mankind, like
         the German <u>Mensch</u>)
       flōs, flōris (m.) flower
       secūris saeva, secūris saevae (f.) the fierce ax

1. - "cinis," though on the surface ending
like turris, truly has a consonant stem as
is shown by the genitive "cineris." Observe
the genitive of any word to learn its stem.

32. <u>Dovetail</u>
    1. The wood of not many trees gives good
       ships: lignum non multus arbor dare
       bonus nāvis.
    2. Ceres thought to give the Romans a
       fertile earth: Cerēs Romānus putāre
       dare fecundus tellūs.
    3. The wicked govern by force only, the
       adroit by force and wisdom: sinister
       gubernāre vīs sōlus dexter vīs et
       sapientia.
    4. Cinderella (the girl of ashes) overcame
       the other daughters by her graciousness:
       puella cinerum superāre alius fīlia grātia.
    5. Black ashes were a sign of penitence:
       cinis niger signum poenitentia.

6. Crowns of red flowers adorn the chambers of the queen: corōna ruber flōs ornāre camera rēgīna.
7. With United Forces (motto of Austria): vīs unitus.
8. In English speech we preserve the Latin word sermō in the form of "a sermon": in Anglicus sermō conservāre verbum Latīnus in forma.

33. Explanation of the Ablative Case
In "ex Britanniā," from Britain, "a Caesare," from the emperor, the Ablative case lives up to its name of "carrying away," "being moved away." From the word which is put in the action, the Ablative moves away or proceeds. Furthermore, the Ablative in Latin swallowed up most instances of an older special case expressing location - Oxoniīs, in Oxford. In a small number of applications this primitive "Locative" was assimilated to the Genitive, as Rōmae - at Rome, domī - at home. Thirdly, it merged with a special Instrumental case expressing either that the noun was cause or means of the action:

gladiō interficere   to kill with the sword
aurō corrumpere   to corrupt with gold

or, at least, that the thing or act put in the instrumental was associated closely with the event of the sentence: sole oriente: with the rising sun; the English "with" itself sometimes means instrumentality, sometimes merely togetherness, sometimes is used in the sense of "against," e.g., "he fought with me" (an ambiguous statement!)

Hence we may say in general: the
Ablative is the most Latin form, first
because it is not found in the languages
of the Western World today, second because it is very rich and varied in usage.
To watch this case wherever it occurs, with
curiosity and tact, is the first step toward conquering the specifically Latin
mentality and style.

Eventually, the Ablative was capable
of explaining all circumstances that modify,
which involve the root notion of separation
or of movement away from. For instance,
the use of the Ablative in comparison
comes from the idea that one who grows
different from others is felt to move
away from them: e.g., equus magis altus
asinō est (the horse stands higher than
the ass).

The uses of the Ablative may be summed
up in the following broad categories:
   I. Movement away from or separation
  II. Cause, Instrument, manner, quality,
       price
 III. Time, place
  IV. Association of one action with another;
       see below Lesson XXIII, Sect. 133.

The following examples are taken from
the Bible. Look them up in an English
New Testament.

   instrument: interficere gladiō, fame
                et morte [Rev. 6:8]
   cause: confortātus fidē [Rom. 4:20]
   manner: quis mīlitat suīs stipendiīs?
            I Cor. 9:7]
   quality: quī sunt mundō corde, beātī
             [Matt. 5:8]

respect: pauperēs spiritū [Matt. 5:3]
price: redimere multō redeem for a high price
       duōbus solidīs for two shillings
time: nocte at night secundum revelātiōnem.
    mysteriī temporibus aeternis tacitī
          [Rom. 16:25]
comparison: prior mē erat [John 1:15]
association: testibus praesentibus,
         with the witnesses present

34. Sentences

1. Timor deī sānctus est.
2. Sermō multōrum hominum cum vitā nōn concordat.
3. Sermō Latīnus est sermō ecclēsiae Rōmānae.
4. Igne ūre Sanctī Spiritūs renēs nostrōs et cor nostrum. [cf. Ps. 25:2, Vg.]
5. Deus creātor hominum est.
6. Iēsus Christus salvātor mundī est.
7. Liberāvistī servum tuum, Domine, ab homine malō.
8. Sermōnēs sānctī Augustīnī clarī sunt.
9. Lēgēs hominum saepe iniustae.
10. Ex puppī Caesar quiētus nautās timidōs gubernat; inter ventōs exclāmat: "Caesarem portātis et fortūnam Caesaris. "
11. Turrim vir prōvidus aedificat nōn in arēnā sed in petrā...
12. Verbum bonum saepe īram hominis plācat.

35. Word List

adiūtor, -ōris (m.) helper
arēna, -ae (f.) sand
beātus, -a, -um blessed
concordāre to agree, harmonize with
mundus, -a, -um pure
mysterium, -ī (n.) mystery
nāvis, -is (f.) ship
pauper, -eris poor
petra, -ae (f.) rock
plācāre to placate
confortātus, -a,-um strengthened

duo, -ae, -o two
exclāmāre to exclaim
famēs, -is (f.) famine, hunger
fidē by faith
fortūna, -ae (f.) luck, fortune
gladius, -iī (m.) sword
militāre to wage war
prōvidus, -a, -um foresighted
quiētus,-a,-um calm

solidus, -ī (m.) shilling   tertius, -a, -um   third
stipendia, -iōrum (n.)   timidus, -a, -um   timid
    stipend, wages   ūrere   to burn, inflame,
tacitus, -a, -um   tacit,   consume
    silent   ventus, -i (m.)   wind
temporibus   at the times

35a. Reading

1. Nēmō hominum sine religiōnis sensū est. 2. Omnēs creātī sumus cum agnitiōne innātā Creātōris. 3. Ergō maiestātem Deī et timōre et amōre et reverentiā adōrāre debēmus. 4. Vīta fugax in mundō est immortālitātis meditātiō. 5. Ubi invenīmus immortālem vītam? 6. In Deō vītam sine morte invenīmus. 7. Quis est praecipua cūra et sollicitūdō vītae nostrae? 8. Nostra cūra est quaerere Deum et aspīrāre ad eum omnī animī studiō. [Adapted from Calvin, Catechism of 1537/38, Section 1].

35b. Word List

Words with obvious English derivatives: religiō, -iōnis (f); sensus, -ūs (m); Creātor, -ōris (m); creō, -āre, -āvī, -ātus; maiestās, -tātis (f); timor, -ōris (m); amor, -ōris (m), reverentia, -ae (f); immortālitās, -tātis (f); meditātiō, -ōnis (f); immortālis (adj.); mors, mortis (f); cūra, -ae (f); aspīrō, -āre,-āvī,-ātus
Other words:
nēmō   no one
homo, -inis (comm.)   man, human being
agnitiō, -ōnis (f)   recognition, knowledge
fugax, -ācis (adj.)   fleeting
inveniō, -īre (4)   to find
quaerō, -ere (3)   to seek, ask
studium, -ī (n)   zeal, study, effort
praecipuus, -a, -um (adj.)   chief, especial,
                 pre-eminent

LESSON VI

36. **Third Declension: I-stems**
In most nouns of the third declension the two
extremes, as shown in turris and gubernator,
blended into a mixed form, some keeping the
"i" in the genitive plural and the neuter
nominative and accusative plural, others not.

I-stems		
small ear	salty sea	the live animal
auris parva	mare salsum	animal vīvum
auris parvae	maris salsī	animalis vīvī
aurī parvae	marī salsō	animalī vīvō
aurem parvam	mare salsum	animal vīvum
aure parvā	marī salsō	animalī vīvō
aurēs parvae	maria salsa	animalia vīva
aurium parvārum	marium salsōrum	animalium vīvōrum
auribus parvīs	maribus salsīs	animalibus vīvīs
aurēs parvās	maria salsa	animalia vīva
auribus parvīs	maribus salsīs	animalibus vīvīs

37. **Word List**
minimum cochlear, -āris   tea spoon
septimus mensis   the seventh month
piscis parvus   a small fish
collis   hill; collis vaticana   Vatican Hill
pulchra vestis   beautiful clothes
exemplar novum   a new model
altus mons, -tis   a high mountain
longus pons, -tis   a long bridge
antiqua urbs, -bis   an ancient city
secrēta ars, -tis   magic art
firma arx, -cis   a firm fortress
albus dens, -tis   a white tooth
pallida mors, -tis   pallid (pale) death

38. The Future and Future Perfect of *Esse*

	future:		*future perfect:*	
3s	erit	he will be	fuerit	he will have been
2	eris	you will be	fueris	you will have been
1	erō	I shall be	fuerō	I shall have been
3p	erunt	they will be	fuerint	they will have been
2	eritis	you will be	fueritis	you will have been
1	erimus	we shall be	fuerimus	we shall have been

39. Imperatives
present:

2s	da mihi panem!	give me the bread!
2p	date dextrās!	give (shake) hands (*lit.* 'your rights')!

future:

2s	estō fīdus!	you are to be faithful!
3	estō fīdus!	he is to be faithful!
2p	estōte fīdī	you (*plur.*) are to be faithful!
3	suntō fīdī!	they are to be faithful!

40. Prepositions with the Accusative

ad — to; toward; for (*expressing purpose with certain verb forms*): ad gubernandam ecclesiam

ante — before: Hannibal ante partam before birth

apud — among; at the house of; nearby, with (in the presence of): apud Deum pāx est

contrā — against; opposite to : etiam contrā malōs iustitia: even against the wicked there is justice.

ergā — toward (on behalf of): ergā amicum fīdus estō: you are (he is) to be faithful toward your (his) friend

extrā — outside of: extrā portam: extrā patriam vita dura: life is hard outside one's native land

inter	between; among: inter arma nullae artēs
intrā	within: intrā murōs una cīvitās
iuxtā	near to; nearby: iuxtā mare multum sal
ob	on account of: ob septem collēs Rōmae
per	through: per aspera ad astra
post	after: post multōs annōs
praeter	besides; except; contrary to: praeter doctrīnam
prope	nearly: semper prope mortem sumus
propter	because: propter īram futūram deī nōn peccāmus
secundum	in accordance with: secundum magnam Chartam Angliam gubernant
suprā	above; over; upon: Caesar non suprā grammaticōs
trans	across: trans Tiberim est urbs Vaticāna
ultrā	beyond: ultrā montēs

41. Prepositions which take the Accusative or the Ablative; their use with the Accusative:

in	denotes motion into, upon, against anyone , thing or place: in Eurōpam īre
sub	denotes motion under: Gallīna congregat pullōs suōs sub alās [Mt. 23:37]
super	over; above; upon: super montem turrim aedificāmus.

42. Sentences
   1. Annus duodecim mensium novus Caesaris fuerat et fuit annus noster per multa saecula.
   2. Pons antīquō mōre ligneus fuit.
   3. Mors iustīs nōn mala.
   4. Dentium albōrum magnus apud Americānōs honor.
   5. Septem artium puerī perītī suntō.
   6. Antīqua urbs Rōma septem collium in rīpā Tiberis fuerat; temporibus christiānīs trans Tiberim in Vaticānō colle magna sanctī Petrī ecclēsia erat atque est.
   7. Verbum Deī ad David: "Es vir secundum cor meum"

LESSON VII

43. <u>Third Conjugation</u>

As the nouns ending in "i" or a consonant make
up the Third Declension, so the verbs ending
in "i" or a consonant make up the Third Conjugation. Instead of guberna -t (First Conjugation), we find such words as:

facit   he does, he makes
mittit   he sends

and these show clearly the principles of the
Third Conjugation.

3 facit   mittit   gubernat
2 facis   mittis   gubernās
1 faciō   mittō   gubernŏ

3 faciunt   mittunt   gubernant
2 facitis   mittitis   gubernātis
1 facimus   mittimus   gubernāmus

Facit results from an I-stem, mittit from a
consonant stem.

Inflect: existit   he exists
               promittit   he promises
               affligit   he afflicts
               afficit   he affects
               efficit   he effects

* * * *

44. <u>Third Declension</u>
As English has many Latin words taken mostly
from the Latin Accusative, English derivatives
help us to memorize these words which disclose
their stem not in the nominative but in the
genitive, accusative, and other oblique
cases.

The stem of "Pāx" (peace) is shown by the
third letter in the English words pa͟cific and
pa͟cifist. Thus the declension:

pāc-is   genitive
pāc-ī   dative
pāc-em   accusative
pāc-e   ablative

Pāx, then, is "pāc" plus "s." A list of similar words follows.

45. Word List   (English Derivative)
  m cinis, cineris ash, ashes incinerator, cinders,
  m flōs, flōris   flower   florist[Cinderella]
  m frāter, frātris brother   fratricide
  f imāgō, imāginis image   imaginary
  m iūdex, iūdicis   judge   judiciary
  f lēx, lēgis   law   legal
  f lūx, lūcis   light   lucid
  m mīles, mīlitis   soldier   militia
  m mōs, mōris   custom   moral
  f mors, mortis   death   mortal
  f nox, noctis   night   nocturne
  m pater, patris   father   patristic
  f pāx, pācis   peace   pacifist, pacific
  m pēs, pedis   foot   pedestrian
  f rādix, rādicis   root   eradicate, radical

46. Sentences
   1. Pāpa mittit legātōs. 2. Facis bonum.
   3. Capiunt piscēs parvōs et magnōs. 4. Mittitis
   flōrēs ad rēgīnam. 5. Legunt chartam magnam in
   scholīs. 6. Cēdunt ex urbe trans Tiberim. 7. Pāx
   nōn facile cēdit bellō sub gubernātōre. 8. Trans
   mare longās epistulās mittis per navem, brevēs per
   aerem. 9. Formae et ovis et lupī in animā hūmānā
   sunt. 10. In marī piscium vīta, aliōrum animālium
   in terrā. [The verb "is" is often omitted in Latin
   since the endings suffice to explain the relations
   between the words of a sentence.]

47. Word List

papa, -ae (m) pope
legātus, -ī (m) ambassa-
    dor, lieutenant
capere to take, seize
    [cf. captive]

legere to read
āēr, -is (m) air
alius, -ia, -iud another
brevis, -e short
cēdere to yield, retreat,
    proceed (cf cede)

47a Reading

Creātōr ineffābilis, quī dē thēsaurīs sapientiae tuae
...elegantissimē partēs universī distribuistī; Tū, in-
quam, quī vērus fons luminis et sapientiae dīceris, atque supereminēns principium; infundere digneris super
intellectūs meī tenebrās, peccātum scilicet et ignōr-
antiam. Quī linguās infantium facis esse disertās,
linguam meam ērudiās, atque in labiīs meīs grātiam
tuae benedictiōnis infundās. Da mihī intelligendī
acumen, retinendī capācitātem, interpretandī subtil-
itātem, addiscendī facilitātem, loquendī grātiam cop-
iōsam: ingressum instruās, prōgressum dirigās, ēgressus
compleās. [Prayer of St. Thomas Aquinas before study.]

47b Reading

Utinam et nōbīs iniiciat Dominus Jesus
 manūs suās super oculōs,
ut incipiāmus et nōs respicere
 nōn ea quae videntur,
 sed quae nōn videntur;
et aperiat nōbīs illōs oculōs,
 quī nōn intuentur praesentia,
 sed futūra,
et revelet nōbīs cordis aspectum,
 quō Deus vidētur in spīritū,
Per ipsum Dominum Jesum Christum,
 quī est glōria et imperium
in saecula saeculōrum. Amen.
    [Origen, In Genesim Homilia 16.1 (PG 12.246B)]

LESSON VIII

48. <u>Third Declension: Adjectives</u>
The adjectives ending in "i" or a consonant
reflect all the constructive problems of the
nouns of the Third Declension. So, this
lesson serves as a recapitulation of the
Third Declension.

<u>Singular</u>	
Masc. & Fem.	Neuter
duplex	duplex
duplicis	duplicis
duplicī	duplicī
duplicem	<u>duplex</u>
duplicī	duplicī

concors	concors
concordis	concordis
concordī	concordī
concordem	concors
concordī	concordī

<u>Plural</u>	
Masc. & Fem.	Neuter
duplicēs	duplicia
duplicium	duplicium
duplicibus	duplicibus
duplicēs	duplicia
duplicibus	duplicibus

concordēs	concordia
concordium	concordium
concordibus	concordibus
concordēs	concordia
concordibus	concordibus

dīves, -ĭtis, pauper, -is, and memor, -is add
"um" instead of "ium" in the Genitive Plural.
[Originally the Neuter was an Accusative,
that is, nouns that were Neuter were nouns that
could only be acted upon and not act; therefore

the Neuter has no special Nominative form.
Its Accusative simply functions as the Nominative, too.]

A few adjectives show three different forms
for the three genders, but only in the Nominative case of the singular.

Masculine	Feminine	Neuter
acer (sharp, heated)	acris	acre
	acris	acris
	acrī	acrī
	acrem	acre
	acrī	acrī

Masculine-Fem. Plural	Neuter
acrēs	acria
acrium	acrium
acribus	acribus
acrēs	acria
acribus	acribus

Masculine	Feminine	Neuter
celer (swift)	celeris	celere
alacer (excited, quick)	alacris	alacre

Other adjectives of the Third Declension,
more numerous than the one-ending or three-
ending, groups, confine themselves to two
Nominative forms.

Masculine & Feminine	Neuter
fortis (valiant, brave)	forte
mitis (mild, gentle, ripe)	mīte
fidēlis (faithful, true)	fidēle
omnis (all, every)	omne
familiāris (familiar)	familiăre
tristis (sad)	triste
vīlis (cheap, low-priced)	vīle

All the words of craftsmanship signifying ability
and ending in -abilis or -ilis have the two
endings "is" and "e."

arābilis,-is -e	that which can be ploughed
fictilis,-is -e	that which can be molded (clay)
facilis,-is -e	that which can be done, easy
later, even	
possibilis, -e	that which can be brought about

49. Present Participles
A powerful group of words are the participles
of the present, like:

gubernāns,	gen.,	gubernantis	governing
amāns	gen.,	amantis	loving
potēns	gen.,	potentis	powerful in, potent
praesēns	gen.,	praesentis	present

When these participles are used as forms of
the verb in Action, they keep the "e" of
their consonant stem in the Ablative, "mē
praesente," (when I was present). However,
when they mark more adjectival qualities,
they conform with all the rest, "in praesentī"
(now).

50. Sentences
1. Medicī colligunt scientiam suam saepe in
   corpore vīlī.
2. Multī hominēs mensūrant duplicī mensūrā,
   alterā in sē, alterā in aliōs.
3. Dominus fortis et potēns est.
4. Magnus est Dominus et laudābilis,
   terribilis est super omnēs deōs.
5. Mīrābilis est in altīs Dominus.
6. Domine, Deus noster, quam admīrābile est
   nomen tuum in universā terrā!

7. Simplex vēritās, mendācium multiplex.
8. Non erit impossible apud Deum omne verbum.
9. Fidēlis Dominus in omnibus verbīs suīs
   et sānctus in omnibus operibus suīs.
10. Ego sum mītis et humilis corde.
11. Admīrābile est mansuētūdō redemptōris
    in peccātōrēs.

Sempiternī fons amōris,
Consōlātrix tristium,
Pia mater salvātōris,
Avē, virgō virginum!

51. Esse: Infinitive, Present Subjunctive
    Infinitives   Subjunctive

esse   to be   sit   sint
fuisse   to have been   sis   sitis
                           sim   simus

52. Relations Between Two
    In "one is better than the other," we use
    the words bet-ter and o-ther with their
    endings to qualify the situation between
    two. This "dual" relation between two
    also survives in father, mother, sister,
    brother. In Latin, one important word
    group sprang from the dual:

uter   which of two
alter   one of two
uterque   one and the other, both
neuter   none of two

These words are declined regularly, uter, utra,
utrum, or alter, altera, alterum, but they
have "-ius" in all the forms of the Genitive
Singular and "-Ī" all the forms of the Dative
Singular.

Alter marī alter terrā vēnit.
The one came by sea, the other by land.

Cum Iēsus et Iudas convenīrent, neuter locūtus
est.
When Jesus and Judas met, neither spoke

Titulus doctōris iuris utriusque sīgnificat
virum perītum legis canonicae atque civīlis.

The title of <u>doctor in both laws</u> signifies
a man is skilled in both the canon and in
the civil law.

Nixon aut McGovern uter victor fuit electiōnis?

* * * * * * * * * *

52a. Prayer of St. Odilo of Cluny (10th Century)

In cuius nomen omne genuflectitur, coelestium, ter-
restrium et infernōrum, eī nunc mea curvō genua,
sive confiteor culpam Patrī luminum, possessōrī
omnium spirituum, imperantī tam terrēnīs quam coelestibus: tibīque, inimīce hūmanī generis, interdīcō,
qui circuīs quaerēns quem devorēs, averte ā mē
machinās tuās et occultās insidiās; quia mēcum est
crūx Dominī quem semper adoro. Crux mihi refugium,
crūx mihī via et virtūs, crūx inexpugnābile signum,
crūx invincibile genus armōrum. Crūx repellit omne
malum. Crūx effūgat tenebrās. Per hanc crūcem di-
vīnum aggrediar iter. Crūx mihī vīta est; mors,
inimīce, tibī. Crūx Dominī nostrī sit sublimitās
mea, sanguis eius maneat in mē redemptiō vēra.
Resurrectiō illius sit mihī dē resurrectiōne iustōrum firma fīdēs et spēs certa; et illius ad coelōs
gloriōsa ascensiō sit mihī ad coeleste desiderium
quotidiāna provectiō, et Sanctī Spiritūs in cordibus nostrīs infusiō sit omnium praeteritōrum nostrorum remissiō. *Amen.* (*Migne, Patrologia Latina,*
142. 1037f)

LESSON IX

53. General Rule for the Comparison of Adjectives

-ior is added to the stem to form the comparative
-issimus is added to the stem to form the
     superlative

Positive	Comparative
dulcis, sweet	dulcior, sweeter
amplus, ample	amplior, more ample

Superlative
dulcissimus, sweetest
amplissimus, most ample

a) Adjectives ending in -er in the Nominative
   Singular
   Masculines form their superlative by adding
   -rimus:

| tener | tenerior | tenerrimus |
| pulcher | pulchrior | pulcherrimus |

b) Six adjectives, facilis, difficilis, similis,
   dissimilis, gracilis, and humilis, form their
   superlatives by adding -limus:

| facilis | facilior | facillimus |

c) Adjectives ending in -dicus, -ficus, and
   -volus form their comparatives by adding
   -entior, and their superlatives by adding
   -entissimus:

maledicus	maledicentior	maledicentissimus
magnificus	magnificentior	magnificentissimus
benevolus	benevolentior	benevolentissimus
malevolus	malevolentior	malevolentissimus

d) More than one adjective effecting the comparison

good	bonus	melior	optimus
bad	malus	peior	pessimus
big	magnus	maior	maximus
much	multus	plus	plurimus
(many)			
near	prope	propior	proximus
	[adv.]		

e) Adjectives ending in -eus, -ius, or -uus,
   that is with a vowel before the ending,
   are unable to develop a direct comparison.
   They use a paraphase:

   idoneus, suitable   magis idoneus   maximē idoneus
   rubeus, red   magis rubeus   maximē rubeus

   Magis - more (greatly) and maximē - most (greatly)
are the comparative and superlative of the
adverb formed from <u>magnus</u>. But <u>piissimus</u>, 'the
most pious,' was too much needed on tombstones;
hence, <u>maximē pius</u> was not used.

f) Adjectives in the comparative degree are
    all declined as Third Declension adjectives:

           Singular
Masc. & Fem.   Neuter
amplior   amplius (note form of neut. nom./
amplioris   amplioris   acc.)
ampliorī   ampliorī
ampliorem   amplius
ampliore (ī)   ampliore (ī)

           Plural
Masc. & Fem.   Neuter
ampliorēs   ampliora
ampliorum   ampliorum
amplioribus   amplioribus
ampliorēs   ampliora
amplioribus   amplioribus

54. <u>The Secret of Formative Endings</u>. A potter or
     carpenter has to use certain terms in his work
     describing very specialized processes; he must
     be able to describe his material and the various
     stages through which it passes. When a potter
     finds his clay manageable, he calls it fictile,
     a thing he can knead. English -able, in man-
     ageable, and -ile, in fictile, docile, and

facile, are derived from Latin -abilis and -ilis,
which in turn sprang from the artisan's language
describing the potentialities of his materials.

The syllable -tor signified a man who is the
action of the very personified, permanently or
professionally: doctor, rector,
monitor, mercător, gubernător, imperător. The
syllable -trīx applies to women:

cantător	cantātrīx	chantress
lavátor	lavātrīx	laundress
imperător	imperātrīx	empress
peccátor	peccātrīx	female sinner (or: anima
		peccātrix=sinful soul)

The syllables -tās and -tūs apply to collectives.
English equivalent is -ity.

cīvitās	community (city)
libertās	liberty
virtūs	manhood, virtue, power
senectūs	old age
iuventūs	youth

Thus from one root many words can be formed.
From the imperative (the shortest form of a
word and the form of speech closest to a mere
cry of oh, ah, [called interjection]) every
other form which we use -- verb, noun, adjective, or adverb -- is built. For example:

arā!	plough!
arat	he ploughs
arō	I plough
arātor	the ploughman
arātrum	the plough
arābilis	ploughable
arāre	to plough
arāns	ploughing

To words like actor, gubernātor, there is
frequently a corresponding feminine noun,
signifying the man's activity: This ends
in -iō [-iōnis] and is found in English in words
ending in -ion. For example:

actiō	action	actor
conductiō	conduction	conductor
gubernātiō		gubernātor
orātiō	oration	orātor
	(prayer)	

Even if there is no name for the person involved
in the action, the action can be expressed in
this way:

mutātiō	transformation, change
allocūtiō	an address
commiserātiō	commiseration
missiō	mission
visiō	vision

55. **Sentences**
1. Hominēs clārissimī non semper sunt fēlīcissimī.
2. Verbum bonum saepe iucundius est quam dōnum.
3. Saepe parvulum peccātum causa maximōrum
     malōrum est.
4. Iēsus amīcus est optimus.
5. Cāritās virtūtum maxima est.
6. Humillimus in terrā maximus erit in coelō.
7. Melior est misericordia tua, Domine, super
     honōrēs mundī.
8. Melius est pauperem esse quam malum.
9. [From an ancient tombstone] Mater innocentī
     fīliō dulcissimē; vīvas in deō.

The following poem, a song of the pilgrims who
went to Rome, dates from the 9th Century. It
was restored to its proper place of prominence
by the greatest modern scholar of medieval
Latin, Ludwig Traube (1861-1907).

Ō Rōma nōbilis, orbis et domina
cunctārum urbium excellentissima,
roseō martyrum sanguine rubea,
albīs et virginum liliīs candida;
Salūtem dīcimus tibī per omnia
tē benedīcimus -- salvē per saecula!

Cf. Sect. 149, below.

55a. St. Cyprian on the Church

Ecclēsia una est,
quae in multitūdinem latius incrementō
  foecunditātis extenditur
quomodo solis multī radiī,
sed lumen unum,
et ramī arboris multī,
sed robur unum tenācī radice fundātum,
et cum dē fonte unō rivī plurimī dēfluunt,
numerōsitās licet diffūsa videātur
  exundantis cōpiae largitāte,
unitās tamen servātur in origine.
Avelle radium solis ā corpore,
divisiōnem lucis unitās non capit;
ab arbore frange ramum,
fractus germināre nōn poterit;
a fonte praecīde rivum,
praecīsus arēscit.
Sic et ecclesia Dominī lūce perfūsa per orbem
  totum radiōs suōs porrigit;
unum tamen lumen est,
quod ubique diffunditur,
nec unitās corporis separātur.
Ramōs suōs in universam terram
  cōpia ubertātis extendit,
profluēntēs largiter rivōs latius expandit,
unum tamen caput est
et origō una
et una mater foecunditātis
  successibus copiōsa;
illius foetū nascimur,
illius lacte nutrimur,
spiritū eius animamur.   (*De unitate ecclesiae*, 5)

LESSON X

56. <u>Adverbs</u>. What is the difference between
"a steady walker" and "to walk steadily"?
When the adjective "steady" becomes the concomitant of a verb, instead of a noun, in
English -ly is affixed; "a steady walker"
becomes "to walk steadily" (see above Sect. 1)

In Latin, likewise, a change takes place.
Pulcher, longus, fortis, being different types
of adjectives accordingly have two different
adverbial suffixes:

pulchrē	pulcherrimē	fortiter	fortissimē
longē	longissimē	celeriter	celerrimē
clārē	clārissimē	potenter	potentissimē

In general, adjectives of the 2nd/1st Declension form adverbs in -ē, while those of the
3rd Declension use -<u>iter</u>. However, this is
not always true and some adjectives have in
fact both adverbial forms.

One adverb is irregular: bonus, bene; but
optimē is formed regularly. Similarly prope
(near). Some adjectives have no distinct
adverbial form: facile. Some use the
ablative case: rarō, primō, postremō. Some
adverbs are combinations of two words both in
the ablative case:

magnōpere (magnō opere)	greatly
hodiē (hōc diē)	today
quomodō (quō modō)	as, how
quotidiē (quot diē)	daily (also: cotidiē)

Also some accusatives are in adverbial use:

multum	privātim, privately
prīmum	sēparātim, separately
sōlum	ōlim, in time past, formerly
tantum	summātim, summarily

All comparatives use the neuter form of the adjective for the adverb:

melius ⎞   ⎛ melior
maius ⎬ from   ⎨ maior
albius ⎪   ⎪ albior
fortius ⎠   ⎝ fortior

Added to these lists should be some adverbs not taken from adjectives or nouns:

nunc, now   semper, always
saepe, often   tunc, then

Any number of adverbs result from combining prepositions and "this" or "that."

proptereā (because of that) therefore
quem ad modum (in which manner) as

57. Sentences

1. Thomas Aquinas dē sānctissimā Eucharistiā doctissimē disputāvit.
2. Sāncta ecclēsia firmiter aedificāta est suprā firmam petram.
3. Hodiē celebrāmus festīvitātem omnium sānctōrum.
4. Ubī bene, ibī patria.
5. Quotidiē orāmus.
6. Bonī semper nomen Dominī sanctificant.
7. Sit nomen Dominī benedīctum nunc et in saeculum!
8. Simon fortissimē rēgī Angliae resistit.

58. Word List

ab intus, from within
aliquando, at some time
crās, tomorrow
ergō, therefore

forsitan ⎱
fortassē ⎰ perhaps
forte, by chance
frustrā, in vain
iam, already
ibǐ, there
ideö, therefore
illǐc, there
illuc, thither
insuper, moreover, besides
ita, so
māne, tomorrow morning
nē, With imp. not
nimis, too much
nōn, not
olim, formerly
paulō minus, a little less
quam, how
quidem, indeed
saltem, at least
sǐc, so
tam, so
tum, then
ubǐ, where
ubǐque, everywhere
unde, whence
valdē, very

59. Prepositions with the Ablative

a) Prepositions taking the Ablative only:

a, ab	from, on the side of ,(with agents) by alienātǐ ā vǐtā deǐ (Eph. 4:18)
absque	without
coram	in the presence of
cum	with (of accomplishment or means)
dē	concerning, from
ē, ex	out of, from

        os ex ossibus meǐs et carō

           dē carne meā (Gen. 2:23)

         ex animǐ sententiā, from the true

           feeling of the heart

argumentum ē contrāriō
prae   before
prō   as, for, instead of, in favor of
sine   without

b)   Prepositions capable of taking both the
Ablative and the Accusative, in their use
with the Ablative (cf. section 40)

in   expresses the place <u>where</u>
                       the time <u>when</u>
                        in stupōre mentis
                        (Acts 22:17)
                       nostra requiēs est in
                       Dominō
                       [in horā mortis nostrī]
sub   under, about
super   over, above, during, about

59a.   St. Augustine on *Fortuna*

In librīs contrā Academicōs non mihī placet tōtiēs
mē appellāvisse Fortūnam; quanvīs nōn aliquam deam
voluerim hōc nomine intelligī, sed fortūitum rērum
eventum in externīs vel bonīs vel malīs. Unde et
illa verba sunt quae nulla religiō dīcere prohibet,
Forte, Forsan, Forsitan, Fortassē, Fortuitō; quod
tamen tōtum ad divīnam revocandum est provīdentiam.
Neque hoc tacuī, dīcēns, etenim fortassē quae vul-
gō Fortūna nuncupātur, occultō quōque ordine rēgi-
tur: nihilque aliud in rēbus cāsum vocāmus, nisi
cuius ratiō et causa secrēta est. Dīxī quidem hoc:
vērum poenitet mē sīc nomināvisse illīc Fortūnam:
cum videam hominēs habēre in pessima consuētūdine,
ut dīcī debet, Hoc Deus voluit, dīcant, Hoc voluit
Fortūna. (Augustine, *Retractiones*, 1. 1. 2)

LESSON XI

60. The Tense Sign: Formation of the Imperfect and the Future

In Latin two other tenses share the same stem with the present tense. These are the imperfect and the future. In English we express these tenses by means of auxiliary verbs:

> Present: he governs
> Imperfect: he was governing
> Future: he shall govern

Latin, however, uses an infix, an extra syllable between stem and ending, for the imperfect, -ba-, in all regular conjugations. In addition, the First Conjugation and the Second also (see Sect. 61) form the future with the infix -bi-:

> guberna <u>plus</u> ba <u>plus</u> t   he was governing
> guberna <u>plus</u> bi <u>plus</u> t   he will govern

The complete imperfect and future active indicative of the First Conjugation are as follows:

Imperfect		Future	
gubernābat	gubernābant	gubernābit	gubernābunt
gubernābās	gubernābātis	gubernābis	gubernābitis
gubernābam	gubernābāmus	gubernābō	gubernābimus

61. The Second Conjugation

The verbs whose stem ends in ē make up the Second Conjugation. Least numerous among the various conjugations, the second includes nevertheless a group of verbs of considerable importance. We find such words as:

docet   he teaches (cf. doctor)
monet   he admonishes (cf. admonition, monitor)
manet   he remains (cf. mansion)

Derived words like doctor, monitor, and mansion
show that the simple consistency of the ā of the
First Conjugation, as seen in laudat: laudātor,
arat: arātor, educat. educātor, and praedīcat:
praedīcātor, is not characteristic of the Second,
where we find:

doceō	docēre	docuī	doctus
moneō	monēre	monuī	monitus
maneō	manēre	mansī	mansus

Thus the ē normally disappears in the perfect
active indicative (docuī) and the perfect
passive participle (doctus). The ē is characteristic, however, of the stem as it is
found in the Present, the Future, and the
Imperfect.

Present

docet	docent
docēs	docētis
doceō	docēmus

Future

docēbit	docēbunt
docēbis	docēbitis
docēbō	docēbimus

Imperfect

docēbat	docēbant
docēbās	docēbātis
docēbam	docēbāmus

A full and regular development of the Second
Conjugation may be seen in the verbs derived
from plēnus, full. They survive in our English
words compline, complete, replete, etc.

impleō, implāre, implēvī, implētus
compleō complēre, complēvī, complētus
repleō, replēre, replēvī, replētus

These rare forms of the Perfect Stem must be
treated as exceptions rather than the rule.

62. The Fourth Conjugation

The final conjugation to be learned has long ī
as its characteristic vowel. As in the Second
and Third, this vowel does not persist throughout as we find to be true of the ā of the First
Conjugation. At some points the student may
confuse the I-stem verbs of the Third Conjugation with verbs of the Fourth Conjugation, as
both have certain common forms. In the present
tense Fourth Conjugation verbs carry long ī in
the Second Singular and the First and Second
Plural, in contrast to the Third conjugation short I-stem verbs which preserve their
"i" throughout. Audit (he hears), one of the
commonest verbs in the Fourth Conjugation, has
numerous English derivatives that give us a
clue to its behavior: audition, auditor,
auditorium, audience, audit, and the like.
Some of the more common verbs of this conjugation include:

audiō, audīre, audīvī, audītus   to hear
veniō, venīre, vēnī, ventus   to come
fīniō, fīnīre, fīnivi, (fīniī),   to finish {from
     fīnītus   {fīnis
serviō, servīre, servīvī, (serviī),   {from
     servītus   to serve {servus
custodiō, custodīre, custodīvī,   {from
     custodītus   to keep {custōs

The present active indicative of audiō is given
beside that of faciō (3rd conj. I-stem) for
comparison:

audit	facit	audiunt	faciunt
audīs	facis	audītis	facitis
audiō	faciō	audīmus	facimus

63. **Formation of the Future Tense in the Third and Fourth Conj.**

The Future Active Indicative in -bi- is found only in the First and Second Conjugations. An alternate way of forming the Future Tense occurs in the Third and Fourth Conjugations, similar in form to what will in Lesson XII be recognized as the Present Subjunctive Active of the First Conjugation. The First Person Singular -am or -iam; the remaining forms take the vowel (i)ē, or (i)e, plus the standard present tense endings. Thus we have:

3rd (cons.)	3rd (I-stem)	4th Conj.
mittet	capiet	audiet
mittēs	capiēs	audiēs
mittam	capiam	audiam
mittent	capient	audient
mittētis	capiētis	audiētis
mittēmus	capiēmus	audiēmus

64. *Word List*

eget* stand in need, be needy
pudet me* feel ashamed
taedet me* be disgusted, offended tired
paenitet me* repent, be sorry
licet me* allow, permit
libet me* please
sedet sit

audit hear, listen
dīligit love
fortitūdō,-inis (f.) strength
iubet command
narrat tell, narrate
cogitat ponder, consider
medicus,-ī physician

65. **Reading**

Audī, Israel - Dominus Deus noster Dominus unus est. Dīligēs Dominum Deum tuum ex tōtō corde tuō et ex tōtā animā tuā et ex tōtā fortitūdine tuā. Erunt verba haec, quae ego iubeō tibī hodiē, in corde tuō, et narrābis ea fīliīs tuīs et cōgitābis ea sedēns in

*See Section 128, below.

casā tuā et ambulāns in itinere, dormiēns
atque consurgēns, et ligābis ea quasi signum
in manū tuā, erunt et movēbunt inter oculōs
tuōs, scrībēs ea in limine et ostiīs casae
tuae. (Deut. 6:4-9, adapted).

66. <u>Exercise</u>   Translate into Latin:

1. Hear, O Father, the words of thy son.
2. The Lord is the strength of my heart.
3. The king of kings dwells in the glory of
   heaven.
4. The Son of God taught the children of men
   the words of life.

Translate into English:

1. Nōn egent quī sānī medicō.(Lk. 5:31)*
2. Taedēbat nōs etiam vīvere. (II Cor. 1:8)*
3. Nōn enim tē pudēbit. (Is. 54:4)*
4. Ancilla tua in manū tuā est, fac eī ut
   libet. (Gen. 16:6)*

66a. From a Prayer of Erasmus for the Unity of the Church

Conditor es / instaura plasma tua.
Redemptor es / serva mercem tuam.
Servātor es / ne sinās eōs interīre, quī tōtī pendent ex tē.
Dominus es / assere possessiōnem tuam.
Caput es / subvenī membrīs tuīs.
Rēx es / da legum tuārum reverentiam.
Deus es / misere supplicum.

Estō omnia in omnibus
Ut universus Ecclēsiae tuae chorus
Concordibus animīs
Et consonantibus vocibus
Prō impetrātā misericordiā grātiās agat
Patrī et Filiō et Spirituī Sanctō,
Quī ad absolūtum concordiae examplum,
Persōnārum propriētāte distinctī estis,
Natūra unum,
Quibus laus et glōria in aeternum. *Amen.*

*See Section 128 below

LESSON XII

67. <u>Subjunctive</u>

The common toast "prosit": That it be help-
ful! and "vīvat rēx": (Long) live the King!
are examples of the subjunctives.

The Latin subjunctive is hard to translate
by itself; it is a frequent and rich form in
Latin, but has nearly been eliminated in English, which uses "would," "might," "could
and "should" instead. The subjunctive describes wishes, hopes and fears, causes, aims
and effects, in short, every action marked
by the speaker's emotions or imagination or
anticipation.

The subjunctive mood can occur in any verb,
like the imperative or the indicative.

<u>Imp.</u>	<u>Ind.</u>	<u>Subj.</u>
	gubernat	gubernet
gubernā	gubernās	gubernēs
	gubernō	gubernem
	gubernant	gubernent
gubernāte	gubernātis	gubernētis
	gubernāmus	gubernēmus

A short explanation of the possible shade of
meaning of an action expressed in our
speech may bring out more clearly why these
three moods must exist beside one another.
Go!, ī!, the imperative, tries to set an
action in operation by the person whom we
address. On the other hand, "It rains,"
pluit, describes, i.e. "indicates" a fact.

The imperative, then, mentions an act of
the future which is desired but which the
speaker himself cannot accomplish; for
the "I" depends on the "you" to whom the
"I" speaks. Whereas the fact given in the
indicative is perfectly independent of
either the speaker or the person spoken to.
That it rains is a fact. It is independent
of anything you or I can do about it. It
depends on the world outside. The sentence,
Christus natus est in Bethlehem, is a story
which happened so long ago that we cannot
alter the fact in the least. But in the
indicative the fact that I and you are talk-
ing about a third thing or person, is omitted.
When I say "it rains" the full truth is:
"I say that it rains." It follows that the
indicative is not the mood of the verb,
but one mood only, because of this omission.

Obviously, there must be a third mood of
speech which stresses the fact that the
utterance depends in some way or other
upon the speaker.

Now the coloring of an utterance by the
speaker's interest in it will spring
either from his personal feelings (a)
or from his reasons (b). (a) If from his
feelings, he may detest, hope, wish, or fear.
This emotional strain: 0 that it rain, 0
that it would not rain, impresses itself
on the utterance and makes it subjunctive,
subdued, to the speaker's appreciation.
(b) If from his reasons, "Because," "lest,"
"if," "when," "so that" and similar con-
junctions link two assertions into one.

```
I may shoot    1.  because you go
               2.  if you go
               3.  lest you go
               4.  in order to show you
               5.  so that you go
```

The speaker, in every one of these five
cases, is considering the "go" as something
linked with his shooting, either as

```
               1.  a cause
               2.  a condition
               3.  a negative aim
               4.  a positive purpose
               5.  a positive aim
```

The speaker qualifies in his intellectual
imagination the interplay between the two
declarations. And so it is his reasoning
that subjugates the "go" to his operation
of shooting. His mentality, then, gives
the decisive color and place to the "you
go" and therefore it is put, in Latin, or
after English "lest," in the subjunctive
mood. In Latin, when the emotion or the
imagination of the speaker permeates a
sentence or clause, this sentence or
clause is found in the subjunctive.

Latin is rather particular about the speaker's
part in speech. If he is passionately or
reasonably interested he must avow it. By
the form itself Latin compels him to admit
his prejudices; English does not. Latin:
Cum eāmus, nōn erimus praesentēs.

The Latin cum eāmus is subjective!

Ut fīlius eat, mittimus pecūniam.

In order that our son may go, we are sending
money!
Optō ut eās. I wish that you would go,

Here the English preserves at least an
indirect subjunctive.

So strong is Latin accuracy that in the
case of fear the speaker's negative attitude makes itself felt by a special negation.

> English: We fear lest you go.
> But Latin: (literally) We fear - O that
> you would not go.
> <u>Timēmus nē eās</u>.

Other Examples

<u>Sit dux</u>, Let him be our leader.
<u>Simus fortēs</u>, Let us be courageous.

Since the English Subjunctive is obsolescent,
we use for a future wish an Imperative with
"please," or a question. "Please go home!"
"Wouldn't you go home?" In Latin the distinction between a command and a wish is
more precisely preserved:

> I say   "Ī" when I command "Go!"
> "eās" when I wish: "Please go."

On Early Christian Tombstones we find:
1. Coca, vīvās parentibus tuīs.
2. Ossa tua bene requiēscant.
3. Sancte Pauline, vīvās et flōreās et
    semper sedeās!

68. Word List

sedeat	may he sit (as a bishop)
flōreat	may he bloom or flower or flourish
vīvet	may he live
requiēscat	may he rest, repose

69. Exercise
Distinguish two formations of the Subjunctive and explain.

1	irrg.	2	3	3 (i)	3	4
gubernet	eat	moneat	vīvat	faciat	mittat	audiat
gubernēs	eās	moneās	vīvās	faciās	mittās	audiās
gubernem	eam	moneam	vīvam	faciam	mittam	audiam
gubernent	eant	moneant	vīvant	faciant	mittant	audiant
gubernētis	eātis	moneātis	vīvātis	faciātis	mittātis	audiātis
gubernēmus	eāmus	moneāmus	vīvāmus	faciāmus	mittāmus	audiāmus

69a. Martin Luther: Decalogus inversus

I   Debēmus in sōlum Deum confīdere.

II   Debēmus in omnibus nostrīs malīs, invocāre nomen Deī, orāre, laudāre, grātiās agere.

III Debēmus verbum Deī magnifacere et venerārī, libenter tum audīre ab aliīs, tum aliōs docēre.

IV   Debēmus habēre Deō et parentibus nostrīs, item illīs quī in nōs habent iūs et imperium, honōrem, servīre eīs, obsequī, colere, et reverērī eōs.

V   Debēmus iuvāre et adesse nostrō proximō in omnibus vītae periculīs.

VI   Debēmus castam et modestam agere vītam, nihil im-modestum neque dīcere neque facere, suam quisque uxōrem dīligere et colere.

VII Debēmus promovēre aliōrum commoda tuērī, defendere.

VIII Debēmus excusāre aliōs, bene de eīs sentīre et loquī, omnī in meliōrem accipere partem.

IX   Debēmus iuvāre proximum, ut suās fortūnās retineat integrās.

X   Debēmus monēre et cohortārī ut in servitiō, quod dominīs debent, remaneant.

Debēmus Deum timēre & amāre!

(Luther, Catechismus Parvus, 1543)

LESSON XIII

70. Infinitive*

These three moods, Indicative, Imperative,
and Subjunctive enthrone one of the three parties
concerned in speech, the "I" or speaker, called
the first person, the "YOU" or addressee called
the second person, and the "it" or "he" or "she,"
called the third person. Quite noticeably, then,
all these moods are lop-sided. The verb, therefore, reacts against these three personal moods
by a fourth mood, through which it is able to
assert its integrity and freedom from personal
domination; to go - īre, to govern - gubernāre,
to send - mittere, to be - esse, to do - facere,
are forms avoiding the dependence on the modality
of any of the three persons, him, you, or me.
For that reason, these forms are called "infinitives" (free of any personal element). An Infinitive is a verb in "pure" action. However,
this purity of action does not kill it or turn
it into a noun; the Infinitive "facere" must
not be mistaken for "factum" (a fact or deed),
nor is "esse" simply "essentia" (being). The
Infinitive keeps the power of all verbal moods
to govern other words, for example:

facere pontem	to make a bridge
īre ad urbem	to go to town
esse praesentem	to be present
gubernāre rem publicam	to govern the republic

Tū regere imperiō populōs, Rōmāne, mementō;
Hae tibī erunt artēs; pācisque imponere mōrem,
Parcere subiectīs, et dēbellāre superbōs.**

(Vergil, Prophecy of Rome's Empire
Aeneid, 6: 851-853)

The infinitive of gubernat is gubernare, likewise

*Cf. Sect. 124, below (on indirect discourse).
**Note that parcere, to spare, governs the dative
(see Sect. 139a).

adorāre. But of mittit and facit, mittere and
facere; likewise petere.

71. The moods now may be put into a logical list.

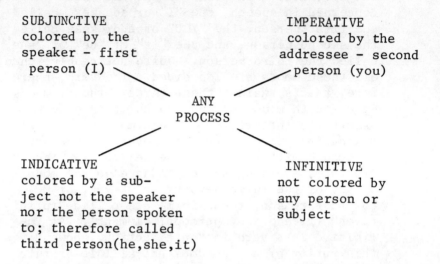

SUBJUNCTIVE
colored by the
speaker - first
person (I)

IMPERATIVE
colored by the
addressee - second
person (you)

ANY
PROCESS

INDICATIVE
colored by a sub-
ject not the speaker
nor the person spoken
to; therefore called
third person(he,she,it)

INFINITIVE
not colored by
any person or
subject

Or when numbered they lead to this series:

I	capit	Indicative, the action is told as the 3rd person's business
II	fac!	Imperative, the action is challenged as the second person's business
III	nē moriar or nesciō an possim	Subjunctive, the action is articu-lated as influenced by feelings of the first person, or the reasoning of the first person
IV	esse	Infinitive, the action is freed from moods, I, II, and III.

"It," "he," and "she" belong primarily to the
Indicative; "Thou" and "you" to the Imperative;
"I" to the Subjunctive. Thus our grammatical
lists which try to assign six personal forms,
three singular and three plural to each mood
are rather misleading. There never was nor is
a first person of pluit, or of fac; and from the
subjunctive of the Perfect we still may see that
"fuerim" needed more clearly a peculiar ending
(contrasted to Future "fuero") than the other
persons which nearly all sound the same in the
Future Indicative and Perfect Subjunctive.

At the threshold of speaking any one of these
four moods is possible:

```
  I   is - you go                facis - you do
 II   ī! - go!                   fac! - do!
III   (a) eās - 0 that you would facias-0 that you would
      (b) dubito an eās -   [go fac ut eas -      [do
          I doubt if you go    see(do)that you(may) go
 IV   īre - to go              facere - to do
```

72. Exercise: give the indicative and infinitive of:

```
    dēputā          give to!
    aberrā          go astray!
    prōmitte        promise!
    signā           sign, mark!
```

73. Declension of the Infinitive(Gerund)
    Gubernare, to govern, may be inflected as a noun
    and still act as a verb.

```
    gubernāre cīvitātēs       obtemperāre amīcīs
    gubernandī cīvitātēs      obtemperandī amīcīs
    gubernandō cīvitātēs      obtemperandō amīcīs
    gubernandum cīvitātēs     obtemperandum amīcīs
    gubernandō cīvitātēs      obtemperandō amīcīs
```

74. <u>Sentences</u>

Ō Domine Deus
Sperāvī in tē;   (From the prayer book of
Ō cāre mī Iesu   Mary, Queen of Scotland and
Nunc līberā mē;   believed to be her own com-
in dūrā catēnā,   position. Said to have been
in miserā poenā   uttered by the Queen, 1587,
dēsīderō tē;   just before her execution.)
languendō, gemendō
et genūflectendō
adōrō, implōrō,
ut līberēs mē.

Fidēs est substantia sperandārum rērum. (Heb. 11:1)
Fidēs docet omnia necessāria ad bene vīvendum.

About the growth of the Gerund with the advance-
ment of deeper religious thinking, the great
Augustine says: "Doctī quīdam temporis recentioris,
cum habērent necessitātem magna et dīvīna quaedam
interpretandī explicandīque, et
essendī et
essendō et
essendum et
essēns dīxērunt. (<u>Grammatici Latini</u>, ed. Keil,
                  V. 494, 25 sqq.)

LESSON XIV

75. <u>How the verb is changed for adjectival use (the Participle)</u>
compare potens in Lesson VIII

1. governing Present Active Part. gubernans
2. governed Perfect Passive Part. gubernātus
3. one who is Future Active Part. gubernātūrus
   to govern
4. one who is Future Passive Part. gubernandus
   to be
   governed

Compare Part: Itūrus, one who will go

1 and 4 are formed from the Present stem. Once one knows the Present, one can articulate these Participles very simply. 2 and 3 are derived from the Perfect (passive) stem. Gubernātūrus and gubernātus are formed in the same way as the words we already know - mercātor, imperātor, and orātiō, mutātiō.

76. <u>Exercise</u>

When one knows any one of these words, one is able to form the others with certainty. Form the other participles of the verbs suggested by these words [see Sect.54]:

orātiō	orātus	orātor
mutātiō	mutātus	mutātor
invāsiō	invāsus	invāsor
conductiō	conductus	conductor
	doctus	doctor
mōtiō	mōtus	mōtor

77. List of the forms of Esse
ens, entis [Sect. 73] esse

Present		Imperfect		Future
Indic.	Subj.	Indic.	Subj.	Indic.
est	sit	erat	esset	erit
es	sis	erās	essēs	eris
sum	sim	eram	essem	erō
sunt	sint	erant	essent	erunt
estis	sitis	erātis	essētis	eritis
sumus	simus	erāmus	essēmus	erimus

	(fuisse)		(futūrus)
Perfect		Pluperfect		Futer Perfect
Indic.	Subj.	Indic.	Subj.	Indic.
fuit	fuerit	fuerat	fuisset	fuerit
fuistī	fueris	fuerās	fuissēs	fueris
fuī	fuerim	fueram	fuissem	fuerō
fuērunt	fuerint	fuerant	fuissent	fuerint
fuistis	fueritis	fuerātis	fuissētis	fueritis
fuimus	fuerimus	fuerāmus	fuissēmus	fuerimus

The Subjunctive of the Imperfect and Pluperfect
may always be found by appending the personal
endings -t, -s, -m, -nt, -tis, -mus to the stem
of the Present Perfect. Infinitives likewise.

78. Exercise
Form the Participles of:
negāre, refuse, negate
adaptāre, adapt, make fit
expectāre, wait for, expect
recuperāre, recuperate, reclaim

79. Sentences
1. Quod (that which) erat demonstrandum. Often
   abbreviated Q.E.D. at the end of a mathematical demonstration.
2. Omnēs hominēs errātūrī sumus.
3. Vōx clamantis in desertō.

80. The Fourth and Fifth Declensions

Two additional declensions exist in Latin which contain a smaller number of words, but some of considerable importance. The Fourth Declension is characterized by ū in the stem; the Fifth by ē. Paradigms follow:

4 Masc.	4 Fem.	4 Neu.	5 Masc.	5 Fem.
sensus	tribus	genū	diēs**	rēs
sensūs	tribūs	genūs	dieī	reī
sensuī	tribuī	genuī	dieī	reī
sensum	tribum	genū	diem	rem
sensū	tribū	genū	diē	rē
sensūs	tribūs	genua	diēs	rēs
sensuum	tribuum	genuum	diērum	rērum
sensibus	tribibus*	genibus	diēbus	rēbus
sensūs	tribūs	genua	diēs	rēs
sensibus	tribibus	genibus	diēbus	rebus

(*or tribubus; **sometimes fem.)

Fourth Declension nouns are generally masculine, although some fourteen are commonly feminine, and four main ones are neuter. The Supine, a special verbal noun (see par. 118, below) belongs to the Fourth Declension.

All Fifth Declension nouns except the masculines diēs (day) and meridiēs (noon), are feminine. The endings of this declension are analogous to, and patterned after, those of the First Declension.

sensus	sense
tribus	tribe
genū	knee [genuflection]
diēs	day
rēs	thing [real]

80a. Reading

Quid est miraculum? Lēx nātūrālis ūnicī cāsūs.
Carnis sunt desertōrum locōrum tentātiōnes; mentis,
illae cultūs humānī. [E.R-H.]

PART THREE: READING LATIN

LESSON XV

81. Introduction

Now the first time, dear Reader, you can act
as a real reader. Nunc prīmum, cāre lēctor,
agere potes vērum lēctōrem.

To help you, the words in the following paragraphs have been marked to distinguish between
the long and short syllables in the forms of
verbs and nouns. Hence, you may know immediately what is a nominative or an ablative in
a noun, an infinitive or a perfect in a verb.

        carta must be nominative
        cartā must be ablative
        misēre must equal misērunt, they sent
        miserē   miserably
        latē is an adverb, widely
        late is the Imperative: hide!
        monēre must be the Second Conjugation
        mittere must be the Third Conjugation
        audīre must be the Fourth Conjugation
        legit must be the Third Conjugation

82. Lectura Prima

From the Peterborough   William of Malmsbury
   Chronicle (1087)   Gesta Regum III, 279

    Thrice King William   Ter quotannīs quibus
wore his crown every   erat in Angliā rēx
year as often as he was   Guilhelmus corōnam
in England. At Easter   suam portābat, Paschā
he wore it at Winches-   apud **Wintoniam, Pentē-**
ter, at Whitsuntide at   costen apud Westmonas-
Westminster, at Mid-   terium, nātāle Dominī
winter at Gloucester.   apud Gloecestram. Ubī
And then were with the   erant cum rēge omnēs
King all the rich men   dīvitēs tōtius regnī

over all England:	Angliae, archiepiscopī
archbishops, and bis-	et episcopī, abbatēs et
hops, abbots and earls,	ducēs, ministrī et mīlitēs.
thegns (thanes) and	(Adapted) (RS 90:2:279)
knights.	

83. Lectura Secunda
De morte turpissimā Godwinī traditoris

Rēx Anglōrum Eadwardus Paschālem solemnitātem
apud Wintoniam celebrāvit. Rēge igitur in hāc
solemnitāte ad mēnsam sedente, cum pincerna vinum
ad mēnsam apportāret, pedem unum ad pavīmentum
offendit. Sed alter pēs pincernae auxiliō fuit
nē caderet. Godwinus autem comes ac gener rēgis
dē mōre rēgī assedēns dīcit: "Frāter frātrī
auxiliō fuit." Rēx īrōnicē respondēns dīcit:
"Frāter meus posset regī auxiliō esse nisi
fuissent mala facta Godwinī." Godwinus per-
turbātus respondit: "non ignōrō, rēx, quia
dē morte frātris tuī Alfredī agitātus generum
tuum habēs suspectum. Sed Deus vērax et
iustus, pānem nōn permittat guttur meum sine
suffōcātiōne transīre, sī umquam frāter tuus
per consilium meum mortī propior aut ā vītā
remōtior fuit." Posteā pānem ā rēge benedīctum,
Godwinus mittit in ōs, et propter malam con-
scientiam ab illō suffōcātus est. Rēx autem
Godwinum exanimem vidēns: "Extrahite," ait,
"hinc canem hunc et traditōrem et in quadriviō
sepelīte. Indignus enim est Christiānā pāce."

Ex Chronicā Matthaeī Paris. Ad annum 1053.
(Adapted) RS 57:1:523

84. Lectura Tertia
dē Normannōrum victoriā

Rēx Anglōrum Eadwardus in Nātivitāte Dominī
cūriam suam apud Westmonasterium tenuit, et
ecclēsiam extrā urbem **Londiniārum ā fundāmentīs**
construxerat in honōre Sānctī Petrī Apostolōrum
principis, cum magnā glōriā dēdīcārī fēcit. Sed

inter dēdīcātiōnis solemnitātēs et ante, rēx
gravī infirmitāte labōrāvit. Tertiā diē quasī
ā morte resuscitātus, graviter et profundē sus-
pīrāns ait: "Deus omnipotens, sī nōn est illūsio
phantastica, sed vīsio vēra, dā mihī facultātem
adstantibus narrandī; sī ē contrariō sit falsa,
rogō facultātem narrandī mihī negēs. Sed mox
ōrātiōne termināta satis clārē dicit: "In
vīsiōne meā pīissimī monachī lectum adībant.
Deī nuntiī exclamantēs: 'Quia principēs Angliae,
ducēs, episcopī et abbātēs non sunt ministrī
Deī sed diabolī; dōnāvit regnum Angliae unō
annō inimicō, demonēsque terram tōtam pervagābunt.'
Cumque populō demonstrātūrus essem ut peccatōrēs
confessionem facerent et misericordiam peterent,
more Ninivītārum secundum lībrum Ionae in sacrā
pagīnā, 'Neutrum erit,' monachī aiunt, 'quia nec
Anglī poenitentiam factūrī sunt nec Deus com-
miserātūrus est. Nullam ergō tantārum calamitā-
tum poterimus sperāre remissionem.'"

Revelationis vēritās posteā Anglīs demonstrāta
est. Anglia aliēnigenārum nunc est habitātiō
et exterōrum dominātiō, nullus Anglus aut dux
aut episcopus aut abbas est, nec etiam ullus
miseriae fīnis.
Matthaeus Pariensis ad annum 1066 (Adapted)

85. Lectura Quarta

Vir erat in cīvitāte Assisiī, Franciscus
nōmine. Erat inter vānōs hominum fīliōs ēducā-
tus iuvenilī aetāte. Post parvam litterārum
nōtitiam lucrātīvīs negōtiīs dēputātus est.
Sed caelestī assistente praesideō nōn aberrat
inter lascīvōs iuvenēs nec inter cupidōs mer-
cātōrēs sperat in pecūniā. Inerat enim iuvenis
Franciscī cordī commiserātiō ad pauperēs
liberālis. Promittit igitur dominō deō ut
numquam pauperī petenti auxilium negātūrus
sit. Usque ad mortem observāvit promissum.
Narrābat posteā quod etiam existēns in veste
saeculārī vōcem dīvīnī amōris sine cordis
mutātiōne audīre nōn poterat.

Suprā humānum modum patientia Franciscī, mūnificentia, ēlegantia mōrum. Vir dē Assisiō
valdē simplex obviāns Franciscō exclamāvit quod
Franciscus magna factūrus esset et propter hōc
ab omnibus fidēlibus magnōperē honōrandus.

Ignorābat autem Franciscus consilium Deī.
Et facta est super eum vīs Dominī et mutātiō
dextrae Deī,*affligēns corpus dolōribus sīcque
adaptāns animam ad sanctī spiritūs unctiōnem.
Nocte vērō palātium pulchrum et magnum cum
mīlitāribus armīs crucis signō signātīs Clementia
dīvīna Franciscō dēmonstrāvit. Itaque māne in
Āpūliam ad proximam cīvitātem Spōlētum ad comitem
līberālem īvit, prō līberātiōne terrae sanctae
secundum vīsiōnem. Sed in viā allocūtiō familiāris
vōcis Dominī facta est: "Francisce, quis potest
melius facere tibī, dominus aut servus, divēs aut
pauper?"

Franciscus: "Et dominus et divēs melius
facere possunt."

Dominus: "Recuperā prō servō Dominum et prō
paupere homine dīvitem Deum."

Et Franciscus: "Quid mihī imperās, Domine,
facere?"

Et Dominus ad Franciscum: "Redī in terram tuam;
vīsiō crucis praefigūrat spirituālem effectum,
non corporālem."

Celeriter redit versus Assisiam secūrus et
laetus et iam exemplar obtemperantiae factus
exspectābat Dominī voluntātem.

Secundum Legendae Sanctī Franciscī Capitulum Primum

---

* cf. Ps. 76:11 (Vg); 77:11 (EV).

86. **Two Vocabularies**
    1. Words whose meaning and phonetics correspond
       strictly with English.

    calamitās, -ātis (f.)   miseria, -ae (f.)
    constructus, -a, -um   pavīmentum, -ī (n.)
    dēdicāre; dēdicātiō, -ōnis (f.)   (pavement)
    demon, -onis (m.)   perturbāre
    diabolus, -ī (m.) (diabolical,   phantasticus, -a, -um
      devil)   remissiō, -iōnis (f.)
    facultās, -ātis (f)   suspectum, -ī (n.)
    illūsiō, -iōnis (f.)   vīsiō, -iōnis (f.)
    infirmitās, -ātis (f.)

    2. Special Word Lists
       Ad Lecturam Secundam
       ait quoth he; aiunt quoth they
       cadere to fall
       exanimis, -e lifeless
       extrahere to drag out/away
       gener, -ī (m.) son-in-law
       guttur, -ris (n.) throat
       habet he has
       indignus honore unworthy of an honor
       mēnsa, -ae (f.) table
       offendere to knock, stumble, offend
       pedem offendere to stumble
       ōs, ōris (n.) mouth
       pincerna, -ae (m.) cup-bearer
       quadrivium, -ī (n.) cross-reads (four corners)
       quia because
       assedēns sitting
       trāditor, -ōris (m.) traitor
       vidēns seeing
       Ad Lecturam Tertiam
       adstare to stand by
       aliēnigena, -ae (m.) foreign-born
       confessiō, -iōnis (f.) confession

cūria, -ae (f.) court
fundāmentum, -ī (n.) foundation
inimīcus, -ī (m.) enemy (the enemy, hence, the
 devil)
labōrāre to toil, labor
meus, -a, -um mine, my
Ninivīta, -ae (com.) a native of Nineveh
pervagārī to wander abroad
princeps, -cipis (m.) leader, chief
quasi as if
sacra pagīna,-ae Holy Writ, Bible
satis enough
suspīrāre to sigh
termināre to end, finish
mox soon
Ad Lecturam Quartam
aetās, -ātis (f.) age
nōtitia, -ae (f.) knowledge
negōtium, -i (n.) business (cf. Sect. 140, 4d)
obviāre to meet on the road
praesidium, -ī (n.) protection
via, -ae (f.) road

86a. Varia Franciscana

1. Mihī absit glōriārī nisi in cruce Dominī.
   (Gal. 6:14, taken as the motto of the Order of
   Saint Francis).
2. Sed videāmus singula diligenter: non enim debet
   nōs taedēre ista cōgitāre, quae ipsum Dominum nōn
   taeduit tolerāre. (Meditātiōnes, 74)
3. Vērus Deī cultor, Christīque discipulus, quī
   Salvātōrī omnium prō sē crucifixō perfectō con-
   figurārī desiderat, ad hoc potissimum attentō
   mentis conātū debet intendere, ut Christī Iēsū
   crucem circumferat iugiter tam mente quam carne.
   (Lignum vītae, Praefātio).
3. Non est dolor sicut dolor suus, exceptō dolōre
   filiī, ad cuius exemplar dolor suus assimilātur.
   (suus = Marīae matris Jēsū) (Bonaventura, Sermo
   in Dominicō diē infrā Octav. Epiphaniae, 1).

LESSON XVI

87.   Relative and Interrogative Pronouns

Beātus vir quī superāvit temptātionem.
Blessed the man who has overcome temptation.

In this sentence, "quī" is a relative pronoun
expressing identity between two persons in the
two clauses of the sentence. In the simplest case
the person who is identified by "quī" is in the
nominative in both clauses, as in our example:
    "vir" is the subject of the main clause
    "quī" is the subject of the subordinate clause

However, in the example: Virum beātum putō
quī est mundō corde, we have expressed the same
relation between the object "virum" in the main
clause and the subject "quī" in the subordinate
clause. Or we may have cases such as:

   Vir beātus quem omnēs amant. Beātī quī nōn
       vīdērunt et crēdidērunt.
   Vērum bonum est cuius omnēs cupidī sunt.
   Obtemperā hominī ā quō gubernātus es.
   Obtemperā hominī cuī deus parcit.
   Bellō quod per longum tempus dūrāvit
       prōvinciae vastātae sunt.
   Sēcūrae cīvitātēs quās cīvēs, nōn mūrī, prōtegunt.
   Reverteris in terram dē quā sumptus es. Quī
       pulvis es, in pulverem reverteris.

Obviously, then, the gender and number of the
relative are determined by the gender and
number of the noun in the main clause. The
Reader, therefore, in looking at a Latin sentence
containing a form of quī, quae, quod, should
always first try to understand the main clause
fully, proceed to identify the noun in the
main clause to which the relative pronoun
points in gender and number, and, finally,
analyze the relative clause and the function of the relative pronoun in it. Wilhelmus
rēx Angliam invāsit quem Edwardus rēx propter
revēlātiōnem expectāverat.

Wilhelmus rēx Angliam occupāvit cuius principēs
   indignī erant.
Wilhelmus rēx Angliam intrāvit cuī mox omnēs
   obtemperāvērunt.
Wilhelmus rex Angliam gubernat cuius rex
   Haraldus in proeliō mortuus erat.
Wilhelmus rex Angliam taxāvit quod facere
   nullus rex anteā potuit.
In this last sentence "quod" identifies neither
William nor England but the verb of the main
clause "taxāvit." (taxed)

Latin possesses two basic interrogative/relative pronouns
which are distinguished from one another in the nominative singular, but in certain other cases are identical
in form: *quī* and *quis*. *Quī* as a relative pronoun may be
translated: who, which, what that. As an interrogative
pronoun, it carries the English meaning of who? which?
what? what kind or sort of? When used to refer to persons, it asks for the character. *Quis* as an interrogative pronoun may be translated who? which? what? When
used of persons, it usually asks the name. But *quis* is
also used as an indefinite pronoun, with the meaning of
anyone, anybody, anything, someone, somebody, something.
A common use is in the form *siquis*, in conditional sentences: 'if anyone....'

The declension of the basic words, *qui* and *quis* follows:

Sing.						
quī	quae	quod		quis	quis	quid
cuius	cuius	cuius		cuius	cuius	cuius
cuī	cuī	cuī		cuī	cuī	cuī
quem	quam	quod		quem	quem	quid
quō	quā	quō		quō	quā	quō

Plur.						
quī	quae	quae		quī	quae	quae
quōrum	quārum	quōrum		quōrum	quārum	quōrum
quibus	quibus	quibus		quibus	quibus	quibus
quōs	quās	quae		quōs	quās	quae
quibus	quibus	quibus		quibus	quibus	quibus

In two ways these basic words can be modified to intensify
the indefiniteness or generality of their reference, thus
producing a rich variety of indefinite, interrogative and
relative pronouns.. First, by doubling: *quisquis;* second,

by adding as suffixes certain intensifying particles, as:
-cumque (-cunque), *-dam*, *-libet*, *-nam*, *-piam*, *-quam*, *-que*,
-vis. Look these forms up in an unabridged dictionary.
Note also such double compounds as *quiviscumque*, *quisquis-libet*.

88. <u>Interrogative Adverbs and Adjectives</u>. The commonest are:

> quandō? when
> quantus? how big?
> cūr? why?
> quot? how many?
> quālis? of what kind or sort?
> quam? how much?
> quousque? how long?

89. <u>Sentences</u>
Quis mīlitat suō stīpendiō? Who goes to war at
  his own expense?   [I Cor. 9:7]
Quid putās? What do you think?
Cuius fēminae vestis est?
Quālis artifex pereō?
Quousque tandem?
Cuī donō novum lībrum?
Quem annum computāmus hodiē?
Quam horam campānae sonant?
Quōrum populōrum regēs et mīlitēs terram sanctam
  expugnāvērunt?

90. The declension of "qui" in verse

Matthieu de Vendômes poem <u>Contrā Davum vitiōsum</u>,
  written about 1170 A.D.
(The verses are in the elegiac meter, in which
hexameters, and pentameters. alternate; follow
our accents in reading them aloud.)

Nón nequit ésse nocéns Davús nátásque nocére;
Dúm nequit ésse nocéns, dégener ésse putát:

<u>Quī</u> fideī, <u>quī</u> iuris inops, <u>quī</u> fraude labōrat,
<u>Quī</u> volat in vetītum, <u>quī</u> pietātis eget.

Cuius honor quod honōre caret, cuius tenor esse
Absque tenōre, fidēs: non habuisse fidem.

Cuī scelus est vītāre scelus, cuī crīmen: egēre
Crīmine, cuī fraudis est puduisse pudor.

Quem leporem timor esse probat, quem praeda leonem
Caupo caprum, vulpem furta, rapīna lupum.

Quō duce mendicat ratiō, quō praeside virtus
Migrat in exilium, deperit aegra fidēs.

Sola vocātivī casūs inflexiō Davō
Parcit; ibī vōx nōn articulāta tacet.

90a. Quid sit credere Deō, vel in Deum, vel Deō
[Peter Lombard, Sententiarum Libri IV, Lib.
III, Dist. XXIII, Cap. IV (pp. 656-657)]
    Aliud enim est credere in Deum, aliud credere
Deō, aliud credere Deum. Credere Deō, est credere vēra esse quae loquitur; quod et malī faciunt; et nōs credimus hominī, sed nōn in hominem. Credere Deum, est credere quod ipse sit
Deus; quod etiam malī faciunt. Credere in
Deum, est credendō amāre, credendō in eum īre,
credendō eī adhaerere et eius membrīs incorpor-
ārī. (Adapted from Augustine)

LESSON XVII

91. Numbers (numerals)

The first three cardinal numbers, unus, duo,
trēs are inflected.

N.	ūnus	ūna	ūnum	duò	duae	duo
G.	ūnius	ūnius	ūnius	duōrum	duārum	duōrum
D.	únī	ūnī	ūnī	duōbus	duābus	duōbus
A.	ūnum	ūnam	ūnum	duōs	duās	duo
Ab.	ūnō	ūnā	ūnō	duōbus	duābus	duōbus
N.	trēs	tria				
G.	trium	trium				
D.	tribus	tribus				
A.	trēs	tria				
Ab.	tribus	tribus				

The full list of the cardinal numbers follows:

ūnus, ūna, ūnum	I
duo, duae, duo	II
trēs, tria	III
quattuor	IV
quīnque	V
sex	VI
septem	VII
octō	VIII
novem	IX
decem	X
ūndecim	XI
duodecim	XII
tredecim	XIII
quattuordecim	XIV
quīndecim	XV
sēdecim	XVI
septendecim	XVII
duodēvīgintī	XVIII
(octōdecim)	

ūndēvigintī	XIX
(novemdecim)	
vīgintī	XX
vīgintī ūnus or	
(ūnus et vigintī)	XXI
trīgintā	XXX
quadrāgintā	XL
quīnquāgintā	L
sexāgintā	LX
septuāgintā	LXX
octōgintā	LXXX
nōnāgintā	XC
centum	C
ducentī,-ae, -a	CC
trēcentī	CCC
quadringentī	CCCC
quingentī	D
sēscentī	DC
septingentī	DCC
octingentī	DCCC
nōngentī	CM
mīlle (uninflected in	
singular)	M
but mīlia	
mīlium	
mīlibus	
mīlia	
mīlibus	

Quīnque is called a "cardinal" numeral
because from quinque as a "cardo," a
hinge, the door swings open into the
realm of words derived from five:

the fifth	five times	five a piece	fivefold
quintus	quinquiēs	quīnī	quintuplex

92. List of Numbers
Accordingly, the numerals may be tabulated in
one list:

	Cardinal	Ordinal	Numeral Adverb	Distribu- tive	Multipli- cative
I	ūnus	prīmus	semel	singulī, -ae, -a	simplex
II	duo	secundus	bis	bīnī	duplex
III	trēs	tertius	ter	ternī, trīnī	triplex
IV	quattuor	quārtus	quater	quaternī	quadruplex
V	quīnque	quīntus	quinquiēs*	quīnī	quintuplex
VI	sēx	sextus	sexiēs	sēnī	
VII	septem	septimus	septiēs	septēnī	
VIII	octō	octāvus	octiēs	octōnī	
IX	novem	nonus	noviēs	novēnī	
X	decem	decimus	deciēs	dēnī	
XI	ūndecim	ūndecimus	undeciēs	undēnī	
XII	duodecim	duodecimus	duodeciēs	duodēnī	
XIII	tredecim	tertius decimus	terdeciēs	ternī dēnī	
XIV	quattuordecim	quartus decimus	quaterdeci- ēs	quaternī dēnī	
XV	quīndecim	quīntus decimus*			
XVI	sēdecim	sextus decimus			
XVII	septendecim	septimus decimus			
XVIII	duodēvīgintī	duodēvīcēnsimus			
XIX	undēvīgintī	undēvīcēnsimus			
XX	vīgintī	vīcēnsimus	viciēs		

*etc.

93. Readings

DĒ PARĪ ET IMPARĪ EX IISQUE COMPOSITĪS.
Omnis vērō numerus aut pār aut impār est.
Pār est, quī in duās aequās partēs dīviditur,
ut duo, quatuor, sex; impār, qui in duās
aequās partēs dīvidī nōn potest, ut tria,
quīnque, septem. Deinde ex imparibus quīdam ex imparibus tantum imparēs sunt, ut
tria, quīnque, septem; quīdam etiam multi-
tūdine constant, ut novem, quīndecim, vīgintī ūnus.... At in hīs, quī parēs sunt,
plura discrimina sunt; at parēs sunt, et
dīvidī possunt. Ceterī vel ex paribus
parēs, vel ex paribus imparēs, vel ex imparibus parēs.... Parēs ex paribus sunt ut
quatuor, quia ex bis bīnīs; octo, quia ex
bis quaternīs constant. Parēs ex imparibus sunt, quī parēs imparī multiplicātiōne fiunt, ut bis ternī sex, aut quīnquiēs

quaternī vīgintī...et hī quī imparem nu-
merōrum multitūdinem parī multiplicātiōne
consummant, ut cum bis ter in sex, et quater quīnque vīgintī fiunt....Atque ex hīs
ipsīs quīdam in duās partēs dīvisī proti-
nus in parēs numerōs recīdunt, quīdam semel saepiusve per parēs replicātī citrā
singulāritātem in imparēs resolvuntur;
nam duodecim et vīgintī semel per parēs
dīvidī possunt, at quadrāgintā octo nimirum bis vīcēnōs quaternōs, inde bis duo-
dēnōs, deinde bis sēnōs omnēs adhuc parēs
efficiunt, novissimē in ternōs imparēs dē-
cidunt. Itaque nēmó longius prōcēdere si-
milī multiplicātiōne potest, quīn ut dup-
licātiōne revolūta adscenditur, sīc per
replicātiōnēs item in plurēs partēs dig-
eritur. Nam vīgintī et bis dēna sunt, et
quīnquiēs quaterna, et deciēs bina, et
quater quīna. (Martianus Capella, De Nup-
tiīs Philologiae et Mercuriī, VII, 748)

Sanctus Hieronymus, Epistula CXXIII (3) ad
Rusticum (PL 22. 1044):

Septiēs cadit iustus et resurgit (Prov. 24. 16).
Sī cadit, quomodō iustus? Sī iustus, quomodō
cadit? Sed iustī vocābulum nōn amittit, quī per
poenitentiam semper resurgit. Et nōn sōlum
septiēs sed septuāgiēs septiēs dēlinquentī, sī
convertātur ad poenitentiam, peccāta donantur
(Mt. 18. 22). Cuī plus dīmittitur, plus
dīligit.

A Tombstone Inscription from the second half
of the 4th century:

Aurelia Agapetilla ancilla Dei quae dormit
in pāce, vīxit annīs (annōs) xxi, mēnsēs iii,
diēs iiii, Pater fēcit.

(Cabrol-Leclercq, 1.2. 1944f. Cemetery of
St. Agnes, near the Mausoleum of Constantia)

94. Reading
Triumphs of Augustus (from the <u>Res Gestae</u>
                              <u>Divi Augustī</u>) *

c.4 Annō ūndēvīcēsimō Augustus rem publicam
pācāvit, quīngenta mīlia civium Rōmānōrum
iurāvērunt Augustō. Bis triumphāvit, vīciēs
semel imperātor appellātus est. In triumphīs
ductī sunt rēgēs līberī novem. Quīnquāgiēs
et quīnquiēs senātus supplicāvit deīs prō
victōriīs Augustī. Consul erat ter deciēs et
scrībēbat monumentum quod narrat facta vītae
suae, septimum et trīgēsimum annum tribūnīciae
potestātis. [1.1-3, 3.16, 4.21-22, 27, 26, 28-30]

c.8 Augustī temporibus civium Rōmānōrum
capita numerāta sunt quadrāgiēns centum mīlia
et sexāgintā tria mīlia. Bis athlētārum
spectāculum populō dōnāvit, lūdōs quater
propriō nomine, sub aliōrum nomine ter vīciēs.
Prō spectāculō terram excāvit in longitūdinem
mille et octingentōs pedēs, in lātitūdine mille
et ducentōs. Ut trīgintā ferē mīlia servōrum
ad dominōs redīrent, imperāvit. [8.3-5; 22.33-
36; 23.43-45; 25.1-3] Adapted.

95. Days of the Week
The medieval calender counts the days of the
week by ordinals.

fēria secunda	Monday
fēria tertia	Tuesday
fēria quārta	Wednesday
fēria quīnta	Thursday
fēria sexta	Friday
Sabbatum	Saturday
dominica	(the Lord's day) Sunday
septimāna	week (containing seven days)
septimāna sāncta	Holy Week (Easter)
quintāna fēbris	every fifth day recurring fever (like malaria)

*Cf. No. 12, pp. 233ff, below.

96. Vocabulary

    a. For Section 93

ascendere to mount up, rise (pass.: be raised)

citrā (prep. with acc.) apart from, except

constare to consist in, be composed of, rest upon (with abl.). Note: this verb is used in such varied ways that it should be studied in an unabridged dictionary.

consummāre (of numbers) cast or sum up, make up or amount to

decīdere cut down reduce, diminish

digerere divide, distribute

discrimen, -inis (f.) that which separates or divides two things from each other, difference, separation, interval

duplicātiō, -ōnis (f.) doubling, multiplication by two

efficere (of numbers) to make out, yield, amount to

fierī (pass. of facere) equal(s) See Sect. 122c below.

impār, -is odd (number), unequal

multiplicātiō, -ōnis (f.) multiplication

multitūdō, -inis (f.) the plural number (also: numerus multitudinis); multiple

novissimē (adv.) last, finally

numerus, -ī (m) number

pār, -is even (number), equal

prōtinus (adv.) immediately, straightway

quīn (conj. with subjunctive) tr. into Eng. as: but that, or without (with participial clause).

recīdere reduce, diminish

replicāre reduce

replicātiō, -ōnis reduction (of a number)

resolvere separate, resolve (into)

revolvere (revolūtus, -a, -um) repeat (participle: repeated)

singulāritās, -tātis (f) unity, the number one

The Names of the Numbers

one	uniō, -ōnis (f) singulāritās, -tātis (f)	five	quīniō, -ōnis (f)	
two	biniō, -ōnis (f) dyas, -adis (f)	six	sēniō, -ōnis (f)	
		seven	numerus sepentārius	
three	terniō, -ōnis (f) triniō, -ōnis (f)	eight	numerus octōnārius	
four	quaterniō, -ōnis (f)	nine	numerus nōnārius enneas, -adis (f)	
		ten	numerus dēnārius, etc.	

    b. For Section 94

alius, -a, aliud other, another

appellāre name, call

caput, capitis (n) head

ductus, -a, -um (having been) led

excavāre excavate

iurāre take an oath

latitūdō, -inis (f.) width

longitūdō, -inis (f) length

ludus, -ī (m) game

monumentum, -ī (n) monument

pacāre pacify

proprius, -a, -um proper, own

scribere write

senātus, -ūs (m) senate

supplicāre implore (cf. suppliant)

tribūnīcia potestās power as a tribune

triumphāre triumph, hold a triumph

LESSON XVIII

97. <u>Pronouns</u>

Intrāte, et <u>hīc</u> deī: come in, here (where we
are), too, are the Gods.

hīc Rhodus, hīc salta! (Don't tell us that you
could dance some wonderful dances in Rhodus):
This <u>here</u> is Rhodus; <u>here</u> dance!

When we are able to point to a thing in our
physical presence, we need not dress it up with
its full name. You and I are in a room together,
and I point to a picture with my finger; then,
the word "this" is all. Vague as "this" is,
compared to the more specific "picture," it
has the advantage of being demonstrated by my
finger. Hence, "this" is labeled, in grammar,
as a demonstrative pronoun, that is to say, as
a word that takes the place of a noun ("<u>prō</u>
nōmine" - "<u>instead of</u> a noun") because it may
be accompanied by a physical or mental gesture
of pointing which suffices to make the hint
specific. The lifting of my voice, or your
recalling of a sentence previously spoken or
written, may render the same service as the
finger. In building up its varieties of "prōnōmina," Latin was strictly logical. The
speaker, the listener, and the world outside
asked for the corresponding three circles em-
bracing the things and persons to which language may point. Instead of naming them explicitly, the speaker may point, in fact, to
three different groups:

1. things or persons going with the speaker
2. things or persons belonging to the realm
    of the listener
3. things or persons existing independently
    of either speaker or listener

The speaker's are "hīc, haec, hoc" – this man, this woman, this house here; and so is "hīc" here where I am, where we are.

The listener's are "iste, ista, istud" – this man, this woman, the house where thou art, where you are.

All that lies *outside* these two realms (called in grammar "third person") is "ille, illa, illud" – the people and things which neither you nor I dominate, that belong to the world of "it,"

This division into three pronouns, according to the true oral situation of speaker, listener, and outside realm, is more logical than the modern divisions of English "this" and "that"; or modern French "celui-ci," and "celui-là." It corresponds to the structure of the three persons and the three modes of Indicative (the objective mode of the world), Subjunctive (my own, the speaker's world), and Imperative (the listener's world). And the reader may look back here, with profit to Lesson XI and XII.

When two people talk together, what is hīc for the one, is iste for the other, and vice versa. Only in the use of ille both will agree. The exchange of these different pronouns in a tale, may serve as a beautiful illustration for the laws of articulated speech. When you say to me, "Come," and I answer, "I am coming" – as we said in our introductory lesson – then we cease to yell or shout, and, instead, begin to play the game of articulated speech in which people will take each other's words and vary them according to their role. Now, this is most true in the use of pronouns. What I call "hoc," would be "istud" for you, illud for some third person who is watching us.

Where the distinction between the three realms
of first, second and "third" person, seems
unimportant, Latin has a fourth, most general
pronoun: "is, ea, id." For instance, when
the speaker points to a complete relative
clause "(cīvitās) quae est maxima mundī," and
wishes to omit Cīvitās, he will write or say:
ea, quae est maxima mundī - the biggest city
in the world. Is, ea, id do not point to any
of three real worlds but to the rest of the
speech, as here to a relative clause. They
relate one part of speech to other parts and
this relation is not as real as the others,
but purely logical.

98.   Formation of These Pronouns.

As to the formation of these pronouns, it is
significant that the neuter ends in -d:

        iste   istud
        ille   illud
        is   id

The same way, we found   quī   quod
                              quis?   quid?

for the relative and interrogative pronoun in
the previous lesson. And other similar words
share this particular neuter ending in -d.
For example, corresponding to "alius," the
other, there is the neuter form "aliud," something else.

CORRESPONDING ADVERB:

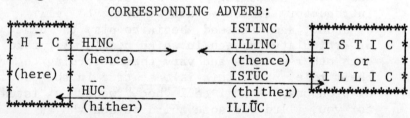

Phrases: haec tempora   our times
          intrāte, et hīc deī   "Enter, here,
            also, are gods."

The pronoun by which the self is stressed is
"ipse": ipse Caesar, Caesar himself; ipsum
bellum, war itself; ipsa animalia, even the
animals.

Goethe's motto: Nēmō contrā Deum, nisi Deus
    ipse.

99. List of Pronouns

singular			*plural*		
is	ea	id	eī	eae	ea
eius	eius	eius	eōrum	eārum	eōrum
eī	eī	eī	eīs	eīs	eīs
eum	eam	id	eōs	eās	ea
eō	eā	eō	eīs	eīs	eīs
iste	ista	istud	istī	istae	ista
istius	istius	istius	istōrum	istārum	istōrum
istī	istī	istī	istīs	istīs	istīs
istum	istam	istud	istos	istās	ista
istō	istā	istō	istīs	istīs	istīs
ille	illa	illud	illī	illae	illa
illius	illius	illius	illōrum	illārum	illōrum
illī	illī	illī	illīs	illīs	illīs
illum	illam	illud	illōs	illās	illa
illō	illā	illō	illīs	illīs	illīs
hīc	haec	hoc	hī	hae	haec
huius	huius	huius	hōrum	hārum	hōrum
huic	huic	huic	hīs	hīs	hīs
hunc	hanc	hoc	hōs	hās	haec
hōc	hāc	hōc	hīs	hīs	hīs
ipse	ipsa	ipsum	ipsī	ipsae	ipsa
ipsius	ipsius	ipsius	ipsōrum	ipsārum	ipsōrum
ipsī	ipsī	ipsī	ipsīs	ipsīs	ipsīs
ipsum	ipsam	ipsum	ipsōs	ipsās	ipsa
ipsō	ipsā	ipsō	ipsīs	ipsīs	ipsīs
idem	eadem	idem	eīdem	eaedem	eadem
eiusdem	eiusdem	eiusdem	eōrundem	eārundem	eōrundem
eīdem	eīdem	eīdem	eīsdem	eīsdem	eīsdem
eundem	eandem	idem	eōsdem	eāsdem	eadem
eōdem	eādem	eōdem	eīsdem	eīsdem	eīsdem

100. Exercise

Note the following list of peculiar genitives and
datives. Form their nominatives and ablatives:

eius	istius	illius	alius	huius	ipsius	cuius
eī	istī	illī	aliī	huic	ipsī	cuī

tōtius	ūnius	utrius	utriusque	alterius	neutrius	sōlius
tōtī	ūnī	utrī	utrīque	alterī	neutrī	sōlī

Ullus and nullus are inflected in the same way as
the words given above. Example:

Tōtī mundō ūnus gubernātor praeest, sōlius regnī
pācis rēx; haec crēdimus, alia aliī populī vēra
esse putāvērunt. Nulla diēs sine līnea. Not a day
without a line.

101.   Compound Pronouns
1.   Idem. In "is quī," "vir quī," "ea fēmina quae,"
two persons in different clauses of one sentence are
identified as one. Sometimes, spoken language
needs underlining." when identity is emphatically
stated idem, eadem, idem, takes the place of is,
ea, id.

Semper idem	Always the same
Idem ipse lātrō	The very same thief once more (himself)
Nē bis in idem	There shall not be two punishments for one and the same crime

Quā mensūrā tū mensūrābis, eādem mensūrā
mensūrāberis.

2.   Uter and its derivative neuter have already
been discussed. Uter, utra, utrum, "which of
two" when enlarged to uterque means "each of
both," as "doctor iuris utriusque." The
syllable "que" is used in the same way in quisque,
quaeque, quidque, everybody.

suum cuīque   to everybody his share

similarly ūnus quisque, ūna quaeque, ūnum quodque
every one.

3. aliquis aliqua, aliquid, somebody, a certain, is so much a compound that after sĭ, nisi,
nē, num, quomodō, or quandō its simpler form
quis, quae, quid suffice to express the un-
certainty of "a certain," that is of somebody
whose name is uncertain or does not matter.
Sometimes it has little more than the force of
the indefinite article in English. (Cf. Sect.87).

Si qua virtūtum memōria post mortem, aliquī
semper memōrēs erunt virōrum innumerābilium,
quī bellō mundiālī vĭtam sacrificāvērunt.

102. <u>Personal Pronouns</u>

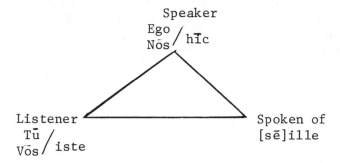

Relation of Personal and Demonstrative Pronouns

The triangle of speaker, listener, theme of
hĭc, iste, ille [see Par. 97, above], also leads
to the terms of me, you, and him. Let us now
analyze the order of these personal pronouns, in
general and in Latin in particular. In real life,
those who speak have names, and the theme on
whom or which they converse also has a name.
Petrus et Marcus dē Christō conversantur. Recor-
dātī sunt, quae Dominus Christus dĭxit eĭs. Petrus,
to himself, becomes, in humble slang, "poor me";
but Mark speaking is "thee" to Peter; and the
Lord is "him." How does Latin express this sub-
stitution of pro-nouns for proper names? In
ordinary conversation, the names are either

given in full or they are omitted and the understanding rests on the endings of the verbs used.
Hence Petrus will say to Marcus: Audī! quod dīcŏ.
But sometimes, the speaker will have to under-
score his own person; then Ego will be added.
Originally this would read: Ego Petrus dīxī.
Later the Petrus disappears and Ego alone stands.
The same is true of Thou, Latin Tū. Originally
it went: Bella gerant aliī, Tū, fēlix Austria,
nūbe; but the name of Austria may be omitted and
the Tū alone remains.

When a person is the theme of the conversation
(third person), and he is doing something to
himself, this "himself" in Latin is "sē" (accusative) "sibī" (Dative). When however the theme
between me and thee, us, and you, is not able to
speak or to act but is a dead object, the
third or thematic person is pronounced as either
"mine" or "thine," in Latin meus, -a, -um and tuus,
-a, -um. This is called the possessive pronoun.
Hosius, the great defender of the Trinity, wrote
to the Arian emperor: "tuum est vincere in
terrīs, meum et nostrum est invocāre deum."

This goes to show that the possessive pronouns so-called (mine, thine, ours, yours, theirs,
his, hers) are really parallel to "he, she, it,"
because the theme of speech must be either other
people or mere things. In the oldest layer of
speech, in the so-called period of animism, the
animals and flowers and the heavens and the seas
were all supposed to speak and to listen. Very
few themes like the infant (=non-speaking) in the
cradle were treated as its, as objects. Animals
were put on formal trial like men, like speaking
subjects. We moderns have reversed this process.
We hardly understand why in Latin trees are
feminine and gems and stones and fire are masculine. We have objectified even ourselves, the

speakers and the listeners, and we try to speak
of ourselves so objectively as though we did not
break the chains of nature by every word which
we speak from the bottom of our heart. Hence,
the order of the pronouns is very sick. We
may even go so far as to write of The Ego!
This cannot be expressed in good Latin. "The Ego"
makes me, the speaker, into an object, a third
person even with regard to my speaking. The
same speech sickness would result from the
phrase "The Thou." Yet, such attempts occur
amongst us. Latin should act as a clarifier so
that we resist such destructive nonsense.
Compare:

| Nominative | Ego | tū | (ipse) |
| Genitive | meī (meus) | tuī (tuus) | suī (suus) |

Our situation in which the speaker and listener
are never objects, but in which the theme may
be either alive or dead, gives the four pronouns:
three personal, the rest possessive.

   The same is true of the plurals: we, you,
they; ours, yours, theirs. The attempt has
been made in Fascism and Communism to speak of
"The We" and "The They" (=the enemies of one's
own class or race). But it is just as illegiti-
mate to speak of "The We" as of "The Ego." A
healthy language protects me and us, thee and you,
him and them; these pronouns may change at any
moment and enter the conversation in another one
of the forms or constellations. When the Bolshe-
viks, for example, speak to us, they speak of
themselves as "we." Rōmulus exclāmāvit ad Rēmum,
quandō lupa duōs frātrēs appropinquāvit. Sed
lupa, Nē timeātis, inquit, quia quamvīs lupa
vōs adiuvābō.

The three pronouns then, are like the prongs
of one fork, and they together constitute the
elementary and complete human claim to speak:
We are ego, tū, ipse, nōs, vōs, ipsī, in al-
ternation. Also, the things of the universe
are mine, thine, his, ours, yours, theirs, in
perpetual change. For instance, fifty years
ago, the air above my neighbor's house, in my
opinion, was his. I would then say: āēr suprā
domum tuam tuum est āēr. But we all know that
nowadays, this same air does not belong to the
owner of the land underneath, but may be passed
through by airplanes: āēr suprā domum tuam
nullius proprietāriī est, sed omnēs per id
volāre possunt." The personal pronouns, then,
and together with them, the possessive pronouns,
are new every minute; they are the most aroma-
tic, fleeting, decisive, and historical element
of speech, as they must remain interchangeable.
If not, life stagnates.

	Singular	
1st	2nd	3rd
ego	tū	[ipse, -a, -um
meī	tuī	suī [or ipsius]
(meus)	(tuus)	(suus)
mihī	tibī	sibī [or ipsī]
mē	tē	sē [or ipsum, -am, -um]
mē	tē	sē [or ipsō, -ā, -ō]

Sē applies both to singular and plural.

	Plural	
1st	2nd	3rd
nōs	vōs	ipsī, etc.
nostrī	vestrī	ipsōrum, etc.
[noster]	[vester]	
nōbīs	vōbīs	ipsīs
nōs	vōs	ipsōs, etc.
nōbīs	vōbīs	ipsīs

103. Reading. The Trinity.

Deus ipse in trinitātis dogmate apparet in
tribus persōnīs, quia pater loquitur: Ego;
fīlius audit   vōcem patris appellantem fīlium:
Hodiē generāvī tē. Spiritus autem quī prōcēdit
ex patre et fīliō, ex locūtōre et audītōre, exit
in mundum vīsibilem et tangibilem et thematicum.
Deus nōn est nōnnisi quī in tribus persōnīs
sermonis apparēre potest. Semper autem vīva
persōna remanent, neque umquam deum tractāre
licet quasi "illud" obiectum nostrae ratiōnis.
Neque enim est Deus significandus quasi meus
aut tuus, Gallicus aut Germanicus, Albus aut
Niger; quia prōnōmina possessīva ad exanima
melius pertinent quam ad vīvum fīlium, vīvifican-
tem spiritum, līberum creātōrem. Nōbīs hominibus
vīta līberā grātiā deī donātur, numquam habētur.
Cf- E. Rosenstock-Huessy, *Speech & Reality*, pp.25ff.

104. Readings

The Lord's Prayer or Pater Noster
[see Part I, a]

Pater noster quī es in coelīs
sānctificētur nōmen tuum;
adveniat regnum tuum
fiat voluntās tua sicut in coelō et in terrā.
da panem nōbīs cotidiānum hodiē
et dīmitte debita nostra sicut nōs
dīmittimus debitoribus nostrīs;
et nē nōs inducʌa in temptātiōnem
sed līberā nōs ā malō.

* * *

Pāx vōbīscum! Tē Deum laudāmus. Nōn huic terrae
creātus sum; patria mea coelum est, Deus magnus
Dominus quia ipsius est mare et ipse creāvit illud.
Dominī est terra et plēnitūdō eius, et ūniversī,

qui habitant in ea. Quid hoc ad negōtium
nostrum? Memor sis nostrī. Omnis anima
mīlitat suō sōlius perīculō [at its own peril
only]. Cum duo inimīcī disputent, saepe
neutrius victōria erit, quia ipsī aliī tertiō
victōriam parant.

* * *

The motto of Self-Reliance, used by Paracelsus:
"Alterius non sit quī suus esse potest."
[cf. Part V, No. 14, below].

104a.   Dē Iustitiā et Iūre secundum Iustiniānum

Iustitia est constāns et perpetua voluntās iūs
suum cuīque tribuēns. Iūris prūdentia est dī-
vīnārum atque hūmānārum rērum nōtitia, iustī atque inuistī scientia. (*Inst.*, 1.1)

LESSON XIX

The Two Verbal Stems

105. Introduction.

Dē nōminibus, dē adiectivīs, dē adverbiīs, dē praepositiōnibus, prōnōminibus, et numerīs omnia quae sunt necessāria nōbīs iam dīcta sunt. Dē verbōrum actiōnis formīs quoque--mittunt, ī, valeās, gubernātūrus, gubernāre, gubernāvisse, potēns, amạndus, factus, posse--multa ex parte tractāta sunt, tamen nunc restat ut pulcram coniugātiōnis harmoniam et ordinem complētum dēmonstrēmus.

Latin verbs have two stems:

gubernat	gubernāvit
est	fuit

Accordingly, the complete organization of the two stems is developed in the following paragraphs.

106. The Present Stem.

I come	I came	I shall come

Many languages proceed in three dimensions of time -- present, past and future. In grammar these three dimensions are called, as we have seen, tenses. Unlike English, Latin verbs have preserved the power of articulation through all three tenses [See Lesson XI]:

	present	past (imperfect)	future
1st Conj.	gubernat	gubernābat	gubernābit
2nd Conj.	movet	movēbat	movēbit
3rd. Conj.	legit	legēbat	leget
3rd I-stem	facit	faciēbat	faciet
4th Conj.	audit	audiēbat	audiet

We see that all these tense forms are built
upon a single stem, called the "present stem."
The form of the present tense for each verb
is determined by the characteristic vowel of
the conjugation to which it belongs: ă, ĕ, i, ī,;
the personal endings are the same. The imperfect
tense, again, differs only in the characteristic
vowel: ā, ē, iē, iē, the tense sign and personal
endings are identical throughout. In the future,
however, we see two distinct formations: one
analogous to that of the imperfect (1st and 2nd
conjugations); and one based upon vowel change
(3rd and 4th conjugations). The rules for
formation were given in Lesson XI, paragraphs
60 and 63. The important point to note here
is the dependence of these three tenses upon
the "present stem."

Two contests: [Matthieu de Vendôme, <u>Ars Versi-</u>
catoria, 174].
1. Certāmen avārī et prodigī:
    Prōdigus sīc invehit in avārum: Prandeō,
    iēiūnās; dō, quaeris; gaudeō, maerēs.
    Potō, sitis; retinēs, ērogō; sperō, timēs.
2. Certāmen mīlitis et clēricī:
    Mīles: Audeō, formidās; fugō, cēdis;
    mīlitō, cessās;
    Clēricus: Surgō, iacēs; valeō, dēficis;
    instō, latēs.

107. <u>The Subjunctive</u>. Sis, eat, vīvat, gubernet.
Wishes and fears in themselves are unfulfilled
dreams of the future. They do not need a speci-
fic Future Tense. Latin, therefore, has for each
simple stem, besides the three Indicatives of
Future, Past, and Present, two Subjunctives, of
Past and Present. The imperative has only
Present and Future.

The Subjunctive of the Present: vīvat, audiat,

moneat, sedeat, contains an "a" except where
the "a" is already in use for the Indicative
(i.e., 1st Conj., gubernat): then "e" is
used (e.g., gubernet). 1st Conj: "e"; 2nd,
3rd, 4th: "a."

The Imperfect Subjunctive is particularly handy
for the tyro, because it may always be formed
by appending the personal endings -t, -s, -m,
-nt, -tis, -mus to the present infinitive. This
is true for any verb, no matter with what vowel
or consonant it ends, e.g., gubernāret, īret,
legeret. From esse we have esset; from gubernāre,
gubernāret; from docēre, docēret; from audīre,
audīret.

Perfect and Present

108.
est	fuit	gubernat	gubernāvit
erit	fuerit	gubernābit	gubernāverit
erat	fuerat	gubernābat	gubernāverat

In Latin, the harmonious balance between the
three tenses, past, present, and future, is
duplicated. To every verbal stem for the
action in process (I am governing) may be
related a second stem, expressing the action
as accomplished: I have governed.

And again this accomplished action can be
expressed by the Perfect stem, (except for the
Imperative which naturally cannot be ordered
when the act is finished "perfectum enim
imperat nēmō"). Any Latin Perfect stem, then,
has three Indicatives and two Subjunctives.
Thus, Latin verbs show two symmetrical quintuplets,
one of the present stem and one of the perfect
stem, namely, three Indicatives and two Subjunctives.

Present Stem	Perfect Stem
gubernat	gubernāvit
Ind: gubernābat	gubernāverat
gubernābit	gubernāverit
gubernet	gubernāverit
Subj: gubernāret	gubernāvisset

Formation of the Perfect Stem
gubernāvit

109.   Not only does the conjugation of the Perfect
duplicate the conjugation of the Present stem;
Latin used reduplication quite literally to
build up the Perfect Stem. "Facit" has as
its perfect, in archaic Latin, "fhefhaked" as an
artist on an excavated vase signed his finished
work. That reduplication is a means of Latin
articulation we already know from sēsē (him,
her, it, accusative) for sē. Other languages
form the plural of nouns by repeating the noun
twice, e.g., Walla Walla. Latin does this,
too: quisquis, utut.* But in the main, Latin
was satisfied to use reduplication for verbs
and to duplicate only the first consonant of
the stem.

pellit	he batters
pepulit	he has battered
mordet	he bites
momordit	he has bitten

    Later, the increasing mass of compounds and of
secondary verbs derived from nouns asked for a
less powerful transformer from Present to
Perfect. The reduplicating verbs, therefore,
became rather like the "strong verbs" of English:

take	took
make	made etc.

---

*[= utcumque indefinite relative]

The verbs ending in the long vowels "$\bar{a}$" and "$\bar{\imath}$" simply appended -v$\bar{\imath}$ to their "$\bar{a}$" or "$\bar{\imath}$": gubernāvit, audīvit. For the rest, often the endings -u$\bar{\imath}$ and -s$\bar{\imath}$ were used instead of reduplication. The rule then is: the perfect stem of almost every verb ending in "-āre" or "īre" in the infinitive is no problem. The perfect stem of other verbs is problematic.

Exceptions: the old "dare" and "stare" though looking like verbs in "-āre" reduplicate "dedit" and "stetit."

Present Stem ⟶	Result	Present Stem ⟶	Result
legit	lēgit	canit	cecinit
facit	fēcit	parcit	pepercit
frangit	frēgit	⎧tradit	tradidit
tangit	tetigit	*⎨ēdit	ēdidit
emit	ēmit	------	meminit
edit	ēdit	videt	vīdit
movet	mōvit	poscit	poposcit
spondet	spopondit	vincit	vīcit
capit	cēpit	currit	cucurrit
tendit	tetendit	venit	vēnit
resistit	restitit	stat	stetit

So every word reaches its own conclusions, depending on sound (phonetic) difficulties and similar influences. This is not so atrocious as it seems because the great majority of verbs is late, ending in -āre, -āvit
                              -īre, -īvit

And certain regularities within the others make things easier.

1. As we have already seen very many verbs especially in long "$\bar{e}$" (2nd conj.) use "u$\bar{\imath}$" for the perfect.

*Compounds of dare.

docēre   monēre   terrēre   paenitēre   patēre   libēre
docet   monet   terret   paenitet   patet   libet
docuit   monuit   terruit   paenituit   patuit   libuit

maerēre   nitēre   florēre   albēre   latēre   rapĭre
maeret   nitet   floret   albet   latet   rapit
maeruit   nituit   floruit   albuit   latuit   rapuit

2. "s" instead of "u" is employed by many verbs,
especially those of consonant ending   (3rd conj.):

dūcit   dūxit   rīdet   rīsit   regit   rēxit
dīcit   dīxit   manet   mansit   sūmit   sūmpsit
vīvit   vīxit   plangit   planxit   tegit   tēxit
sancit   sanxit   labitur   lapsus est   auget   auxit
fulget   fulsit   indulget indulsit   laedit   laesit
invadit invasit flectit   flexit   cēdit   cessit
sentit   sensit   dīvidit   dīvīsit   trahit   traxit
gerit   gessit   ūrit   ussit   iubet   iussit
vincit   vīnxit

3. Some verbs make no change at all for the
perfect stem:

Pres.	Perf.	Pres.	Perf.
statuit	statuit	minuit	minuit
vertit	vertit	luit	luit

To this group, practically, belong the very
numerous compounds of:

currere	cucurrit	concurrit, recurrit
		succurrit, accurrit
		occurrit
tendere	tetendit	intendit, attendit, contendit

While the parent verbs reduplicate in the perfect, their compounds do not.

4. Latin often builds up its present stems from
the pure stem by certain additions or insertions.
Then, these specific elements which belong to
the Present are dropped before the Perfect can
be built. For example, in the Present stem
"sc" is frequently inserted to emphasize that

the action is getting under way. Discipulus
discit.

di-sc-it	dĭdicit	cre-sc-it	crēvit
no-sc-it	nŏvit	cogno-sc-it	cognōvit
	obdormi-sc-it	obdormīvit	

"m" or "n" often enters a Present stem and must
leave in the Perfect, e.g.,

tangit	tetigit
vincit	vīcit
-cumbit *	cŭbuit
fundit	fūdit
rumpit	rūpit
linquit	līquit
relinquit	relīquit

*Found with the "m" only in compounds such as
  accumbo; the form of the parent verb is cubo.

109a.   Ecologia secundum Johannem Calvinum.

Custodiae hortī praefectus est Adam. Id nōbīs
ostendit nōs possidēre quae Dominus nōbīs ad
manum contūlit, ut frūgālī et moderātō ūsū con‡
tentī, quod residuum erit servēmus. Agrum quī
possidet, fructum annuum ĭta percipiat nē pati‡
ātur fundum per incūriam decĭdere: sed posterīs
qualem accēpit, vel etiam melius excultum, tradere studeat. Fructibus īta vescātur nē quid
vel per luxum dilapidet, vel per negligentiam
corrumpī ac perīre sinat. Porro ut inter nos
vigeat ista parsimonia, et in bonīs quae Deus
nobis fruenda dedit, sedulitās: cogitet quisque sē in omnibus quae possidet, esse Deī oeco-
nomum.

* * * * * *

Deus nōn clam vivit in sēipsō duntaxat, sed
vigōrem suum profert in gubernātiōne tōtius
mundī.

LESSON XX
The Passive Voice

110. <u>Passive Forms</u>. Cīvitātēs gubernātae sunt. The cities have been governed. Sentences of this sort are already familiar to us from our study of the Participles. This is a passive sentence. The cities are not governing but are experiencing government. Latin, like English, has an auxilliary Passive for all Perfect forms, e.g.:

Perfect	: gubernātī sumus	we have been governed
Pluperfect	: gubernātī eramus	we had been governed
Future Perfect	: gubernātī erimus	we shall have been governed

In the Present system unlike the Perfect, Latin has a fully articulated formation:

	Ind.	Subj.
Present	: gubernātur	gubernētur
Imperfect	: gubernābátur	gubernārētur
Future	: gubernābitur	

For all the five Passives formed on the Present stem the endings are identical: -tur, -ris (-re), -r; -ntur,-mini, -mur. The Present Passive is here given beside the Active for comparison:

Act. Ind.	Pass. Ind.	Act. Sub.	Pass. Sub.
gubernat	gubernātur	gubernet	gubernētur
gubernās	gubernāris (-re)	gubernēs	gubernēris
gubernō	gubernor	gubernem	guberner
gubernant	gubernantur	gubernent	gubernentur
gubernātis	gubernāminī	gubernētis	gubernēminī
gubernāmus	gubernāmur	gubernēmus	gubernēmur

111. <u>Exercise</u>.
Give the other five forms of gubernābātur, gubernārētur, gubernābitur.

112. Passive Imperatives.
"Recordāre!" Recall! The Imperative of the
Passive "Let yourself be ruled" ends in -re:
gubernāre. Therefore, it looks like an active
infinitive, or like the rarer form of the Passive
Second Person Singular. The plural "Gubernāminī!"
shows the same imperfection. Reminisciminī!

113. Passive Infinitives. Latin has three active
and three passive infinitives, as follows:

	Active	Passive	
Present:	gubernāre	gubernārī	
Perfect:	gubernāvisse	gubernātum esse (-am, -ōs) (-ās, -a)	
Future :	gubernātūrum esse (-am, -ōs) (-ās, -a)	gubernātum (uninflected) īrī	

Thus the First Conjugation. The Second and
Fourth are analogous: monērī, monitum esse,
monitum īrī; audīrī, audītum esse, audītum
īrī. However, there is a shorter form in the
Third Conjugation: mittī, capī, legī, etc.,
for the present passive infinitive. The formation of Future Passive Infinitive arises from
the tendency in Latin to use an impersonal
passive construction for what in English would
be a generalized statement in the active voice.
Sperāmus nōs amātum īrī, we hope that we shall
be loved.

114. Deponent Verbs

Recordāre	Recall!
Reminiscere	Remember!

Here you see true passive Imperatives with
active meanings. Some verbs in Latin are
inflected three-quarters as passives and one-
quarter as actives. They truly are in a
middle voice, neither active nor passive, the
person is half-acting and half-reflecting, and

the verbal articulation takes no sides in the muddle.

delectātur	he takes delight
verētur	he is afraid

These show the situation of a middle voice rather clearly. These verbs are called Deponentia (Deponent Verbs). They inflect like passives all through their articulation. However, they are not entirely deprived of the possibilities of the Active Voice. They preserve the present active participle and the future active participle: sequēns and secūtūrus, (which in all verbs lack corresponding Passive Forms) Therefore, existing side by side are sequēns and secūtūrus, secūtus and sequendus, three of them with an active, and sequendus only with a passive.force.

sequitur	he follows
sequēns	following
sequendus est	he must be followed
secūtūrus est	he will follow

laetāmur	we are glad
laetāns	glad

nunc est laetandum	now let us be glad
laetūrus est	he will be glad

The Passive is the only form used for the rest.

recordātur	he recalls
hortāminī	you exhort
adipiscātur	may he acquire
venātus est	he has hunted
reminiscere	remember!
adeptus est	he has acquired
proficiscor	I depart
profectus sum	I have departed
fruitur	he enjoys
fruitūrus sum	I am going to enjoy

When the meaning is unambiguous, the participle
reverts to its passive meaning, e.g.:

adeptā libertāte   When liberty was attained

admirantur   they admire, they wonder
sequētur   he will follow
oriēns   the rising Sun. Orient
nascor, nātus est, nascī

Some of the Deponents mix an active Present
stem with a Passive Perfect:

audet   ausus est   audēre   to dare
gaudet gāvīsus est   gaudēre to rejoice
solet   solitus est   solēre   to be accustomed

The possession of an <u>active</u> participle for the
Perfect makes all the Deponents highly valuable
for the pattern of a long sentence. Instead of
many actions having to be coordinated, they now
can be organized more artistically: Post
Christum nātum saepe hominēs gāvīsī natālia
Dominī celebrāvērunt.

Equī viridī herbā prīmō vēre fruitī celeriter
incrassantur. Hence, some other regular verbs
use their Passive Participles in an active sense:

pōtus   having drunk
conātus   having dined
pransus   having breakfasted
iurātus   having sworn

Our word "jury" is a vestige of this pleasant
opportunity to speak of those who have sworn as
"iūrātī."

For verses of Alexander de Villa Dei on deponent
verbs governing the ablative case, cf. Sect.
138,3

The peculiar character of the Middle Voice
enables Latin to use passive forms where our
logic balks:

navigandum est:	one has to navigate
itur ad urbem:	literally, going is done toward the city (people flock to town)
desperātur:	the people despair
curritur:	one runs

Latin takes advantage of this strange potentiality to say "īrī": going to be done, to develop
a special Passive Infinitive of the Future:
spērāmus nōs amātum īrī, We hope that we
shall be loved. (cf. 113).

115. The Supine. In Paragraph 116, we find the form
gubernātum īrī as the future passive infinitive.
The word gubernātum is called a "supine." When
we see the form audītum we can immediately
identify it as the masculine ascusative or the
neuter nominative or accusative singular of
the perfect passive participle of the verb audit
"he hears." While this is correct, there is a
possibility that audītum may be one of two forms
of a construction peculiar to Latin. Take for
example the sentence, Legātōs ad Caesarem mittunt
rogātum auxilium. Translated, it reads, "They
send ambassadors to Caesar to ask help." Here
rogātum expresses purpose, and this form is
in use after verbs of real or figurative motion.
"Dare nuptum": 'give in marriage' literally
"give to be married."

Compare: Puellās laudātās esse audīvī.
    I have heard the girls to have been
        praised.
    Exspectō puellās nuptum īrī.
    I expect the girls to be going to be
        married.

The participial construction changes, the
supine construction remains unchanged.

Ab infīnītīvō distinguō supīnum. Supīnum
eō differt ab infīnītīvō quod construitur cum
verbō importante mōtum ad locum, ut: "vādō
nātātum" (I go swimming), sed nōn infīnītīvus.

The supine, in addition to an accusative
form, has an ablative.
    Mirābile dīctū

The action through which a certain quality,
in our example that of being astounding (mirā-
bile), is produced, is often put in this second
supine.
    iucundus audītū
    horribile vīsū
    facile dīctū

As the examples show, the second supine ends
in "ū," whereas the first supine ends in "um."

The supine got its strange name (which is:
to lie knocked out) from its indifference to
the "voice" of the word. One, indeed, cannot
tell whether in admirābile audītū the process
of hearing is understood in an active or in a
passive sense. The supine attitude of the
supīnum is due to the fact which we mentioned
before that there is, besides active and
passive, the middle voice, or "Medium" for
the verb.

In the following famous example from old
Cato, the difference in usage of the two
supines is well-illustrated.
    "Pater familiās prīmitus cubitū surgat,
    postrēmō cubitum eat. The father of
    the family shall be the first to rise
    from sleep, the last to go to sleep."

dēmonstrātum	for demonstrating
īre nuptum	for getting married
petītum	for seeking
quaesītum	for asking

That the Supine belongs to the Fourth or ū
Declension is more completely disclosed by
the second usage of the supine, the "Ablative
of the Supine":

incrēdibile dīctū	incredible to say
mirābilis vīsū	miraculous to see
difficilis cognitū	hard to know

116. Homō et Serpēns.

Cum homō per desertum īret, invēnit serpentem
frigōre afflictum, iacentem quasī mortuum. Quem
compassus cum homō in sinū suō fovēret, anguis
iam calēfactus, circumvolvit virum resumptīs
viribus eum intoxicātūrus.

Quī serpēns cum homō conquestus esset dē
ingrātitūdine, rēspondit: Tū scīs, quod nātūra
mea est quod non noceō nisi calēfactus, et hinc
venēnum effundere necesse habeō. Nōn inculpēs
mē, sī nātūram meam secūtus sum; sed tibī imputā,
quī mē calēfēcistī et fōvistī. (Ulrich, p. 189).

116a. **Verbs compounded from esse.** In Latin, esse, the
verb to be, has a usefulness beyond all its multi-
farious functions as a simple verb and as an auxilliary in the perfect passive system. With certain
prepositional prefixes it forms an exceedily ver-
satile class of verbs. In Psalm 23, we read "nihil
mihi deerit"; in Cicero, *De natura deorum*, 1.42:
"superstitio, in qua inest inanis timor deorum."
Among these verbs perhaps the most varied in meaning is **interest.** Look up the following in an unabridged Latin dictionary, and note how they are
used: abesse, adesse, conesse, deesse, inesse,
interesse, obesse, postesse, praeesse, praeteresse,
proesse, subesse, superesse.

LESSON XXI

Organization of the Verb for Practical Purposes

117. The Four Conjugations. In Lessons I, VII, and XI, the student has been introduced to the fact that most Latin verbs are grouped into four convenient classes or "conjugations." At this point it will perhaps be useful to examine and characterize these four conjugations. The First Conjugation provides the dominant pattern for the Romance Languages; it contains 1,800 simple verbs and 3,620 verbs in toto. Very few started out as verbs; most are secondary, derived from nouns or other words. This is also true of the Second Conjugation which contains 180 simple verbs, 570 in toto. thus these verbs in *ā* and *ē* have a secondary character. Among the derivative verbs, those in -āre are often transitive, expressing action: e.g., agitāre, to drive; ablactāre, to wean; bellāre, to war; nigrāre, to blacken. Those in -ēre express state of being: e.g., torpēre, to be full of torpor; horrere, to be full of horror; albēre, to be white; lucēre, to be full of light , to shine. The Fourth Conjugation consists of about 60 verbs, mostly descriptive in character. Many of them are derived from nouns.

The Third Conjugation consists of 570 original verbs and 1830 composite verbs. In contrast to the verbs of the other conjugations, those of the Third are pure verbal stems which convey original experiences of processes. We have seen that this conjugation affords greater variation in forms than the others, there being two primary divisions, the consonantal stems (e.g., mittō) and the I-stems (e.g., capiō). In this respect the Third Conjugation is analogous to the Third Declension. Note how Latin derives words from a primary form:

Primary Form	Derivatives
dūcere, draw lead	dūx, leader dūcātus, dukedom dūctilis, ductile
regere, direct	regnum, reign, rēgīna, queen regnāre, be king
pendere, weigh	pensum, weighed, pondus, weight; pensāre, weigh, judge, estimate

Those examples just given represent Third
Conjugation verbs from which nouns, adjectives,
and other verbs are formed. An example of
derivation from an adjective as primary form
is that of sacer, consecrated. Derivatives
include: sancīre, to sanction; sānctus, sacred,
holy; sacrāre, to sanctify; sanctificare, to
make sacred; sacrificāre, to sacrifice, per-
form sacrifice. Thus we see the primary
character of Third Conjugation verbs as against
the commonly derivative character of those of
the other conjugations.

118. The Principal Parts. In Lesson X, four forms
were given for each verb. This is the minimum
number of forms the student must know in order
to construct the entire conjugation of a given
Latin verb. While there are some variations,
most Latin-English dictionaries carry the
principal parts as follows:

I Present Active Indicative, 1st pers. Sing:mittō
II Present Active Infinitive   :mittere
III Perfect Active Indicative, 1st pers. sing:mīsī
IV Perfect Passive Participle, nom.sing.masc:missus
or First Supine   :missum

In regular conjugations, like the First, the
dictionary gives the following sort of entry:
amō, 1, The student will know from this that
the other parts are regularly formed.

In the case of deponent verbs or defective
verbs, corresponding alterations are made in

the listing of the principal parts, e.g.: vereor
verērī, veritus sum; odī, odisse.

119. <u>Exercise</u>. Look up the principal parts of the
following verbs: adiuvō, dēlectō, iubeō, legō,
fruor, faciō, ēgredior, pūniō, experior.

Classify the following verbs by the number of
their conjugation and supply the other principal
parts: capere, regere, amāre, iuvāre, audīre,
adipiscī, habēre.

120. <u>Reading</u>   Mundī Dīvisiō [1]
Omne hoc quicquid est cuī Mundī Coelīque
nomen indidimus, ūnum id est, et ūnō ambitū
sē cunctaque amplectitur.

Partibus differt, unde sōl oritur, Oriēns
nuncupātur, aut ortus; quō dēmergitur, vel,
Occidēns vel Occāsus; qua decurrit mediō diē,
Merīdiēs, ab adversā parte, ubī numquam
appāret, Septentriō, secundum septem stellās
ursī majoris quī septem triōnes id est septem
bovēs [2] appellābantur.

Julius I Pāpa ad episcopōs orientālēs: [3]
Nolīte errāre, frātrēs meī cārissimī, doctrīnīs
variīs et extraneīs. Instıtūta Apostolōrum
habētis: hīs fruīminī, hīs circumdāminī, hīs
dēlectāminī, hīs armāminī ut hīs frētī, circumdātī,
dēlectātī, armātī contrā cuncta inimīcōrum iacula
persistere valeātis.

---

[1]From Pomponius Mela, *De Chorographia*, 1.3
[2]Charles' Wain (Wagon) or the Plow.
[3]Cf. Sect. 122, p. 126, below.

LESSON XXII

121. Defective Verbs
"Bis duo sunt 'odī,' 'nōvī,' 'coepī,' meminīque
Quae retinent sensum praesentis praeteritīque."

Two verbs exist only in the Perfect forms:

meminit he remembers (takes genitive case)
odit   he hates

    Meminit shows the typical reduplication of a
Perfect stem. Its present stem is preserved
in reminiscitur; however, this deponent has
enlarged its stem with the inceptive suffix
-sc-. "Memoria," memory, is a reduplicated
word of the same meaning. "Memory" and "remember"
both imply, indeed most strongly, the hanging on
of our thought when the action is over; and obviously the language took care most emphatically
to advertize its principle of Perfect reduplication in their formation. Odit, he hates, is
also found only in the Perfect, Pluperfect, and
Future Perfect. Its subjunctives are, or course,
ōderit and ōdisset. Oderint dum metuant, "Let
them hate me if only they fear me." said Emperor
Tiberius of his subjects. And the Greek hero
Odysses got his name from his tenacity in
resentment.

    The verb nōvit is not found solely in the
Perfect. It has a Present, Imperfect, and
Future as well. The only reason that it must
be singled out for explanation is that in the
Present, noscit, it means, "he learns"; nōvit,
the Perfect, means, "he has learned" or "he
knows," which is of course almost a different
verb in English. [cf., Sect. 109, 4, above].

122. Some Irregular Verbs

    (a) velle and its derivatives: In the English

expression "willy-nilly" we have a corruption
of the Latin volens-nolens ("willing or unwilling). We will also recall that the battle-
cry of the Crusaders was Deus vult or Dieu le
veult, God wills it. The verb vult, "he wills,"
is irregular in Latin as is its English equivalent.
It has, most significantly, no imperative. Its
forms follow:

Pres. Ind.	Pres. Subj.	Impf. Ind.	Impf. Subj.
vult	velit	volēbat	vellet
vīs	velis	volēbās	vellēs
volō	velim	volēbam	vellem
volunt	velint	volēbant	vellent
vultis	velitis	volēbātis	vellētis
volumus	velimus	volēbāmus	vellēmus

Fut. Ind.	Pres. Inf.
volet	velle
volēs	
volam	Pres. Part.
	volēns
volent	
volētis	
volēmus	

From velle we have the noun voluntās (the will)
and the adjective voluntārius (voluntary). Derived from velle are the verbs nōlle and mālle.
Nōlle combines velle and the negative; mālle
stands for magis velle.

Nōlle means "to will not" or "to be unwilling."
Mālle means "to prefer." Their conjugation in
the present indicative, together with that of
volō, follows:

Sing.				
	3	vult	nōn vult	māvult
	2	vīs	nōn vīs	māvīs
	1	volō	nōlō	mālo

Plur. 3	volunt	nōlunt	mālunt
2	vultis	nōn vultis	māvultis
1	volumus	nōlumus	mālumus

Name and complete the following tenses:
nōlit, mālit, nōllet, māllet, nōluī, and māluī

Nōlle is richer than velle or mālle in that is
has an imperative. Nōlī and nōlīte are the im-
perative of nolle. Compare the letter of Pope
Julius I [Sect. 120].

"Nōlī turbāre circulōs meōs" verba Archimēdis
mathēmaticī sunt cum mīles invāderet domum ut
occideret eum.

"In Evangeliō secundum Johannem legimus:
"'Quī sitit, veniat et bibat, quī potest capere,
capiat. Nōn dīcit: velītis, nōlītis bibendum
vōbīs est atque currendum; sed quī voluerit,
qui potuerit currere atque potāte, ille vincet,
ille satiābitur."

                              --Hieronymus.

(b) Ferre: One of the most frequently used
Latin verbs is ferre, to bear or carry. In
English we find the abbreviation "cf.," meaning compare [Latin: confer]. When the Danai,
i.e., the Greeks, as an offering to Minerva
(Athena) put a horse before the city of Troy,
Virgil [A., 2:49] says a Trojan exclaimed "Quicquid id est, timeō Danaos et dona ferentēs."
"Whatever it is, I fear the Greeks even bearing
gifts." In this phrase, used proverbially today, the verb ferre is immortalized. Every
one of the principal parts of ferre is sur-
prising:

1) fert [3rd sing., present active indicative]
   is comparable to est and vult in having no
   vowel before the "t." In a corresponding
   manner are formed fers and fertis [2nd
   singular and plural].

2) ferre, the infinitive, is comparable to esse, velle, nōlle, mālle. Generally one can find the imperative of a verb by dropping off the -re from the end of the infinitive. This method will work for ferre, but the imperative is seen to be fer, a word ending in a consonant rather than the much more common vowel. Es, dīc, dūc and fac conform to this style.

Fer aequō animō, Bear it with equanimity.
Dīc cŭr hīc, Tell why [you are] here.

3) Tulit [3rd sing. perf. act. ind.]: est and fuit are a pair with which we are familiar already. Fert also employs an entirely different stem, tul-, from tollere, to articulate its perfect. Examples of compounds:

Present		Perfect
refert	he reports, relates	rettulit
affert	he brings in, matters	attulit
prōfert	he is useful	prōtulit
effert	he carries out, raises [also extellit]	extulit
confert	he compares, contributes	contulit
suffert	he takes up, removes [more often tollit]	sustulit

4) Lātus, -a, -um [perf. pass. part.; supine, lātum] is taken from a third stem lāt-.
   Examples of compounds:

offert	oblātus	English:	offer, oblate
confert	collātus	English:	confer, collate

We also have the English words oblation and collation from Latin oblātiō and collātiō. Best known English derivatives are relation and elation from Latin relātiō and ēlātiō, respectively.

(c) <u>Fieri</u>: Passive of <u>Facere</u>. Just as
    facere has a peculiar imperative in
    <u>fac</u>! it has a very unusual passive
    system, fit [3rd sing pres ind]. E.g.,
    fiat lux, Let there be light.
    Christiānus fit, non nascitur.

In the simple tenses <u>fit</u> might be considered
the opposite of a Deponent, since almost all
of its endings are active but meanings passive.
The present Infinitive however is passive in
form, <u>fierī</u>.

LESSON XXIII

A. How to Organize a Latin Sentence

Any language depends for its flexibility on
its wealth of inflections. No wonder, then,
that Latin takes advantage of its many cases,
participles and infinitives for its phraseology.

123. Ablative Absolute: Adeptā lībertāte pācem
observābant diū. Here we must render the two
short words "adeptā lībertāte," as "When
freedom was gained," or"with freedom gained,
they kept peace for a long time." Rēbus bene
gestīs domum rediērunt, when their enterprise
was carried out well, they went home. The
participial constructions of these two examples
are called "ablātīvī absolūtī," or in English,
Ablative Absolutes. English has a borrowed
construction called the "Nominative Absolute,"
used only in formal speech. Scan the previous
lessons for ablative absolutes.

124. Indirect Discourse.* Medieval and Classical
Forms. In English we can have the sentence:
"He told her that he loves her." The substance
of what he said is given, but the exact words
are not quoted by the speaker, hence "indirect."
In medieval Latin, speaker and thinker put
their words and ideas in much the same form
that we do. Dīxit puellae quod amābat eam.
Putāvit puella quia erat amāta [that she was
loved]. Quod and quia, then, are used for
English "that."

However, Latin possessed a more refined way
of exploiting its wealth of inflection, the
accusātīvus cum infīnitīvō [accusative with
infinitive] construction, the commoner pattern
for indirect discourse of classical Latinity.
After the words for "thinking," "judging," and
"speaking," putāre, dīcere, loquī, dēmonstrāre,

---

*Cf. Sect. 70, above (on the infinitive).

arbitrārī, clāmāre, iudicáre, etc., the subject
of the thought or utterance stands in the
accusative case, the verb in the infinitive
mood. Vir puellae dīxit sē amāre eam. Puella
Putāvit sē amātam esse. Scan the previous
lessons for examples of the accusative with
infinitive construction.

In the following five sentences the subordinate clause depending on the verb of
thinking or judging or speaking has its subject in the accusative case even though the
same subject may be found in the main clause
in another case. When this construction with
the infinitive is used at all, its subject
has to be added under all circumstances and
in the accusative case.

1. Coriolānus prīmō dīcit sē numquam contrā
   rem publicam bellum gestūrum esse.
2. Posteā autem Rōmānōs armīs esse puniendōs
   putāvit.
3. Triangulum numquam plŭs duōbus rēctīs
   angulīs continēre posse geōmetricī
   dēmonstrant.
4. Mē Latīnum sermōnem partim intelligere
   partim ignorāre sciō.
5. Iudicēs Iohannae iudicāvērunt eam nōn
   rectē virī vestem induisse.

Differently and nearer to our usage one says:

1. Dīcitur divēs esse.
2. Vidēris nescīre.
3. Normannī in Americam vēnisse trāduntur.

As you analyze these latter examples, you will
note that the verbs of thinking, judging, per-
ceiving are all used in the passive.
"The Normans are thought to have come...."

125. Conditional Sentences

Sī vīs, potes. Sentences with _sī_, if, offer no
peculiarities in general. However, it is worth-
while to look more closely at the one case in
which an impossible condition is expressed: "If
I were king...," "if the house had not burnt..."
Sī rēx essem, paupertātem abolērem. Sī domus
nōn conflāgrāsset, in eādem cīvitāte mānsissent.
Here the assumption is unreal: I am not, and
never was king; the house did burn. Therefore,
the main clause and the dependent clause as well
are put in the Subjunctive of the past, in both
Latin and formal English. This sort is called
'Condition contrary to fact,'

Sī homō nōllet crēdere nisi ea quae cognosceret,
certē nōn posset vīvere in hōc mundo. Quomodō
enim aliquis vīvere posset nisi crēderet
alicuī. Fortassē dīceret patrī suō non esse
eum patrem suum.

--Thomas Aquinas.

B.   Idiomatic Phrasings

126. nē ...quidem: When a word is to be emphasized
in the sense of "not even," Latin brackets it
by a _nē_ and a _quidem_. Nē tū quidem mihī per-
suādēbis, Even you shall not persuade me.
Nē puerum quidem vincit. _Quidem_ alone means
the same thing positively: Ego quidem nōn
cēdam, I, at least, shall not give up.

127. Nam/_enim_/nempe: _Nam_, for, becomes _enim_ when
following the first word of the sentence.
E.g., Nam hiems fīnīta, but Hiems enim fīnīta,
For winter was over. _Nempe_ (perhaps equivalent
to _enimque_) means "however," "indeed," "no doubt,"
"assuredly," "I am sure," etc.

128. <u>Impersonal Verbs</u> [See Sect. 64, 66, above]:
<u>Pluit</u>, it rains, is a simple description of
raining without mentioning the author. "Rain- ·
ing takes place," would be a correct translation.
In a similar way, in

paenitet	it irks
taedet	it wearies
pudet	it shames
libet	it pleases

and other emotional expressions remain impersonal, i.e., they do not betray the source of
the emotion. But they should be translated
into a personal form of English. The present
and the perfect forms are:

Present		Perfect
paenitet mē	I repent	paenituit
taedet tē	Thou art tired of	taeduit
pudet eam	She is ashamed of	puduit
libet eōs	They like	libuit

Licet mihĬ, I am free to, easily came to be
used as a conjunction: licet faciat bene,
efficit mala, though he may do well, it turns
out evil.

129. *Diminutive.* Latin is able to put its tenderness (or
sometimes sarcasm) into the articulation of a single
word. Diminutives are generally formed by the suffix
-lus, or *-culus* (found in all three genders).

os osculum	kiss (little mouth)		
mulier muliercula	little woman		
oculus ocellus	lit. 'little eye' = apple of one's eye		
rex regulus	chieftain		
domna domicella	little dame	sacrificus	
filia filiola	little daughter	sacrificulus	priestling
puer puerulus	little boy	sacramentum	
homo homunculus	mannikin	sacramentulum	sacramentlet
ceremonia ceremon-		tabula tabella	tablet
iuncula	little ceremonies	ager agellus	small field

There are also diminutives of this sort:

vitulus, calf	vitellus, little calf
vēlum, veil, curtain	vexillum, flag
ala, wing	auxilla, armpit

130. <u>Verbal Prefixes</u>: In Latin, as in Greek, German
and to a lesser extent English, simple verbs
are commonly modified in meaning by the use
of prefixes. We have seen many examples of
this practice in previous lessons. Some of
these prefixes are the same in form as prepositions which govern nouns and pronouns. Others
are never found as prepositions, only as prefixes. Still other prepositions are never
found as verbal prefixes.

a. prepositions only: clam, coram, causā,
ergā grātiā, licet, sine, simul, -tenus
[literally, "extension," is a "postposition,"
Rōmārum tenus, as far as Rome], usque, ultrā,
vice(m) [with gen., in place of, instead of].

b. Prefixes only: dis-, ne-, per-, re- [red-
before vowels], sē- [sed before vowels] e.g.,

dissolvere	dissolve
sēcludere	seclude
revolvere	to turn about, revolve
pollicērī	to promise
negligere	to neglect

c. prepositions and prefixes: ab, ad, ante,
circā, cis, contrā, cum [prefix form con-],
dē, ex, in, infrā, inter, intrā, iuxtā, ob,
per, prae, prō, propter, praeter, prope,
post, suprā, super, sub, trans.

d. **verbs compounded with prepositional prefixes,
with object in the dative case. Normally,
verbs bearing the following prefixes take
a dative rather than an accusative case:**
*ad-, ante-, con-(cum), in-, inter-, ob-,
post-, prae-, sub-, and super-.* **For ex-**
ample: Puer Iesus Mariae obtemperāvit.
(para. 17, above).

131. <u>Verbs frequently compounded with prefixes</u>: The following Latin verbs are prolific in compounds with one or two prepositions (e.g., in-ac- + cessible:

gerit	gestum	legit	lectum	facit	factum
ducit	ductum	it	itum	cedit	cessum
agit	actum	dat	datum	fert	latum

Pliny, *Panegyric*, 49.3, on the love of a good king by his countrymen: "Haec arx inacessa, hoc inexpugnābile munimentum, nōn egēre munimentō."

132. <u>Exercise</u>: (1) form as many compounds from these words as you can recall from English usage.
(2) Analyze the following English compound words:

indigestion	tradition
reduction	effect
exactitude	reiteration
predilection	contradiction
exit	intercede

133. <u>How to Compare Two Actions or Things or Qualities</u>:

Fac aliīs prout vīs aliōs facere tibī, Do unto others as you would have others do unto you; Dīligēs proximum tuum tanquam tēipsum [Mk. 12:31], Thou shalt love thy neighbor as thyself; Fiat voluntās tua sicut in caelō et in terrā, Thy will be done on earth as it is in heaven. In these three examples prout, tamquam, sicut all mean the same thing. In the same sense may be used: velut, quomodō, ita... ut, ut, quasi.

When two quantities, of one and the same quality, are compared, we may say: Plūs quam perfectum est, more than is perfect; Plūs quam par est, more than is fair; Quī amat patrem aut matrem plūs quam mē.... Or that which is compared is put in the Ablative case, Quī mē amat plūs patre aut

matre suīs. Or, the year before this year,
annus hōc annō prior.

A knowledge of this construction enables
us to interpret a strange pun on a tombstone
correctly. The ancient Christians spoke of
their death day as their birthday (nātāle)
into heaven. And they were baptized mostly
late in life. Thus we read, "Postumius
fīdēlis quī gratiam sānctam consecūtus est
pridiē natālī suō." (He was baptized on the
day before his birthday.)

Atque (or ac) is used in comparisons with
about the same sense as quam:
    aequuus ac tū sum
    aequus atque
    potius ac

"Dēpōne potius ac cēde temporibus," Erasmus
to Charles V (1516). "You would do better to
abdicate before you give in to the times."

Another form of comparison uses the positive
degree of the adjective plus prae and ablative.
E.g., prae aliīs prōdigiōsa est blasphēmia.
[Calvin, Inst., 3:5:3].

134. How to express perfect equality: Perfect
equality may be expressed in Latin by a
series of special pairs:
    equality of size   tantus...quantus
    equality of number   tot...quot
    equality of recurrence totiens...quotiēns
    equality of quality   tālis...quālis
    equality of degree   tam...quam

135.   O Quanta Qualia

O quanta quālia
  sunt illa sabbata,
quae semper celebrat
  superna cŭria,
quae fessīs requiēs
  quae merces fortibus,
cum erit omnia
  deus in omnibus.

Nostrum est interim
  mentem ērigere
et tōtīs patriam
  vōtīs appetere,
et ad Ierusalem
  ā Babylonia
post longa regredī
  tandem exsilia.

Vēra Ierusalem
  est illa cīvitās
cuius pāx iugis est,
  summa inucunditās:
ubi non praevenit
  rem desiderium,
nec desideriō
  minus est praemium:

Illic molestiīs
  fīnitīs omnibus,
securi cantica
  Sion cantabimus,
et iugēs grātias
  dē dōnis grātiae
beāta referet
  plebs tibī, Domine,

Quis Rēx, quae cŭria,
  quāle palātium.
quae pāx, quae requiēs,
  quod illud gaudium,
huius participēs
  exponant glōriae,
si quantum sentiunt
  possint exprimere

Illic ex Sabbatō
  succēdit Sabbatum,
perpes laetitia
  sabbatizantium,
nec ineffābilēs
  cessābunt iubilī,
quos decantābimus
  et nōs et angelī

Perennī Dominō
  perpes sit glōria,
ex quō sunt, per quem sunt,
  in quō sunt omnia.
ex quō sunt, Pater est,
  per quem sunt, Fīlius,
in quō sunt, Patris et
  filiī Spiritus.

--Peter Abelard

LESSON XXIV

136. <u>Negation</u>.

Vĕra hominis virtūs noscitur ex potentiä
negandī. Man's most manly function becomes
known from his power to say "No." If anybody, in everyday life, should forget or
overlook the productive and destructive processes that are carried out through speech
and thought, the existence of the word "no"
should remind him of his blunder. Nulla rēs
omnī modō nōn est sicut rēs frigida undique
frigida nōn est, sed minus tepida quam aliae.
Nothing really exists not at all, as little as
a cold thing is all cold; it only is less warm
than other things. Everything in the physical
world has a breath of warmth in it; when we
call it cold, we judge its temperature in relation to warmer things. Whenever we say 'ho,
this is not," we really throw a thing out of
our realm of thought. We ask it to leave us
alone; we decide the place which that which we
deny holds in our world. It, however, has not
simply disappeared. It only shrinks in importance. Cum negēmus strīgās esse, illae rēs ex
quibus aliī strīgās esse iudicāvērunt, ā nobīs
aliter explicantur. (When we deny the existence of witches, we explain that which leads
other people to believe in witches, in a different way.) When we say: There is no God, we
only say that the processes which lead the rest
of mankind from the day of man's creation to
this belief, do not suffice, in our eyes, to
condense them into one universal name valid
for all. We deny God's name, not the reality
of the soul's processes which flood the heart
so that the mouth speaks: negāmus nōmen deī;
nōn possumus negāre animae commōtiōnēs quibus
efficitur ut ex abundantiā cordis ōs loquātur.

There is, then, a special awe and daring
about negation. Antīquīs hīc verbōrum,

quibus negāmus, tremor atque stupor perspicuī
erant. Quia ūtitur verbīs Nōn, Nĕ, Num,
Quīn, homō iudex mundī et reformātor sociĕtā-
tis sĕ gerit.

No wonder that, in Latin, the waves of
passion which lead most freely to the use
of negation, lead to such a characteristic
style. There is a peculiar No in religious
deprecation: Nĕ hoc fiat! Again, in solemn
cursing we have; Nĕ habĕtō vītam quī hoc
fĕcerit. In logical doubt: dubitō an ita
rēs sĕ habeat. Legal absolution: nōn fecit.
Practical exclusion: Aaron Burr aquā et
ignī interdīcitur. Ironical question: Num
expectātis pecūniam sine labōre? Furthermore,
once a thing has been treated negatively, by
denying its existence or its value, as in
those modes of speech listed here, the affirmation is more difficult, and asks for deep
breathing and a certain emphasis. We may,
then, expect a special form of affirmation
which differs from simple naive babbling
and uncontradicted statement by being "post-
negative." Prōcēdāmus nunc ad singulōs
negātiōnum ūsūs.

137. Ways of Expressing Negation
    1) The negative particle is one of the few
classes of words in Latin that is tied down
to a strict word order within the sentence.
The negating form must precede the word or
sentence it negates. The confusion result-
ing from disregarding this rule would be
considerable. For example:

nōn nēmō putat   some think (not nobody)
nēmō nōn putat   everybody thinks (there is
                 nobody who does not think).
Before "Posse" the "nōn" must immediately
precede the verb: īre nōn possumus, We
cannot go.

2)   The "n" in "no," "negation," not, and
our physical contracting of the muscles of
the nose when we refuse or deny, perhaps,
are linked.

3) The Latin word for "don't!" is "nē!"
Fear, fright, stopping, warding off, for-
bidding, produce it. E.g.:
nē veniäs! don't come!
timēbat, nē caderētis, he feared that you might
fall.

4) Derivatives of nē:

    (a) nēquam, an exclamation nĕ-quam.
        Literally, don't how, "a not even
        how." This word developed into
        an adjective undeclined in the
        positive degree, "a ne'er do well."
        Comparative: nēquior; Superlative:
        nēquissimus.
        Derived noun: nēquitia, -ae.

    (b) nècesse (nē plus cessem from cĕdere).
        Literally "no evading," necessary,
        hence the adjective necessārius.

    (c) negat, he says no [ait, he says yes].

    (d) negōtium est, no leisure is; hence:
        negōtium, business; cf. negotiation.

    (e) negligit, neglēxit, neglectum; in-
        finitive, neglegere, to neglect.

    (f) nescit [nē plus scīre] he does not
        know

    (g) nefas, sacrilege [fas, right]

    (h) nōlō I do not want (nē volō; but
        nōn vult]. [Cf. Sect. 122]

5) Derivatives of shortened form ne:

neuter	from	uter
numquam	from	umquam
nusquam	from	usquam
nūllus	from	ūllus
némŏ	from	nē homŏ (no man)

Similarly,

neque, nec "and not," "but not"
nequit, nequīre [neque eō it, neque eō
īre, literally, "and not to get that
far," i.e., not to be able] to be unable.
Nequeō, I cannot. This is retransformed
into queō, I can.

6) The short "ne" is used to introduce a
question.

facisne hoc?	Do you do that?
Venitisne?	Do you come?
Vīcitne?	Did he conquer?

This "ne" is appended to the verb. However, when the question expects an affirmative answer, Won't you come? the
-ne is affixed to an added "nōn."

Nōnne sequeris?	Don't you follow?
Nōnne patitur?	Doesn't he suffer?
Nōnne retulistis?	Did you not report?

Ūnus phīlosophus fuit trīgintā annōs in sōli-
tūdine ut cognoscere nātūram apis. Sī ergō
intellectus noster est ita dēbilis, nōnne
stultum est crēdere dē Deō nisi illa quae
homō potest cognoscere per sē?

In a double question "an" is used. This
"an" was originally "at ne."

Rogāvit utrum venīrēs an manērēs.

He asked whether you came or stayed.

7) In its weakest form, "nē" becomes
"en-" or "in-" and is used to negate the word
to which it is prefixed: ratus, ratified/
inritus, not ratified, in vain [g]nomen,
name/ignōminia, (no name), blame

insomnis, sleepless
ignōrant, they are ignorant, do not know
ignārus, know-nothing
ignāvus, inert
inaudītus, unheard of

8) Litotes. "Cum fīlius ūnicus morerētur,
Goethe exclāmāvit, 'Nōn ignōrāvī mē mortālem
genuisse.'" Latin loves to express a "yes"
by two "no's":
nōnnullī, some
artēs nōn ōdit nisi ignārus
nē dubitēs, be sure (do not be uncertain)
nesciō an scrīpserit, Literally: "I don't
know if not"; but the meaning simple is:
perhaps (or probably) he wrote the letters.
non dubitō quīn (quī nē) veniat. I am sure
that he is coming.
9) A negative being always a risk in close
social contacts, positive expressions seem
preferable. E.g., "satis," enough, often
serves as a veiled "no." "caret," often-
times stands for English "he has not." Also,
"male," "minimē," "vix" (scarcely), and
"parum" (too little), take the place of
direct negation. "Minus" is most widely
used as a polite form of "no," especially
in answers. Hence, quō minus, "so that not"
became a negative conjunction like nē: impedīvit ventus, nē nāvis Angliam appelleret.
Or: Impedīvit ventus quōminus nāvis Angliam
appelleret.
10) After nē, quōminus, num ("if not"),
nisi, sī, all compounds of the stem ali- drop
this part of their formation. E.g., aliquid
becomes nequid: Sī quid... stands for sī
aliquid...
Videant consulēs nē quid detrimentī rēs
pūblica capiat, was the general formula for
an emergency decree of the Roman Senate. Quid
here stands for aliquid. Thus it may be read
in the Rēs Gestae Dīvī Augustī, chapter I.*
Sī quis is the regular formula in law in the
statement of the conditions which establish
a crime or a contract. It stands for aliquis.

---

*See, p. 233, below.

11)   <u>Sophisticated Affirmation</u>:   "Gubernat,"
"est," are simple statements. Such a statement is changed into an affirmation when
someone has negated or questioned its reality
before:
    Num pluit?   You don't say it rains?
    Sīc; pluit.   Yes, it does.

To express a pure "yes" after the statement
of a negative, or a doubt or a question was
a serious problem for the Latin tongue. At
first they had to build a whole sentence:
sīc est, īta sē habet, or they used a pug-
nacious term, "immō"; yea (or nay) verily,
as in Dant'e letter: "inglōrium immō ignōminiō-
sum": inglorious nay ignominious. Only about
the time of Abelard and the First Crusade
would "sīc" regularly by itself carry the full
meaning of a calm "yes." <u>Sīc et Nōn</u> is the
title of a famous dialectical book of Abelard,
meaning "Yes and No," in the modern, absolute,
usage of negation and affirmation. However,
any scientific affirmation only follows in
the wake of negation. It is re-affirmation.

12)   <u>Haud</u> is a negation that mainly negates
one word of a sentence, not the whole action.
E.g., haud male, not badly.

13)   In similis/dissimilis, iungere/disiungere,
vestire/divestire, the prefix <u>dis</u>- turns the
main notion into its very opposite. This at
first sight might seem puzzling, since <u>dis</u>-
generally means not more than "away from,"
"in two." The complete negation of these
frequent words is easily understood when we
look at a word like "diffident." A man is
diffident who is "not confident"; <u>dif</u>- here
negates <u>con</u>-. He does not go together with
("con" equals "cum") the other fellow; he
parts with him. In this way consimilis is
denied by dissimilis. We may then say that
compounds with <u>dis</u>- negate compounds with <u>con</u>-.

LESSON XXV

138. <u>Significant Verbal Constructions</u>: Latin verbs
sometimes are followed by cases that we would
not expect. Note the following examples:

    1)   Accusative Case:
        Tē certiōrem fēcimus herī.
        We informed you yesterday.
        Sequēbantur puerī equitem extrā oppidum.
        The boys followed the horseman outside
          the village.
        Regnum coelōrum patitur violentiam.
        The kingdom of heaven suffers violence.
        Iubēbant eum sē sequī.
        Iussus est eum sequī. [Passive]
    2)   Dative Case: (Cf. Sects. 130, 139)
        Mihī persuāsum est ut pluat.
        I am convinced it will rain.
        Quod hostibus pepercit, Augustus Caesar,
          quandō scrībēbat rēs ā sē gestās,
          glōriātus est, Dēbilibus parcere
          virtūtis initium.
        Fuērunt eī rēs magnae
        He had a great fortune.
        Confītentī hominī dōnantur peccāta.
        To a man who confesses, his sins are
          forgiven.
        Dūcī Normannōrum Angliam facile ·
          expugnārī posse vīsum est.
        Vidēris aegrōtus esse parentibus tuīs.
        Anglīs quidem līber iudiciārius Guilelmī
          rēgis magna innovātiō vidēbātur.
        Tē audī; tibī obtemperā. [Cicero, <u>Ep. Fam.</u> 2.7.2]
    3)   Ablative Case:
        Potiuntur baronēs Londiniō ut rēgem
          cōgerent sē oboedīre.
        Fāma Normannōrum orbis terrārum seculō
          ūndecimō resonābat.
        Normannia, Sicilia, partibus Ītaliae
          expugnātīs ipsā urbe Rōmā nōn
          abstinuērunt.

Multīs precibus pāpa ūsus est ut urbem
relinquerent et domum in sua redīrent.
Egent fugitīvī cīvēs vestibus.
Consulātū Caesarēs rārō fungēbantur;
at tribunicia potestāte semper
vestītī erant.
Deus carminibus nostrīs dignus est.
Multī, audaciā quādam innāta frētī,
quibus-libet ratiōnibus ūtuntur,
ut suam intentiōnem quamvīs prāvam
consequantur.

Alexandri de Villadei, Versūs dē Verbīs
dēponentibus quae rēgunt Ablātīvum:
"Vescor" cum "potior," "fruor" addās,
"fungor" et "ūtor."
Ūtimur ūtilibus fruimur caelestibus
caelīs
Vescimur aeternīs, potior dape, fungor
honōre
Frētus quamvīs abstinēre egēre consequī
resonāre. [cf. Sect. 114].

4) Genitive Case:
Suādēre principī multī labōris est.
Johannis Lockeī interfuit fīlium
amīcī linguam Latīnam novā methodō
docērī; putābat Locke Latīnum
sermōnem vīvā vōce inter discipulum
et magistrum exercendum esse. Ob-
liviōnis condemnāvit suam ipsius
in scholā viam discendī Latīnam
linguam.

Bonae cīvitātis interest cīvēs lēgibus
nōn sōlum parēre sed etiam consentīre.
It is in the interest of good government
that the citizens not only obey the
laws but consent to them.
Interest hominis nūllīs mendāciīs
mentem replēre.

But: octo mīlia passuum intersunt
inter Boston et Cantabrigias.
Here "interesse" is used in its
physical sense.

139. <u>Word Charades</u>:   Homonyms are words of the
same appearance in speech (homographs, words
of the same appearance in writing), but of
different meaning like "ear," our organ of
hearing, and "ear," head of grain.   Certain
forms in Latin look alike though real
homonyms are much rarer than in English.
The most frequent homographic equations
occur through conjugation and declension.   E.g.,

  ēdŭcō may be either from ēducāre, educate,
  or ēdūcere, lead out;
  sĕcŭris may be either the nom. sing. of
  sĕcūris, axe, or the dat. or abl. plur. of
  sĕcūrus, -a, -um, safe.
  occurrere may be either the pres. act. inf.
  or the shortened form of the perf. act. ind.
   3rd. plur., occurrērunt.
  reliquere is either pres. act. inf. or 2nd
  sing. pres. pass. ind. (for relinqueris)

One very frequent equation results from the
favorite Latin formant in -or:
        gubernātor,governor
        victor, victor
        conditor, founder
These words form their gen. plur, in -um:
        gubernātōrum, of the governors
        conditōrum, of the founders
        amātōrum, of the lovers
At the same time each parent verb has a perf.
pass. part.:
  gubernātus, gen. plur. m. & n. gubernātōrum
  conditus, gen. plur. m. & n. conditōrum
  amātus, gen. plur. m. & n. amātōrum.

Thus the word <u>gubernātōrum</u> may be translated
'of the governors' or of the governed.'
Generally, however, only one interpretation
makes sense.
Gubernātōrēs ergā gubernātōrum possessiōnēs
maximam cūram habēre debent.
Gubernātōrum iustōrum gubernātiō dōnum magnum
patriae.
Conditōrum memōria sāncta sit.
Oppidōrum privātim conditōrum numerus infīnītus
invenītūrīs in Americā.

Further examples of homonyms:

<u>misĕrĕ</u>: (1) <u>misērunt</u>;   (2) adv. of <u>miser</u>
<u>mala</u>:   (1) the bad, neut, plur.:(2) the apples
<u>lĕgis</u>:   (1) you read;   (2) of the law
<u>[g]nŏvī</u>: (1) of the new;   (2) I know

Since "quisque," "quidque" means everybody,
everything, but <u>que</u> may be appended to any
word in the sense of "and,"
  cuiusque may mean (1) of everybody; (2) and
            of whom
  quoque   may mean (1) also: (2) and where to.

Finally, we should mention the words beginning
with <u>in-</u>. In indict, impugn, in- means "into,"
"against," whereas inept, illicit, inadmissible
show that they are negatives of apt, licit,
admissible.

139a. Special Verbs with the Dative Case

Ōrāmus, Pater coelestis, tē succurrere favēreque nōbīs.
Delictīs nostrīs ignosce et parce filiīs tuīs. Imperā
nōbīs, Domine: tibī parēbimus. Nihil nōbis laedet vel
minābitur. Nōbīs per evangelium tuum dē amōre Christī
prō omnibus hominibus cotidiē persuādēs. Nē tibī peccātīs
nostrīs displiceāmus, sed docē nōs tibī manū cordeque servīre, et malignō resistere, et neminī invidēre, et promis-
siōnibus tuīs credere. Tibī sōlī semper placeāmus. Audi,
Pater noster, precātiōnem nostram. Tibī omnis glōria, hon-
or maiestāsque in saeculum saeculōrum. Amen.

LESSON XXVI

PRONUNCIATION I: SOUNDS

140. Pronunciation should be taught by ear. The student who is using this book independently should seek out a competent Latinist for pronunciation, for the written word never gives more than an approximation. The pronunciation scheme used in this textbook is the modern one, based upon strictly scientific principles, which has come to the fore in the last two generations. It proposes, as nearly as possible, to restore the sounds of classical diction of two millenia ago. But there are several other schemes which differ from it in varying degrees. The most important is the pronunciation of the Roman Church, used in the Mass, the tradition of the singing community. For example, the <u>excelsis</u> of <u>Gloria</u> in excelsis Deo is "scientifically" pronounced ex-kellsees, "ecclesiastically" and "musically" exchellsees. Beside these two currently-used schemes, there is the scholastic pronunciation, with its continental and its British variants, as developed since the sixteenth century. The execrable pronunciation of Latin in English-speaking countries in vogue since the late 17th century, and only supplanted by the "scientific" form in recent times, is traditionally attributed to the stern schoolmaster of the English West-minster School, Dr. Richard Busby (1606-1695). Busby expurgated the Latin and Greek classics "solely for the pious purpose of enabling his own pupils to imbibe the beauties without being polluted by the impurities of the ancients" [DNB, viii, 31]. In like manner, to prevent his pupils from being corrupted by continental vices on their "grand tour" through the medium of a common language, Busby is supposed to have "Englished" the pronunciation of school-boy Latin, thus making English and Continental Latin mutually unintelligible. Busby's pronunciation became the norm in the

British Isles. Older American and British
Latinists still sometimes exhibit this "English" Latin pronunciation, especially in
vowels and in consonants like C, G, and J.

Whatever may be the truth of this story,
the fact remains that Latin pronunciation
tends to be colored by the native language
of the speaker. Therefore, the remarks on
Latin vowels and consonants given in this
book must be taken as approximations at best.
For a full discussion of Latin pronunciation
the student is referred to Sturtevant, The
Pronunciation of Greek and Latin, 1940.

The Latin Vowel System
The Latin vowels may be conveniently classified by the following chart:

		front	central	back
high	close	ī machine [Fr. il]		ū brute [Ger. gut]
high	open	i sit, pin		u put [Ger. dumm]
mid	close	ē they [Fr. élève; Ger. Beet]		ō boat, stove [Ger. Sohn]
mid	open	e met, ten [Fr. dette]		o mob [voll]
low			ā father [It. or Ger. a, not Fr.]	

In addition, y (in Greek words), among those
Latins of the classical period who knew Greek,
was pronounced much as French u̲ or German ü̲.
Otherwise it was treated as i̲.

The chief dipththongs, which are always
long vowels, include:

ae   as in English m̲y̲, a̲i̲sle

au   as in English o̲u̲t, h̲o̲w̲

oe   as in English b̲o̲y̲, o̲i̲l

eu   as in the British pronunciation of "Oh,
        No̲" or in the slang expression "y[eah-
        oo]"

It should be noted that o̲e̲ and a̲e̲, in many
Latin words, became interchangeable in writing:
praelium/proelium, paena/poena, poenitet/
paenitet, caelum,/coelum

Exercise. Pronounce the following words
containing short or long vowels.

1. ab, ante, atque
    sāl, quā, chartā, pācem
2. neque, sed, et, ex
    dē, nē, rēvēra, lēgibus
3. in sine, quid
    sī, sīc, quī, dīc, illī
4. quot, ob, novem
    flōs, rōs, dōnum, nōn
5. sub, ut, urbs
    plūs, rūs, lūx, lūcis, crūcem

142. Latin Consonants. Little need be said about
consonants. "C" is always hard. Caesar, in
Latin, did not sound like Caesar in English,

It should be pronounced as if the word were
spelled kysar (in English). Cicero is pronounced kikero. Pecūnia (money) reads
pequnia. Cicero is pronounced kikero.
Pecūnia (money) reads pequnia. Hence it
appears that, in the beginning of writing,
Latin used:

  k   in kano, Kaesar
  c   in cervus, Cicero
  q   in pequnia, Marqus.

But all three were employed for one sound only,
their use depending on the vowel or consonant
that followed. This sound was written on the
vowel or consonant that followed. This sound
was written:

  k   before "a" or consonant,
  c   before "e" and "i,"
  q   before "u" and "o."

And it is still true that the following vowel
shades our pronunciation of the "guttural
tenuis" as "k" is called. The contrast between
the front k in "key" and the back k in "coat"
is evidence of this fact. The Semitic alphabet,
from which the Greek and the Latin alphabets
were derived, writes these as two distinct
letters ꓳ and ꓑ having distinct sounds.
The hearing of the ancients, then, was more
susceptible to the subtleties of sound than
our ear, blunted as it is by writing and reading. However, even today we preserve this
immemorial tradition by giving the three
different signs: "q," "k," "c," three names
that contain their specific vowel. We pronounce:

    a "q" standing alone: 'kyoo"
    a "k" standing alone: "kay"
    a "c" standing alone: "cee"

The sound "g" in Latin is always hard, as
in the English words "go" or "good," "angry";
it never dwindles down as in Italian "Gior-
gione" or English "bridge" or "gem."

"J" and "i" are not distinguished in Latin
texts though there is a difference in pronunciation. Hence the spelling of the word
"iacere," to throw, and of its many compounds
differs from their actual pronunciation con-
siderably. The simple "iacit," he throws,
was pronounced as if spelled (in English)
<u>yacit</u>. Its compounds, though spelled with a
single "i" have a sound equivalent to -yi-:

abicit	pronounced	"abyicit"
reicit	pronounced	"reyicit"
conicit	pronounced	"conyicit"
obicit	pronounced	obyicit"
subicit	pronounced	"subyicit"

[Compare English abject, reject, conjecture,
object, subject.] Many dictionaries distinguish between i and j. In the signature
alphabet used in binding older books j is commonly omitted.

143. The Grammarian Scaurus on K. Q, C.

'K' quīdam supervacuam esse līteram iudicāvērunt quoniam vice illius 'c' satis fungī posset.
Sed retenta est,...quoniam nōtās quāsdam sīgnifi-
cāret, ut... 'kaput' et 'kalendās.' ['K' lītera]
tamen antīquī...ibī tantum dum erat, in quō
aut 'k' lītera 'c' nomen suum retinēre posset,
singula [lītera] prō syllabā scrībēbātur,
tamquam satis [syllabam]...nōmine [līterae]
implērent, ut puta: ... 'cēra' - 'c' simplex
et 'ra.' ...Ita et quotiēns 'kānus' et kārus'
scrībendum erat, quia singulīs līterīs prīmae
syllabae notābantur, 'k' prīma ponēbātur, quae
suō nōmine 'a' continēbat, quia, sī 'c' posuis-
sent, 'cenus' et 'cērus' futūrus erat, nōn

'cānus' et 'cārus.' ...'Q' lītera aequē
reteṛta est propter nōtās, quod per sē posita
sīgnıficat 'quaestórem,' et quia cum illā
'u' līterā conspīrat, quotiēns...prō vau
līterā [pónitur], ut 'quis' et 'quālis.'

Quīdam prō 'quis' scrībunt 'cuis,' quoniam
superfluam esse 'q' līteram putant. Sed nōs
cum illā 'u' līteram ... consentīre iam dēmon-
strāvimus. 'C' autem in dātīvō pōnimus, ut
sit differentia: 'cuī' et 'quī,' id est
dātīvī singulāris et nominātīvī et vocātīvī
plurālis. [from Keil, Grammatici Latini,
VII.14-16, 27f, altered.]

144. Syllabification of Latin Words

Within the word, division is normally made as
follows:
(1) between vowels (unless they constitute a
    diphthong);
(2) after a vowel, if it is followed by a
    single consonant or a normal initial
    consonant cluster; the following single
    consonant or consonant cluster then
    begins the following syllable;
(3) after a normal final consonant cluster
    (unless identical with an initial cluster
    as in Rule 2)

145. The Wolf's Spelling
[From a manuscript in Brussels, 536]

Presbyter quīdam docuit lupum līterās. Presbyter dīxit A, et lupus similiter. Presbyter
dīxit B, et lupus similiter. E dīxit presbyter, et lupus dīxit similiter. "Modō con-
gregā," ait presbyter, "et syllabicā." Et
respondit lupus: "Syllabicāre nōndum sciō."
Cuī presbyter: "Ut tibī melius vidētur, sīc
dīcitō." Et ait lupus: "Mihī optimē vidētur,
quod hoc sonat: 'agnus.'" Tunc presbyter
ait: "Quod in corde, hoc in ore."

LESSON XXVII

PRONUNCIATION II: ACCENT IN PROSE AND VERSE

146. <u>The Lineage of Intonation</u>. From Lesson XXVI
we have seen that the Romans generally used
sounds which are also found in modern European
languages. The real difference between classical antiquity and the Christian era stems from
the fact that the sounds were dealt with in a
different manner. And no wonder! For the
daily blurring of sounds, syllables, words, and
sentences through two thousand years has used
up the linguistic material like a stream wash-
ing out the rocks of its bed. Furthermore,
the proportions among the various uses to
which language is put have completely changed
today.

What do we mean by this change of proportions? In antiquity the main use of language
was in prayer, in military command, in law,
and in singing: whereas, today language is
infinitely more used for the ephemeral purposes of everyday speech: press, private
letters, telephone calls, broadcasting and
the like.

Now, these different branches of human
speech are intoned in different ways. The
history of intonation leads from plain chant
to whisper. Religious intonation, and
similarly, legal and military and crafts-
man's use of language, are most <u>explicit</u>.
In fiction, gossip, talk, correspondence,
commerce, journalism, the half- and quarter-
tones prevail. In this realm we speak by <u>impli</u>-
cation. To be explicit means to raise the voice
and to keep it on an even and evenly impressive
level. Prayer is uttered in plain chant.

Hebrew prayer and the Roman Catholic Mass
simply preserve this oldest layer of human
speech; they help us to understand the original
principles of Latin pronunciation. This primary intonation we call <u>plain chant</u>.

Plain chant is an attitude halfway between
the singing of an artist and everyday speech.
In plain chant, as used in the Mass and in
the synagogue, we probably have the manner
of speech that is nearest the primeval values
of speech. Compared to plain chant our oral
efforts are a kind of shorthand in speech.
The way in which we articulate and move
our larynx, tongue, gums, etc., is a mere
shadow of the light that flooded the old
language when man first cried to God.

We may summarize these levels of intonation
as follows:

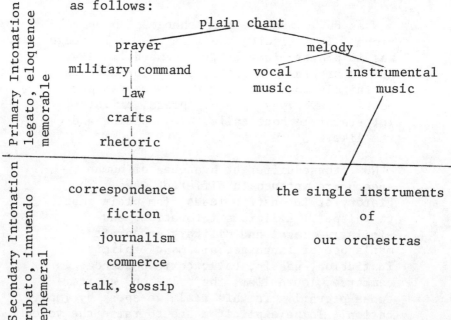

Genealogical Table of Levels of Intonation

This diagram will be elaborated, in a slightly
different form, in Lesson XXIX.

147. The Accentuation of Latin Prose.

The earliest Latin was marked by a strong
initial stress accent. Subsequent development saw the shift of accent toward the end
of the word and the addition of pitch to
stress on the accented syllable. Probably
the stress accent was never lost, although
writers of the classical period (to A.D. 300)
in their insistence upon musical pitch and
quantity in Latin verse (after Greek models)
do not mention it. At all events, stress
reasserts itself in the Latin of the Church
and characterizes the poetry of the Middle
Ages.

In classical dactylic hexameter (the epic
meter), a study of the relation of poetic
beat (ictus) to the normal accent of the words
themselves indicates that the greatest degree
of harmony occurs in the words of the two final
poetic feet of the line. This suggests that,
in addition to stress word accent, there was
also phrasal or sentence accent, and that it
tended to be final rather than initial. Furthermore, the degree of harmony between word
accent and poetic ictus increases markedly with
the poets of Silver Latinity.

In the light of this evidence for a continued
stress accent throughout the history of Latin,
the traditional distinction between "qualitative" (stress) and "quantitative" (pitch)
accentuation must be reinterpreted. Classical
poetry, then, had both pitch and stress,
while the Latin poetry of the earlier epoch,
and of the later (Christian) epoch, was one
chiefly of stress accentuation.

The traditional rule for the accentuation of
Latin words may be briefly stated. Naturally,
however, there is superimposed upon these

word accents a phrasal and sentence accentuation
determined by the thought itself. The three
final syllables of a Latin word are named:

```
a     -     gri     -     co     -     la
   propaenultima     paenultima     ultima
   (antepenult)      (penult)
```

The next-to-the-last syllable (paenultima,
penult) determines by its character the accent
of a Latin word. If it is long, it always
carries the accent; if short, the accent
reverts to the preceding syllable (propaenul-
tima, antepenult). Longa paenultima accentuā-
tur. The following table, then, summarizes
the possible places of accentuation:

```
words of 1 syllable     nōn     accent on ultima
words of 2 syllables    a-qua   accent on paenultima
words of 3 or more syl.:
    paenultima long     rē-gī-na accent on paenultima
    paenultima short    a-gri-co-la  accent on
                                     propaenultima.
```

While the "rule of the paenultima" is the key
to Latin prose accentuation, there are also certain regular features about Latin vowelling that
help us to spot long syllables:

(1) As we have seen, a syllable can be long because it contains a long vowel (single vowel
or diphthong), e.g., lau - dis, or because
the vowel, while short, is followed by two or
more consonants ("long by position").

(2) All nominatives ending in -a, -um, -is
have final short syllables, e.g., rĕgĭna,
bellum, fortis. Ablatives in -ā, -ō, -ī,
-ē, -ū are all long. Note that the ablative
in short -e (third declension), is not in-
cluded here, but the ablative in long -ē
(fifth declension). E.g., rēgĭnā, lignō,

crēbrŏ, febrī, rē, ūsū, but NOT rēgimine.

(3) The infinitives of the first, second,
and fourth conjugations, possessing a long
characteristic vowel, have a long paenultima,
e.g., gubernāre, docēre, audīre. [But on
stare and dare see Sect. 109, above]. The infinitive of the third conjugation has a short
e in the paenultima, e.g., legere, bibere,
reddere, facere.

(4) Any vowel followed by another vowel is
always short, e.g., am-bi-gu-us, an-nu-us,
tri-du-us, rē-gi-us, ē-gre-gi-us, mal-le-us,
i-dŏ-ne-us. This rule of course does not
apply when two vowel letters constitute a
diphthong, e.g., cae-lum; or in certain words
from the Greek, e.g., he-rŏ-us (of a hero).

A further characteristic of Latin pronunciation was the tendency to slur final vowels
and endings in a vowel plus m. (This tendency
is not unknown in modern European languages,
e.g., in French.) The verb "est" is hardly
uttered at all. Consequently we have such
common elisions as the following:

bellum est   = bellumst
difficile est = difficilest

We shall see in a moment the importance of
elision for Latin poetry.

Exercise. Read the following passage with
particular attention to the accented syllables:

Maiŏrum bellŏrum memŏria nōn trāditur quem
eōrum quibus Kōmānī terrās, quae hodiē His-
pānia, Portugālia, Francia, Ītalia, Graecia,
Albania, Jugoslavia, Hungaria, Germania,
Hollandia, Belgium, Britannia, Helvētia,
Austria, Turcia, Aegyptus, Syria, Palaestīna,

Mesopotámia, Mauretánia, Rumánia, Checoslovácia,
Bulgária, nóminantur, in únum imperium rede-
gérunt. Hispáni̦ Portugalénsés, Francisci,
Itali, Graeci, Albani, Jugoslávi, Hungarici,
Germáni, Batávi (=Hollandi), Belgae, Britanni,
Helvétii, Austriaci, Osmanés (=Turcensés),
Aegyptii, Syrii, Palaestinensés, Arabés,
Berberi, Rumáni, Bohémi, Bulgári habitant
in fínibus imperii Rómáni antiqui.

Meridiés medium diei.

149.   The Accentuation of Latin Verse.

We have already reviewed some of the evidence
of poetic accent to show the persistence of
stress throughout Latinity. This is not however intended to minimize the obvious contrast
between the dactylic hexameters of a Virgil or
the elegiac couplets of a Propertius on the
one hand, and the great hymns of the Western
medieval Church or the hearty lyrics of the
wandering scholars on the other. Yet all are
links in the great chain of Latin poetry.

The prototype of medieval Latin verse is
Augustine's Alphabetical Psalm against the
Donatists. Here is the first stanza.

Abundantia peccátórum solet frátrés conturbáre.
propter hóc dominus noster voluit nós praemonére
compáráns regnum caelórum reticuló missó in mare
congreganti multós piscés omne genus hinc et inde.
quós cum tráxissent ad litus, tunc coepérunt séparáre,
bonós in vása misérunt, reliquós malós in mare.
quisquis nóvit évangelium, recognoscat cum timóre.
videt reticulum ecclésiam, videt hoc saeculum mare;
genus autem mixtum piscis iustus est cum peccátóre;
saeculi fínis est litus: tunc est tempus séparáre;
qui modó retia rupérunt, multum dílexérunt mare;
vása sunt sedés sánctórum, quó nón possunt pervenire. *
[CSEL 51:1]

*For translation, see F. L. Battles, *Aurelius Augustine: Alphabetical
Psalm against the Party of Donatus* (1974).

Furthermore, the heightened prose commonly
taught in the schools of rhetoric of Augustine's day was often of a poetical turn, even
containing rhyme. We find, for example, rhymed
passages such as the following in Augustine's
sermons:*

Quomodo ergo debet gaudendo vigilare Christi amicus
  quando   et   dolendo vigilat   inimicus?
Quomodo in tanta Christi gloria inardescat vigilare Christianus,
  quando   erubescat dormire   paganus?
Quomodo decet eum, qui hanc domum magnam intravit in tanta eius festivitate vigilare.
  quando iam vigilat qui   disponit   intrare.

As in our conventional modern poetry, the line
of medieval Latin poetry is bound together by
regular qualitative stress and rhyme, e.g.:

    diēs īrae, diēs <u>illa</u>
    solvet saeclum in <u>favilla</u>.
    teste David cum <u>Sybillā</u>.

Sometimes regular qualitative stress alone is
used to give form to the poem, e.g., Ō Rōma
nōbilis [See above Sect. 56].

Much medieval poetry was set to music, thus
transforming it from plain chant to song.
Thereby the words themselves were freed from
their ancient plain-chant character, that is,
of being pronounced with full voice but without
musical tune. The transition from plain chant
to musical speech is seen in the development of
the Alleluia, culminating in Adam of St. Victor.**

In contrast to this, the binding of the poetic
line in Classical times was through a recurring
pattern of longs and shorts, marked by a pitch
<u>accent, but probably</u> not devoid -- as we have

---

*Cf. Part V, No. 23, below: *Cantiones Augustini*.
**F.J.E. Raby, *A History of Christian Latin Poetry from the
  Beginnings to the Close of the Middle Ages* (1927), chs.
  7.2, 4, 11, traces the development of the sequence.

seen -- of a concurrent stress accent. In the
hexameter, for example, a long syllable is
followed six times by short ones:

```
     #           #          #              #
Quidquid  a- gis pru- den-ter a- gas et
  *              *         *        *
                             #
                           res-pi-ce fi-nem.
                             *          *
```

This verse, read as prose, would be accented as

```
     #                  #                    #
Quid-quid a-gis pru-den-ter a-gas et re-spi-ce
  *          *         *                  *
fi-nem
  *
```

   Accented syllables are marked *; syllables
"long by position" are marked#.
The larger number of such syllables in the poetic
form of the line reveals a significant difference between poetry and prose. Poetry is continuous, organic, closely knit; its building-
block is the line or verse. Prose rhythms
stem rather from the individual words and, of
course, the phrasal groupings. To express it
in another way: in poetry, the whole wishes to
be apriori.   In prose the single words form
the apriori; the whole is aposteriori.

Prose: quos animus fuerat tenui excusare libello

Poetry: quosani musfue rattenu excu sareli bello.

Elision, which was shown to be fairly common in
Latin prose, is an even more prominent characteristic of Latin poetry. Hence the verse:

   Scribendi recte sapere est et principium
   et fons
is read for the meter as though it were written:

Scriben direc tesa perstet principi et fons.
The weak "est" is found also in Latin verse.
Hence, the line :
    id tibī iudicium est, ea mens; sī quid
    tamen olim scrīpseris
reads
    idtibi iudici umstea menssi quid tamen
    olimscrip seris.

A modification of the classical hexameter is
the "elegiac distich" or "couplet," which may
be considered a regular hexameter coupled with
a truncated hexameter, so-called a "pentameter."
E.g.,
    do-nec e/ -ris fē/ -līx, mul/ -tōs nu-me/
    -rā-bis a/ -mī-cōs,
    Tem-po-ra/ sī fu-e/ -rint// nu-bi-la/
    sō-lus e/ -ris.

Actually in the "pentameter" the third and
sixth feet of the regular hexameter seem to be
cut to a single syllable.

150.   Exercises.

(1) Where does a slur (syncope) occur in the
     following verses:
     Aut prodesse volunt aut dēlectāre poetae
     aut simul et iucunda et idōnea dīcere vītae.

     Difficile est propriē communia dīcere; tūque
     rēctius Iliacum carmen dēdūcis in actūs
     quam sī prōferrēs ignōta indictaque prīmus.

(2) The great Virgil, in his famous Aeneid,
     managed to keep his introduction clear
     of too many slurs. Try to establish its
     rhythm by applying our rules:

     Arma virumque canō Troiae quī prīmus ab ōrīs
     Ītaliam, fātō profugus, Lavinaque vēnit
     lītera; multum, ille et terrīs iactātus et
                             [altō

vĭ superūm*, saevae memōrem Iunōnis ob īram.
[A.I.1-4]   [*superum = superōrum]

151. <u>Virgil in Shakespeare</u>.
In the play Henry VI, Part 2, [1.4.64] the
quoted oracle [Ennius, <u>Annales</u>, 174-6; from
Cic., <u>Div</u>., 2.56.116]

Aiō tē, Aeacida, Rōmānōs vincere posse

shows an ambiguous grammatical construction in
the Delphic oracle which had misled King Pyrrhus,
the descendant of Aeacus. Also in the same play
[2:1:24, from Virgil, <u>A</u>., 1.15]:

Tantaene animīs coelestibus īrae?

152. <u>Readings</u>.

(1) Medieval verses in classical meter by
Rodulfus Tortularius (d.c. 1122):

Ōceanī missam dē litore perlege cartam,
   mittit Rodulfus quam suā curā tuus. [Ep.4.1.f]

Sī nōn est sapiēns, quem passiō commovet ūlla,
   est reor hōc nūllus tempore vir sapiēns.[3.449f]

Donec adhuc adolēs, assūme probōs tibī mōrēs,
   quōs nunc arripiēs, semper habēre volēs.[4.69f]

Multa tacēns audī, dubitāns quasi, plurima
                                    quaere.[11.219]

Pauca loquī, sed plūra studē sollers operārī,
Nec proferre vetō tempore verba suō. [11.177f]

Tōtā mente Deum, tē sicut amātō propinquum...[11.91]

(2) On the medieval poet Primas and his epitome
of the Old and New Testaments:[1]

---

1. Meyer, pp. 78-79.

Magister Hugō Aurelianēnsis, quī dīctus est
Prīmas, versificātor ēgregius fuit hīs temporibus [1181 to 1189]. Huius ingenium fuit ultrā
hūmānum versificāre elegantius et repente. Ex
quō inter ceterōs versificātōrēs vir ipse illustrīs habitus est eximius et excellēns, cuius
extant operà mīra. Dum in cūriā Rōmānā super
eius in arte versificandī ingeniō, quaestiō
verterētur, dīctum est alium poetam meliōrem
esse. Dumque amīca contentiō inter multōs
verterētur, màteria, sub quā ambo versificāre
debērent, papae mandàtò per collegium cardinālium data est. Erat autem māteria breve compendium Novī et Veteris Testamentī. Quī
igitur pauciōribus eam versibus comprehenderet,
ille habērētur eximius. Prīmas duōbus, alius
quattuor eam comprehendit versiculīs. Hī autem
fuērunt Prīmatis versus:

Quōs / anguis / tristī / vīrus / mulcēdine /
                                pāvit,
Hōs / sanguis / Christī / mīrus / dulcēdine /
                                lāvit.

Note that each word of the two lines has its
corresponding rhyme.

A less perfect verse on Mary and Eve reads:

Quōs male prīma parēns transgressus vulnere strāvit,
Hōs tuā fīne carēns virtūs   plenē reparāvit.

153.   Quintus Ennius and Johannes Secundus:
       1700 Years of Latin Poetry

Quintus Ennius was the first genius who permanently introduced Greek hexameters into Latin
for his great song of the history of Rome, the
Annales.   Johannes Secundus, a Dutch youth,

deserves the title of last real genius of Latin
verse. From Ennius to Secundus there is a
space of about seventeen-hundred years: Ennius
lived from 239 B.C.; Johannes Secundus from
A.D. 1511 to 1536. Ennius died at seventy-two;
Secundus at twenty-five.

Ennius spiced his hexameters with allitera-
tion, that is, the recurrence of the initial of
the same sound in two or more words of the same
verse. For example, when the trumpeter is
shot dead, he writes:

Quomque[cumque] caput caderet, carmen tuba
sōla perēgit...[Ennius, Annales, 499]

Here, four times a word begins with the metallic
"k" sound. The unbeatable record of seven
alliterations in one verse was reached by
Ennius in his notorious verse on the murder of
King Titus Tatius:

Ō Tite, tūte, Tatī, tibī, tanta, tyranne, tūlistī.
        [Annales, 108; Prisc., 947]

In another word order this could read:

Ō Tite Tatī tyranne, tū ipse tibī tanta tūlistī.

There are many more t's in the verse besides the
seven underlined above.

In two lines worthy of being learned by heart,
Ennius condensed the twelve "deī Congenitālēs,"
the genuine Roman deities, six godesses, six
gods. Jupiter, the leader, is relegated to
two short syllables in the form of Jovis:

Iuno, Vesta, Minerva, Ceres, Diana, Venus, Mars,
Mercurius, Iovis, Neptunus, Vulcanus, Apollo.
[Annales, 60-1]

Finally, as a specimen of archaic Latin,
we give his words for his own tombstone, quoted
often as truly proud:

Nēmō mē lacrimīs decoret nec funera flētū
faxit.* Cur? Volito vivos** per ōra virum.***

_____

*faxit = faciat **vivos = vivus ***virūm =
                                        vivōrum

At the other end of seventeen centuries of
Latin poetry, there await you the love songs of
Johannes Secundus (Jan Everaerts, 1511-36), whenever you should be in need of finding expression
for your feelings in that matter. Here, in the
meantime, are two less specific examples of his
mastery:

Senex dīvus dē sē

Pauper eram iuvenis; nunc tandem aetāte senīlī
Ditescō: hei miserō tempore utrōque mihī.
Ūtī, cum poteram, nummōrum copia deerat
Copia nunc superest larga, sed ūsus abest.

154.   From Johannes Secundus to the Lydia

The last selections from the long history
of Latin poetry take us back from Johannes to
the Appendix Vergiliana which contains a beautiful expression of how all nature mirrors the
poet's love, the exquisite Lydia.

Dead at twenty-five, Johannes Secundus left
behind him a rich and varied literary legacy.
Perhaps best known of his works are the Basia
(Kisses), often translated and imitated, but
never equalled. These had much influence on
the love poetry of subsequent generations in
England, France, and other lands. From his

lesser known Epigrammata it is fitting to quote
what he wrote when mortal illness gripped him
in Spain:

In discessum suum ex Hispania cum regionis
aere offensum gravissime laborare

    Hesperiae fines arentes linquimus aegri,
      Et petimus blande dulce solum patriae,
    Et quorum in manibus melius moremur, amicos:
      Cur invisa meum terra moraris iter?
    Cur mihi tot montes, cur saxa obstatis eunti?
      Vere quid in medio me fera pulsat hiems?
    Ninguida diluvium mittit liquefacta Pyrene,
      Et madidus pluvias Juppiter addit aquas.
    Parce meo cineri iam non, Hispania, vivo!
      Quid iuvat (heu) manes sollicitare meos?
    An vero, paucis cum sis fecunda poetis,
      Laudem de tumulo quaeris acerba meo?
    Ut lubet, ipse tamen fugiam terraque marique,
      Ne mihi sis etiam post mea fata gravis.

He summed up the magic of beauty in three words,
exclaiming at the end of a poem: "O vis superba
formae!" "O proud power of beauty!" Goethe
in old age jotted it down as a surrender, beautiful because so simple, to that power that
governs man.

Johannes Secundus is a worthy successor to a
tradition of romantic love poetry much earlier
exemplified by the Lydia, which a modern critic
adjudges, "a love song which perhaps has no
equal in Latin poetry."[1] Peter Dronke, from
whom a portion of this poem is quoted, sums up
the mood of the piece: "The opening takes us
into a world in which romantic love is radiant,

---

1. Augusto Rostagni, Virgilio minore (1961),
    quoted by P. Dronke, Medieval Latin and the
    Rise of European Love-Lyric (1965), vol. I,
    p. 174.

epitomized in the joy and beauty which Lydia
and the fields and streams around her seem to
reflect reciprocally....Love is something
common to deities, men and beasts--why then
should only mankind know love as pain? If
men can share in the all pervading cosmic love,
why is their love not as uncomplicated as that
of the world around them?"[1]

Invideo vobis, agri formosaque prata,
hoc formosa magis, mea quod formosa puella
est vobis - tacite nostrum suspirat amorem;
vos nunc illa videt, vobis mea Lydia ludit,
vos nunc alloquitur, vos nunc arridet ocellis,
et mea submissa meditatur carmina voce,
cantat et interea, mihi quae cantabat in aurem.
Invideo vobis, agri: discetis amare.

Perhaps these fragments which "bracket" the
long Latin poetic tradition will serve to
introduce our reader to an unfailing stream, a
stream that still invigorates the imaginations
of men,[2]

_____

1. Ibid., pp. 174f. The portion of the poem
    here quoted is given on p. 173.
2. With this chapter we cease to mark long
    vowels.

Part Four: Keeping a Language Alive

How the Renascences of Latin Are Achieved

CHAPTER XXVIII

Evolution of Language

155. Introduction: From Plain Chant to Broadcast.
In c. 3000 BC, Plain Chant, music and speech
were undivided. Gestures (dances) and plain
chant went together in all community cere-
monies. This we may call the 'loud voice.'
Between individuals, the full gesticulation
used in public was probably omitted; the 'still
small voice,' as the Bible calls it [1 K. 19:12]
was used. This still small voice comes to the
fore. After 1500 BC, speech and music separated.
A nucleus of plain chant remained for prayer,
law and oratory. This may be called the
'hieratic layer.' After music split off, it
eventually separated into instrumental and
vocal music. (See diagram in Lesson XXVII.)
At the same time the still small speech split
into poetry (epic, lyric, drama) and prose
(mathematics, history, philosophy). For Latin,
about 500-600 BC, the written language entered
the scene as a language-changing power. After
oral speech became supplemented by written documents, four types of expression, together with
their combinations, resulted: (1) oral, impro-
vised; (2) oral, memorized; (3) written read
aloud; (4) written, read silently.

We modern men think that type 4 is the regular type. Originally, it was used only for
doctrinal, scientific, or historical traditions.
Type 3 has been used for poetry, and for all
hieratic texts once they are written down, although even then most of them are recited in
plain chant; this means they have been handed
down from generation to generation by immediate
oral transmission, while the written documents

have been used only as an 'aide-memoire' -- not
to tell the whole story of how to pronounce
the texts.

Type 2 is the genuine way of speaking in
slogans, proverbs, formulas: 'How-do-you-do?
'Talk' develops by jocose variations of such
a formula of quotation.

Type 1 bears the genuine power of creative
language, now restricted to prophetic language,
'speaking in tongues.' This faded at the end
of the pre-Christian era, in the last oracles
and sibylline books and similar ecstasies.
Women, in their dirges, were especially apt
to preserve pregrammatical, ecstatic cries
and yells. When Paul said: 'Let the women
be silent in the church,' (1 Cor. 14.34), he
was probably turning against the shouting
and yelling still in use today among Jewish
women at time of death. Thereby he paved the
way for the real emancipation of women to
public speaking; whereas before they represented
an inarticulate element.

Thus, at the beginning of our era, the various withering services and cults all over
the globe were reunited in one form of public
worship that comprehended in itself all styles
of speech. The Christian Church regenerated
the realm of hieratic plain chant once more
by taking over the psalm-singing of the synagogue. The result is that today in the synagogue service and in the Roman Mass the oldest
type of human speech, plain chant, is still
preserved. And in singing Latin we can even
now trace the relation of plain chant Latin
to that virgin state of language, before
the separation of the various ways of expression.*

---

*With Vatican II has come, in the Roman Church,
a shift away from Latin to the Vernacular in
liturgy, parallel to what has happened in the

But the Church also had the sermon (= daily speech) and lessons (i.e., meditative reading), and the whisper of the confessional. Any living religion must keep all ways of speech alive. When one can tell from the radio voice that this <u>must</u> be a sermon, here is the death-knell of religion.

Today we once more differentiate; we not only have: (1) music -- written and played, (2) plain chant, (3) speech -- written and spoken; we also have broadcasting* -- a fourth something because it is subject neither to the conditions of ordinary speaking nor of ordinary writing and reading. All oral speech relies on the presence of the speakers, on their being able to supplement speech by gesture, facial expression, etc. All writing relies upon the absence of the speakers. What with radio? Now, everybody today is familiar with the problems of broadcasting. Hence, it is the simplest thing to deal with the specific difficulties of broadcasting first, then draw attention to the troubles our ancestors had with the other phases of language -- all very clearly visible in Latin. Yet we, too, have these very same problems, but have -- in the midst of our new problems -- pushed the former ones into the background.

---

liberal synagogue, and to the elimination of Greek and Old Church Slavoic in New World Eastern Orthodoxy.

* These lines were obviously written before television eclipsed radio among the mass media. As in the case of the cinema, television gives us the illusion of a present speaker, yet two-way discourse is obviously not possible.

Since Speaker, Listener and World Spoken
of are involved in every conversation or act
of communication, there must always be three
elementary difficulties in every phase of
speech. It may be difficult to identify the
speaker, to reach the listener, to clarify the
object. Ceremonial ('danced') speech posed
this difficulty when the young were initiated
into the mysteries of the tribe. Everywhere
we find secret language and the idea of 'revelation' conceived as a slow, tortuous process.
At the time of 'plain chant,' people did not
think what was being spoken of as "plain."
The orgiastic attitude of the dancer, the
medicine man's wearing a mask, etc., were
thought necessary to prepare the listeners
to receive the communication.

We, on the other hand, are so blunted as
to overlook the common sense in all these
procedures. We go to church, or to court,
or to a class room; by the very locale itself
we are fully prepared to get one specific
kind of communication. In the times of plain
chant the awe now conveyed by the building
had to be imparted by the speaker's dress and
the listener's contrition.

Let us now analyze speech and writing.

156. The Special Difficulties of Broadcasting,
Writing, and Speaking.

1. Broadcasting
   a. station and program: where does the
      program come from geographically?
   b. tuning in at right moment and in right
      manner
   c. no static interrupting

2. Writing
   a. which script: Arabic, code?
   b. date of letter; edition of book.
      When?
   c. interpretation

3. Speaking
   a. which language?
   b. which pronunciation?
   c. usage

* * * * * *

Why is the problem in broadcasting geographical; in printing and writing, chronological? All language creates a present
between a past and a future. As long as
people speak together, they share a single
present. Broadcasting triumphs over all distance by being always simultaneous. Writing
triumphs over chronology by being with us
after any elapse of time. Thus, there are two
paths, two 'afters' in any written communication. One is that past after which the writer
sat down and wrote; the second past is that
after which we sit down and read that which
he has written. Therefore, the writer's
place between past and future must be stated
explicitly by dating the document, by marking
the edition. Ordinarily, we are as little
aware, in our paper age, of this inherent
necessity of taking a stand on the writer's
'date,' as we are of the shortcomings of the
indicative. (See XII, Sect. 68). We are
reminded of it, however, when faced by the
problem of interpretation (2c). Since in
writing all gestures and intonation are ab-
sent, many words are ambiguous as to the
amount of emphasis they should carry. The
text remains a dead letter unless we agree
on how to interpret a written document.

Now it is interesting to see that in our era of the printed word we are reversing the process. In matters of importance, to write is now more normal than to speak. Hence, American intonation represses all inflection of tone and speaks as though the words were written, without once lifting or changing the intonation. Compare an Italian born in Italy, and an Italo-American born and raised in this country. The descendant of Latin in Europe still speaks as though he had never been exposed to the invention of printing. His manner of speech was actually fixed in 1450, just before the printing press was invented.

The Italo-American, however, like all other Americans, tries to imitate by his larynx the even flow of the printed page. The American intonation is 'print-conscious' probably because millions of immigrants have learned the language as adults, from the printed page. Most people speak as if they had learned reading before speaking. The Puritans allege religious persecution as the cause of this. This is actually true for the greater share of our words and ideas: we have mastered eleven-twelfths of our vocabulary through reading alone.

Let us now turn to the difficulties of speaking. Oral expression has its own problems; these are in the limelight in the development of Latin. The Imperial Language of victorious Rome, more than nearly any other language, most successfully solved these problems. Three thousand years ago thousands of idioms were spoken. Latin has survived all the many Italian dialects and languages. Latin has been a monopoly-winner as much as has English; but more than that.

The stream of language inspired individuals
through individual channels, descending in
four or more derivations: (1) through the
family and the economic centers for the language of cooperation, the technical words of the
crafts, etc.; (2) through the temples for
religion; (3) through the army, for the law;
(4) through the market place for trade and
ideas. At every moment, then, language was
imperilled by idiomatic segregation and disintegration. A great and lucid example of
this danger is the fact that the Christian
Church in Rome for its first two hundred
years spoke Greek in its prayers. But in
every home in Italy a special idiom was
spoken. And we still find villages in the
Alps today, where two or three families or
houses will differentiate themselves in their
pronunciation from the next four or five home-
steads. Also, on different occasions the same
words had a very different meaning. This is
the ambiguity of metaphors and analogies,
from time immemorial.

Hence arise the two great problems of
antiquity: even after unity of language has
been determined pronunciation and usage must,
also, be clarified. At the beginning of a
conversation there are formal words about the
weather and about personal health. 'Howdoyoudo? Fine' is not an exhibiting of truthful-
ness, but of pronouncing together, or tuning
in. The very patient who goes to see her
doctor about her nerves will answer his polite
question about her well-being by saying,
'Fine.' Then she will let off steam by saying, 'Oh, I feel rotten.' This is not stupid.
The exchange of this little poem:

Hoddoyoudo? Howdoyoudo?
Fine and you? Not so bad.

is not expected to be true but to be stereo-
typed. We say 'fine' when we feel rotten because it is not a question of telling the truth
but of making the other person both speak and
listen. Only a stereotype can serve this purpose. Hence, the value of standard phrases
in speech. Now in Latin these standard phrases
still have the unction of a responsible social
act; whereas our paper age is apt to belittle
them too much.

This sameness of usage was possible because
language was in the making for many centuries.
In conversing, people could continually derive
new shades of meaning from concrete roots,
repeatedly forming diminutives, adjectives,
verbal nouns and the like. The tremendous
wealth of grammar served this creation of
common usage, ad hoc, i.e., on the spur of
the moment. The effort of speaking on important subjects must have been as great as
when we today write a book. Modern man in
America, as we have seen in the case of the
Italo-American, has fallen completely under
the spell of printing and broadcasting. He
is unaware of the frailty of speech when up-
rooted from its social conditions.

The modern American registers words with
his brain; hence, he mistrusts them. For
the brain has been given us for analysis and
criticism. Consequently, this same American
may have recourse to gambling, drinking, or
speeding, in order to fill the gap that
creative speech once filled before it was
restricted to printing and broadcasting.

In olden times, the whole man was moved
when communication reached him. A man
listening to plain chant, to recitation,
experienced social recognition, intellectual
revelation, emotional satisfaction, and

personal responsibility -- all at the same
time. He had no reason to be afraid lest he
be cheated by advertising or propaganda or
ranting. It was under this fourfold pressure
that the speaker spoke, initiating the newcomer
into the central secrets of the life of the
community to make him a full-fledged partner
in this community. It was under this same
pressure that the listener received the news
about the universe. And the news reached
the listener with remarkable precision and
vigor. He was sufficiently wondering at,
sufficiently impressed by, the creative
spell of this communication to become a
bearer of the torch himself. This explains
the remarkable durability of our linguistic
traditions. If we analyze the spell cast
over the people when speaking together, we
can see that it was law-giving, teaching,
moving, and creative -- all at the same time.

Now it is a biogenetic law of society
that we must all pass through the phases of
man's evolution, although perhaps in an abbreviated process. To arrange for this biogenetic curriculum is education. Latin is
the classic of evolutionary education because
we realize all the phases and layers of human
speech by learning Latin. Without Latin, we
remain under the spell of broadcasting and
printing, powers of the modern era which en-
danger our loyalties because we have need to
debunk them so often.

To sum up. Education means to present
every man with the potentialities of the
whole race. Speech is that energy which
makes us partake in the six or seven thousand
years of civilized life on earth. Latin
provides us with evolutionary vitamins that
are lacking in our daily linguistic food.

Latin, then, can be a powerful weapon in our perpetual struggle for the reunification of mankind.

LESSON XXIX

Some Remarks on Etymology

157. Introduction. The Italian dialects spoken in
different parts of the peninsula -- Oscan,
Umbrian, Latin, etc. -- came into existence
when the Indoeuropean intruders clashed with
the various aboriginal tribes of Italy. The
language of the invaders (this at least is
the probable interpretation of the facts)
underwent the influences of different tongues,
tribes, and localities, or, to say the least,
of different experiences and destinies. Into
this period of which no written documents
exist, we are taken back by the science of
etymology. This science, which explores the
sources and true origin (= etymon) of words,
may tell us about the sources of modern English words like gerrymander or gawdy. However, the greatest triumphs of the etymolo-
gists may be expected where he is the only
guide whom we have, as in the period before
the split between Latin, Greek, Sanskrit,
German, Slavic, Lithuanian, and Persian
occurred.

The science of etymology, founded by Franz
Bopp in 1816,* is devoted to discovering the
relations, transition and laws, often ob-
scured, that connect the Latin language with
Greek, German, Sanskrit, Etruscan, or any
other language, and it reveals the ties that
exist between Latin words that, at first sight,
seem to be but disconnected atoms. The thousands of words that comprise a language

---

*Franz Bopp (1791-1867) published a treatise
on the inflectional endings of verbs in Sanskrit,
Greek, Latin, Persian, and Germanic in that year.

are not isolated. They are shot through
with a common life; sometimes this is quite
evident and transparent; nobody will doubt
that <u>amor</u> and <u>amare</u>, <u>objectum</u> and <u>subjectum</u>,
must have something in common. It is more
difficult to perceive that <u>alumni</u> and <u>adoles-
cents</u> are called by two closely interdependent
names.

   Though it is impossible to go into the
details of Latin etymology, let alone Indoeuropean linguistics, the student of our book
is entitled to get a realistic picture of a
language in process and of Latin in action;
you have seen again and again, through these
pages, that to speak is not to lie or cheat
or to sell or to be smooth and soft-spoken
or to rhyme; all these are more or less
superficial and peculiar abuses of the human
power to speak. At the core, language and
literature constitute a heroic campaign of
man's spirit to provide peace and unity
between all potential interlocutors, and
that means among all men. This genuine
struggle of the spirit of man against the
perpetual decay of the forms and means of
expressing his most intimate experiences to
his neighbors may be traced in the network
of etymological relationships. Therefore,
some remarks about these belong here.

158. The Latin Root "-al." English "old" corres-
     ponds to Latin <u>altus</u>. <u>Altus</u> means "high"
     according to the dictionary. How may the
     same word express two such distant ideas as
     "old" and "high"? Latin <u>altus</u> means "grown
     up." Later <u>altus</u> was restricted to physical
     height, meaning "high," and a special com-
     pound with the preposition <u>ad</u>, <u>ad-ultus</u>, was
     used to signify the inner maturity of the
     "adult"; while "adolescent" was the young man
     in the process of growing up.

Of all these different participles, <u>altus</u>,
<u>adultus</u>, <u>adolescens</u>, the verb <u>alêre</u>, to
nourish, is the source. It had the active
meaning of "feeding" or "making grow." <u>Alma
mater</u>, then, is the nursing mother. The
child nursed by the mother, the <u>alumnus</u>,
preserves in the ending <u>-umnus</u> a primeval
passive form of the participle otherwise destroyed in Latin, but known to us from the
Greek, as in words like "phen-o-<u>menon</u>," "Melpo-
<u>mene</u>," "prolego-<u>mena</u>." Thus, the word for the
babe and suckling tells the truth about a
buried past in which Latin shared its passive
with other Indoeuropeans. On the other hand,
the response of the nursling, the <u>alumnus</u>,
was expressed by enlarging the short and consonant stem "al-," into the fuller stem that
ends in "ê," and thereby expresses being:
"<u>(ad)-olêre</u>" means to "grow up"; hence, <u>adoles-
cere</u> is a second additional growth stressing
the initiative and the process of becoming
by the syllable "-esc." Further derivations
became: <u>indoles</u> = ingrained or ingrown nature;
<u>proles</u>, <u>prolis</u>, fem., contracted out of
<u>pro-oles</u> = out-growth, offshoot, progeny,
descendants (prolific).

Thus all the words, <u>alimentum</u> (nourishment),
<u>alimonia</u> (nourishment, grain), <u>alumni</u>, <u>adoles-
cents</u>, and <u>proletarian</u>, are derived from the
same alma mater, the root which means "growing"
and "nursing."

159. <u>Juppiter, or the God that was Tuesday</u>. Another
connection of Anglo-Saxon, Latin, and Roman
leads us into the center of Rome's rise to
political power. This connection is hidden
away in the name of the God which the Roman
worshiped as "the Biggest and the Best," on
the Capitoline Hill. It is a story in three
chapters, one dealing with the God as an
Indoeuropean deity, the second as a God of

the inhabitants of Latium, the "Latins," the
third as the God of the city of Rome.

i

In <u>Tues</u>-day, the English language preserves
the Indoeuropean God. Tiwaz, Zeus in Greek,
was the God of daylight, of the sky, of lightning, of war. In Latin the word <u>diēs</u> is of
the same root. In Latin, to the Germanic
"Tiw" should correspond a name that begins
with a "d." For a "t" in German usually
corresponds to a "d" in Latin. (See Section
164, below, on <u>t</u>ooth =<u>d</u>ens, <u>t</u>en = <u>d</u>ecem.)
The chief Roman God, however, is known to
us not as *<u>dieus</u>; he is called <u>Juppiter</u>.
The sound in the beginning of the word has
been changed against the general rule.

Etymology never becomes more exciting than
when it is chasing a panting exception through
time and space,

ii

We know, indeed, that the exceptional form
<u>Juppiter</u> was preceded by the regular form
*<u>Dieus</u>, *<u>Diovis</u>, in which it is not diffi-
cult to recognize the Greek Zeus and the Germanic Tiu, Tiw, Tiwaz. In fact, the first
capital of the Latins, Alba Longa, had an
altar of Diovis, as of the central Indoeuropean, and therefore Latin, deity. This cult
seemed so dignified that it survived the
destruction of Alba Longa itself in the 6th
century BC. The Roman Republic carried on
the cult and put in charge of it a family
of Rome's own gentry, the <u>gens Julia</u>. And
the service was continued at a place one or
two miles distant from the ruins of Alba
Longa.

This new cult-center was eleven miles from
Rome, its now destroyed predecessor Alba
Longa twelve miles, whereas Anglia where the
God Tiw (= Mars) was worshiped, was a thousand
miles away. Common sense, then, would suppose
that the difference between the worship of
Tiw and the two cults in Latium must be overwhelming, whereas it would suppose the Gods
of Alba Longa and Rome to be almost identical.
Common sense always judges by what is seen,
as distances or mileage. Gods however, as
powers, defy space, and the measurement by
inch or mile. Tiw, Diovis, the God of Alba
Longa, and Juppiter, the God of Rome, belong
to three layers of religion. And the Roman
religion restored a genuine feature of Tiw
with great vehemence. Such, however, was the
impetus of the Roman Lutherans, against the
decay of Alban religion, that the purified
God lost its initial, the "d," in the process.

The God of lightning, as worshiped by the
Indoeuropeans, had led them into battle.
In Alba Longa and Latium, the tribal cult
of the ancestors played a great part. The
God Diovis cared for the dead and as time went
on, more and more myths and all too human
stories were told of the God himself. The
spirits of the dead forefathers of the tribe
were placated by him.

iii

When the Romans established the religion
of the Capitoline Hill to Juppiter Optumus
Maxumus, they concentrated all their faith
on their God's dealings with the living. The
one ancient feature by which the God's lightning had governed defeat and victory, his
eagle's flight had given luck or disaster,
was accentuated. And this was done with the
furious rigidity of people who felt shocked

by the wild legendary growth around the god
of their government. Violently, the Roman
Republic erased every bit from the official
cult that interfered with their god's central
quality of being the present god. By a grue-
some and hairsplitting ritual, all the priests
of Juppiter were forbidden to come in touch
with a grave or a corpse or anything not
representing the Roman militia. The priest
could only be shaved by a member of the militia.
All the legends about the god's past and his
role as the god of the dead were suppressed.
The myths were replaced by the city's annals.
We have mentioned already the astounding fact
that the first great poem of Rome, by Quintus
Ennius, is no mythological song, but is called
annales, the annual history of the city. Historical greatness, here and now, animated the
Roman religion. The general who marched in
triumph up the Capitoline Hill incarnated
Juppiter. He was the god, in real presence!
Myths give way to history; dreams to actual
experience.

   This radical shift away from ancestral
worship to the faith in the real presence of
the "biggest and best" divine power made it
impossible to put the service in the hands
of one family, as the gens Julia had been
allowed to serve the Alban deity. The Juppiter of Rome was no clannish god but the god
of the whole republic. And the Romans took
great care that their deity should not be
mistaken for the old god of the peasants, a
deity on the tribal and mythological level.
The new creed of the republic required a clean
break between old and new. Though tolerating
the old religion, as any wise ruler will, they
coerced it. Thus, in the time when the greatest
son of the gens Julia, Gaius Julius Caesar, was

born (<u>circa</u> 100 BC), his family when building the altar, true to Alban ritual, could
not inscribe it "Iovi."

The inscription (<u>Corpus inscriptionum
latinarum</u>, XIV, 2387) reads:

'Vediovi ['Patri' is a later addition]
 lege albana'

Who is 'Vediovis'? Long overlooked, his
relationship to Tiw and Juppiter, as established by etymology, discloses why Rome was
able to become the master of a world that was
chained to the past and whose god *Dieus had
decayed to become a god of the defunct. The
Romans lowered the rank of the god of the
Latins by adding 've' to the name. The
syllable 've' in Latin, when put before a
word, spoils its beauty or normalcy. <u>Sanus</u>,
for instance, meaning 'sane,' when enlarged
by 've' into <u>vesanus</u>, comes to mean 'not
too sane' or 'little <u>sanus</u>.' <u>Vecors</u> means
'of little heart.' Ve-Diovis, then, in the
Rome-tolerated cult of the Julii; compares
with the genuine Diovis or *Dieus as Charles
the Fat does with Charlemagne. It belittles
the god of the ancestors; he is not the regular or normal *Dieus any longer.

Thus, the prefix 've-' was an energetic
means of separating the creed of the old
timers from the new political faith. Nor
was this all.

For the Romans, as we know, spoke of *Dieus
as Juppiter. This too, did not happen by
accident. *Diovis and Jovis were members
of a class of words having no special form
for the nominative case. (In <u>civis</u> or <u>navis</u>,
for example, the nominative is simply the

genitive case, repeated). The Romans exalted
their god by a remodelling of his name and
their way of doing this was unique. The
name 'Juppiter' is a formation of the Romans
-- over against the Latins -- in at least
three respects.

First, it is a vocative turned into a nominative. Its literal meaning is: 'O Father Zeus.'
This form, used in prayer, froze or petrified
into the nominative. Secondly, the way this
vocative was formed represents another peculi-
arity. This vocative is articulated by the
absence of any formative ending whatsoever,
and in this respect this vocative preserves
a primitive quality of nouns, otherwise unknown in Latin. Throughout this book we
have stressed that the absence of a formative ending is the significant quality of
the verbal imperative in Latin. 'Dic,' 'Fer,'
'I,' 'Ama,' as imperatives are the pure stem
without any addition. They are the shortest
possible form. The form 'Juppiter' stands
out as an absolute twin to the imperative of
verbs. Indeed, the vocative, 'O Father
Zeus,' and the urgent cry, Da! Give!, belong
to each other when the god is considered the
one and only center of the republic's prayer.
For the name of the god whose real presence
was to oppose the mythological figure of
Latium, no better starting point could be
chosen than the bare vocative. Of Diovis,
one might tell tales of the past; of Juppiter,
one could speak only of present and future
things.

Consequently, the distance from the Alban
deity was further increased. Vediovis and
Diespiter are already as far apart as Diovis
junior and Diovis senior. Now, however, the
third and last feature in the singular formation of Juppiter has to be mentioned. For

the tying together of *Dies and piter in the
ritual and in the new nominative taken from
the ritual shifted the phonetic hurdle or
pronunciation from the beginning to the end
of the newly-combined word. In the words,
'divinus' and 'dies,' the 'd' could be properly
cared for because the later parts raised no
difficulty. In 'diespiter,' anybody who wishes
to pronounce it correctly will have to think
of the collision of the consonants 'v,' 's,'
and 'p.' The word *dieus was now determined
from its end instead of from its beginning.
As a result of this new emphasis, the initial
'd,' once the greatest sound of the whole
original Indoeuropean stem, withered away.
*Dieuspiter, Diespiter, evaporated into
Jupiter, Juppiter. And as Jupiter, the
Roman Yahweh certainly no longer ran the
risk of being mistaken for the Alban God.

   *Dieus now had evolved into two names that
may, at best, be called second cousins to
each other: Vediovis and Juppiter. Though
they have a common stem, the names belong to
two different religions and to two different
forms of givernment, one good for the clans
of old, the other appropriate for the triumphant
march of the Roman Empire. The elision of a
consonant, then, may mark an epoch in the history of the world. And the science of etymology may see deeper into the process than any
other observer.*

---

*See Havet, Mémoire Linguistique, V.; Carl
Koch, Der Römische Juppiter (Frankfurt am
Main, 1937); Sommer Handbuch, 3rd ed.,
pp. 202, 374; Walde-Hofman, 350; Ovidius
Naso, Fasti, III.435ff.

160. English 'b-' : Latin 'f-'
  The most frequent English word, 'to be,'
is extant in Latin in two equally important
words that display their identity with 'be'
only after a somewhat intricate study of
etymological laws. The Latin words are:

  'fui' (I have been; hence also 'futurum'
  'fio' (I am becoming); also 'fore,' a
    word used as future infinitive for
    'esse'

Fio is a present, fui, a perfect stem of the
word that is preserved in English 'be-ing,'
and which supposedly, in the primeval Indoeuropean unity, was *bhuijo.

  Bhuijo, a mere supposition as this form
must be called (the linguists add an asterisk *
to such a word so that everybody can see immediately that the poor thing is a mere hypothesis -- *bhuijo, then -- has a large clan:
English 'bee,' the building animal, is related, as well as 'to build.' 'Bottom' is
a great grand nephew, and German 'Bühne'
(=stage) as well. On the Latin side, 'bottom'
corresponds to fundus, which, like 'bottom,'
means the are of growth. The most hidden,
yet one of the most fecund applications in
Latin is the 'b' which we know so well in
the formation of the Future of long -a and
-e stems: amā-b-is, docē-b-is contain, as
the future tense should, this revered exponent
of 'becoming.'

161. Real and Apparent Etymological Resemblances
  Sex-appeal repeals the dis-section of man
and wife into two persons. This is literally
true. For sexus is derived from sec-are, to
cut into two. Similarly, another derivative
of this root is saxum, the part of the mountain that is split off, the rock. Sexus,

then, must be conceived as the two halves
into which human nature is 'cut.' Securis
we already know as the cutting instrument,
the axe. Sica is the small cutting knife,
the dagger; sicarius, the murderer. Seg-
ment, section, sector, are further derivations
in mathematical and political usage today.
On the other hand, it is important to note
that secundus is not related. Secundus hails
from an older sequundus, as it appears in
sequitur (= follows), pedisequa (= one who
follows in the footstems of a master).

This example of secundus (second-), wherein
our imagination would easily have leaped to
some relation with sec-are, and to 'cutting
into pieces,' shows how carefully one has to
act before admitting superficial similari-
ties into the society of true etymological
relations.

Some warning is therefore to be sounded
at this point. Just as sec-are and sequitur
are not related, so no bond exists between
legere (reading, gathering, picking) and
legare (dispatch), thus 'legate' and 'leg-
ation.' Legare is derived from lex, legis
(law). Here the noun is the first growth,
the verb the second. With legere, on the
contrary, the verbal idea of 'picking'
came first; the noun, legion, the picked
men of the army, is a secondary creation.
Thus we see illustrated two contrary developments:

```
    n o u n              v e r b
      legio <------------ legere
      lex   ------------> legare
```

Our remarks on homonyms have already drawn
your attention to the fact that a long and
a short vowel of the same color are still
as far distant as two quite distinct and
alien sounds.

The following words have nothing to do with
each other etymologically:

(1) bellum (war : bellus (pretty)
    bellum was originally *duellum
    (fight between two, split)
    bellus was benulus, from bonus (good)
(2) littera (letter) : litus, litoris
                            (seashore)
(3) mica (crumb) : micare (shine),
                derived from meare

On the other hand, who would expect that
the English word 'seed' is a cousin of the
Latin God and Star, Saturnus, the planet of
'Saturday'? However, this is true: Latin
serit, sevit, satus, serere, correspond to
English 'sow.'

162. Correspondence of Latin and Germanic Consonants

a. As a general rule, Latin 'c' corresponds
   to English 'h.'
   'canis' - 'hound' ' 'centum' - 'hundred'
b. Latin 'h' corresponds to English 'g.'
   'hostis' - 'guest'; 'hortus' - 'garden'
c. Latin 'g' corresponds to English 'c' or
   'k'
   'gnoscit' - (he) 'knows'

The rule of this correspondence may be
symbolized by a circle in which the sounds,
'c,' 'h,' 'g' chase each other. For these
sounds, by the way, we may use a more general term. For 'c,' 'g,' 'h' are no isolated
triplets. As much as 'g,' 'k' and 'h' are

produced by our gums and throat, another
triplet is performed when we press our lips.
When we do this, putting the emphasis on our
lips, there come forth the sounds 'b,' 'f,'
or 'p.' When we put the pressure on our
teeth, there are produced 'c,' 't' and 'þ'
('th').

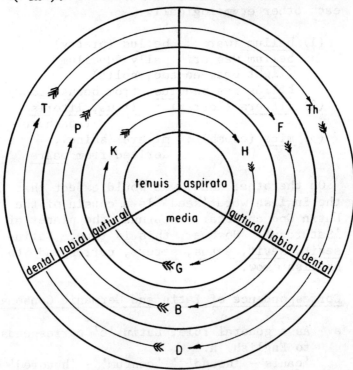

Circle of Consonantal
Relations between Latin and
Germanic

Our diagram shows the cross-classification
of the three triplets of consonants. On the
one hand 'k,' 'h,' 'g' are gutturals; 'p,'
'f,' 'b,' labials; 't,' 'th,' 'd,' dentals.
On the other hand, 'k,' 'p,' 't' are called

tenuis, because they are thin, strained sounds;
'g,' 'b,' 'd' are media; 'h,' 'f,' 'th' are
aspirata (and affricata). This circle, in
which the sounds chase one another etymologically, in their developments from the level
of sound in Latin to the level of sound in
German and English is formed by the Tenuis,
Media, and Aspirata:

   a.   L:tenuis---E:aspirata
   b.   L:aspirata---G:media
   c.   L:media---G:tenuis

Examples:
   a. Tenuis turns to aspirata

tres	three
pater	father
pes, pedis	foot
cervus	hart
mater	mother
frater	brother
septem	seven
octo	eight

   b. Aspirata turns to media

ruber (IE: rythros)	red
faba	bean
hanser	goose
haedus	goat

   c. Media turns to tenuis

deus	tues (in Tuesday)	
dens, dentis	tooth|	root
baculum	peg	
gena	chin|	like
ager	acre|	cast
radix	root	
ligare	like	
gerit,gestum	cast	

LESSON XXX

On Latin in General

163. <u>Is Latin a dead language?</u>
       Latin is called a dead language because no
modern community uses it in its daily social
intercourse.

However, Latin lives in the Romance Lan-
quanges, Spanish, Italian, French, Protuguese,
Roumanian, and Ladin; these sprang from Latin's
"peasant idiom" (<u>sermo rusticus</u>). Latin has
lasted through twenty centuries in the undy-
ing works of its orators and schoolmen, his-
torians and poets, lawgivers and grammarians;
it has lasted, in a more dignified and complete
way, by serving as the official language of
the Roman Catholic Church. Together with
Greek, Latin has given to all the sciences
the roots of their hundreds of thousands of
technical terms. Year after year, the mines
of Greek and Latin have been exploited for
the new concepts of the Niagara of modern
science. For this reason, the two languages
may be called our learned languages.

As such, the Latin language shares the
fate of any language; it incessantly changes
in order to hold its own in a changing world.
Its words spread into the innumerable varieties of forms as we have already seen in:

arare
aratrum
armentum
arator
arabilis

And this process is the life of language.
Words that do not increase in area of meaning

and variation, will decline and petrify and
finally become archaic and forsaken, and
therefore be more and more pushed aside.
Language is alive; nothing alive can remain
what it is; it must partly die, and partly
vary, in order to survive.

Of this ineluctable law of survival,
'dead' Latin is an outstanding example. What
we call 'dead' in its evolution, is one great
demonstration of its life. For Latin changed,
in the first millenium of our era, into the
Romance Languages; its full grammatical forms
slowly became so destitute of life that the
texts allegedly written in it practically
turned more and more into French, or Italian,
or Spanish, with only a faint veneer of the
classical constructions. Where a Roman had
said gubernavimus mundum, an Italian says
habemus gubernatum mundum. This is a new
principle. And, after A.D. 700, the confusion between the shells of the written
tradition, and the new forms of the spoken
language had become unbearable. Normal
daily life soon gave up the trimming of anything 'Latin.' However, the dead parts were
not completely thrown overboard. They now
began to serve a new, more specific purpose.

Church and State, from 800 to 1500, after
disentangling the core of 'Latin' from the
new branches of the Romance Languages, restored it to life as the language of the
ruling classes in the courts and cathedrals
and schools, as medieval Latin. This, again,
was a rich language, giving life to new forms
for higher life. What Augustine said of the
term essendi (XIII, Sect. 73) -- that it is
necessary for the interpretation and explica-
tion of great and divine truth, to push ahead
with new linguistic developments -- is true of

medieval Latin in general.

Again, this language broke down when the
governing classes that spoke it, in Church
and State, broke down in the Reformation.
The Reformation gave authority to the vernacular in Law and Religion. The Bible and
the Common Law were translated into the idiom
of the commoners. State and Church (instead
of Church and State as heretofore) now spoke
the vernacular, and thereby the vernacular,
Romance as well as Germanic, English as
well as French, became new and much richer
languages. With a congregation reading
and singing the national version of the
Bible, and a laity reading the common laws
of the land in their own language, the
national languages really became new compounds. 'Glory' and 'penitence' and 'posse'
and 'legacy' entered the vernacular. Thus
the vernacular and the legal and religious
heritage of the Middle Ages were blended
together to form the literary English, French,
German, etc., of modern times. These literary or "high" languages of today are as
different from their medieval progenitors
as they are from medieval Latin, but they are
the children of both.

Exercise: Sort and assign the following
words of modern English to the Latin of (a)
Church and (b) State: negotiate, intestate,
conversion, penalty, confession, criminal,
Chrism, divine, service, communion, altar,
congregation minister, posse.

The time when English took over the medieval Latin of Church and State was the time
of Henry VIII. Ever since, English has
been soaked and shot through with medieval
Latin, to an extent unknown in Chaucer's day.

The English of Shakespeare and Milton was a
new vernacular, originating (as we have just
said) as much from medieval Latin as from
Middle English.

Was Latin finally dead in 1500? It died,
it is true, at that time, with the new blend
achieved. But to "die," for a language, does
not necessarily mean to remain dead and unused.
Now the academic professions and the sciences
turned to Latin. This new movement was led
by the very leaders of the fight against medieval Latin, the so-called Humanists. In killing
one brand of Latin, they called forth another.
All our technical terminology -- vitamins and
automobiles, glands and botany, aviation and
telescopes -- are products of this warfare
for a new language of the sciences. And the
community in which this new language was
developed and used was the international republic of scholars. The letters of John Locke
(some of which are printed in our texts in
Part Five) may convey an idea of the life in
this Latin republic.

The stream always seems to be divided and
split and thereby lost in the soil; and each
time one part of it is dyked and damned and
used for a new and universal purpose.

164. The Periods of Latinity
With our eyes now sharpened to this phenomenon,
we may easily observe that this same development was at work even before the appearance of
the Romance Languages. Several centuries before, as early as A.D. 200, classical Latin
was superseded when the pagan faith of the
classics was destroyed. After A.D. 200,
the Biblical Latin of rising Christianity slowly
suffocated the 'Bostonian' Latin of Cicero,
that is to say, the golden Latin that had bor-

rowed its gold from Athens. The new Christian
language in Rome was Greek, too, for a long
time. However, this Greek did not hail from
Athens, but from the Jewish Bible and the
letters of Paul and Peter and John, and the
gospels of their companions. Upon this "Greek"
base, the new mansion of ecclesiastical Latin
was erected. No classical Roman could have
said, Credo in Deum or Te Deum laudamus,
Hosanna or Amen or Alleluia. The central
block of this new language is the 'Vulgate,'
the Latin version of the whole Bible of which
our texts contain a chapter from Job. The
bulk of what we have termed Singing Latin got
its style from this linguistic layer.

With all these precedents, we can see how
the so-called "golden" or "classical" Latin
of Cicero, Vergil and Horace was produced in
exactly the same manner. Here, too, an inten-
tional effort was made to erect a dam against
the disintegration with which Latin was threat-
ened in Caesar's time, just as any language
is threated at any moment in its history.

The men around Caesar Augustus, whose Res
Gestae are printed in full among our texts,
did not simply write or speak one of the
many Italian dialects. 'Latin' to them was
not the language of the geographical province
of Latium, nor was Roman contained in the
walls of the city of Rome. Latin, as the
language of the Roman Empire, was no longer
a dialect but a high and sovereign instrument
and expression of political victories. All
the victors of old had grafted upon it much
of their style and literature. Latin may
at that time be called the 'legal heir of
victory.'

And so in summing up we may outline the
history of Latin in the following epochs:

a. 'Golden' Latin   200 BC - AD 300
b. 'Ecclesiastical' Latin   AD 200 - 700
c. 'Scholastic' Latin   to 1500
d. Academic Latin of the
   Sciences, beginning   c. 1450
e. End of Liturgical Latin
   in the Roman Catholic
   Church, beginning   1963

Epochs a-d are conscious reactions against
disintegration and splitting and natural
decay of language. 200BC, AD 200, 700, or
800, 1450: the degradation of the language
into something too local, too idiomatic, too
flat, was reclaimed by countermovements which
restored Latin as a universal language. This
was achieved each time with the help of Greek
influence and authority. Parts of the old
linguistic domination were lost, to the
Romance Languages and to the vernacular; but
these losses were balanced by the successful
move toward unity on the political, the legal,
the religious, the scientific, and the artis-
tic level.

The stream of language, then, is divided
into the current that follows the laws of
inertia and natural consumption, and the
current that reveals the laws of human effort and social renascence. Incessantly,
the social renascence leads to new centraliz-
ing and universalizing literatures.

As to the stimulating injections from the
Greek, we must be very brief. The models
were presented by:

(1) Greek poetry to victorious Rome
(2) The Greek form of the Bible (called
    Septuaginta as far as the Old Testa-
    ment goes, for 72 translators supposedly
    wrote it) to Christian Rome

(3) The Greek philosopher Aristotle and
    Byzantine Greek to Medieval Latin
(4) The Greek Plato and all other Greek
    scientists, to the academic clan

These models stimulated these four social
efforts toward a unifying spirit and its
unifying expression in a Latin literature.

Or, to put it this way:
(1) Horace and Vergil learned from Greek
    poetry
(2) The early Latin Fathers from Greek
    Christianity
(3) Thomas Aquinas and the Schoolmen from
    Aristotle
(4) Erasmus and John Locke and John Stuart
    Mill from Plato

Under Greek stimulation a perpetual rebirth
of Latin took place. The 're-births' correspond, as conscious efforts, to the perpetual
running down of the unified language once it
is created and falls among children and wet-
nurses and classroom exercises.

Naturally, the movements we have mentioned
overlap. Classical Latin may still be found
as late as A.D. 500 in Martianus Capella's
Nuptiae (of which we have printed the chapter
on numbers), or in the sentence we have
chosen from Roman Law. And Ecclesiastical
Latin went on until 1150; only then was
'Medieval,' or more correctly, scholastic
Latin triumphant. To show the slow change:
In ecclesiastical Latin, 'theology' was a
pagan occupation of pagan philosophers; only
about 1120 was it permissible for a priest
or monk to dare call his own writings 'theological.' So distinct is every stratification
of Latin from every other one! Similarly, the

word 'academic' is a purely 'academic' pro-
duct; before 1450, it had no ring. Since we
wish to be on our guard against oversimplifi-
cation, we must remember the overlapping.

	BC 200	AD 200	600	1100	1300	1600	1700
Classical....							
Ecclesiastical...							
Scholastic..............							
Humanistic.....							

Neither the pioneers nor the dogmatists can
be traced to clear-cut dates.

165. Chronological Survey of Latin Disintegrations
and Renascences

a. Indoeuropean Language splits into many
families; of these, the Italic further
splits into dialects, one of which is
spoken in Latium; Roman is a subdivision
of Latin:

D = split into regional dialects

R = Classical Latin, under Greek influence; 200 BC - AD 500

b. Classical Latin

D = decaying into Rustic, military,
provincial

R = Ecclesiastical Latin AD 200-1100

c. Ecclesiastical Latin

> D = disintegrating under the pressure
> of the many Germanic tribes

> R = Carolingian and Scholastic Latin
> 800 - 1600 (mostly 'Medieval' Latin)

d. Scholastic Latin

> D = disintegrates under the pressure of
> its daily use in the schools and
> courts of the lower grades

> R = Humanistic Latin of the Republic of
> Scientists; 1450-1900

And today? People who know nothing but
their mother tongue or another 'modern'
language are deprived of their birthright
as full human carriers of evolution. Latin
is the Magna Charta of emancipation of a
man's thinking. The processes through which
Latin has passed during a period of three
to five thousand years tell the story of
social evolution more lucidly and succinctly
than any other material. Having done away
with classical Latin, we rediscover Latin
as a classic of linguistic evolution. Latin
teaches man to think of himself and his civili-
zations in timespans worthy of human beings,
in milleniums.

166. <u>Clemens Scotus on the Division of the Latin
Tongue</u>

XXXVIII.Δ.Quot sunt divisiones Latinae
linguae? M. Quatuor, ut quidam dicunt: id
est prisca, Latina, Romana, mixta. Prisca
est, qua vetustissimi Italiae sub Iano et
Saturno sunt usi, incondita ut se habent
carmina Sabinorum; Latina quam sub Latino

rege Tusci et ceteri in Latio sunt locuti et
qua duodecim tabulae fuerunt sciptae; Romana,
quae post reges exactos a populo coepta est,
qua Naevius, Plautus et Virgilius poetae et
ex oratoribus Gracchus, Cato et Cicero efful-
serunt; mixta quae post imperium latius pro-
motum simul cum moribus et hominibus in Romanam
civitatem irrupit integritatem verbi per soloe-
cismos et barbarismos corrumpens. Cavendum
igitur est unicuique qui Latinam sequitur
loquelam, ut integritatem ipsius linguae, sicut
ab eruditis doctoribus est constituta, cognos-
cat. Quid enim aliud putandus est qui integritatem linguae, qua utitur ignorat, nisi
brutis animalibus deterior? Illa enim
propriae vocis clamorem exprimunt, iste
deterior, qui caret propriae linguae notitia.

from Tolkiehn, pp. 22-23

167. On Custom and Precedent in State and Church

a. Justinianus imperator: Consuetudo praece-
dens et ratio quae consuetudinem suasit,
tenenda est. Diuturni mores consensu
utentium approbati legem imitantur.
Imperator Constantinus: Consuetudinis
ususque longaevi non vilis auctoritas
est: verum non usque adeo valitura est
ut aut rationem vincat aut legem.

b. Papa Gregorius ad Augustinum Anglis praedi-
cantem: Novit fraternitas tua Romanae
ecclesiae consuetudinem in qua se meminit
enutritam. Sed mihi placet, ut, sive in
Gallicorum sive in quaqua ecclesia aliquid
invenisti quod plus omnipotentis Deo
possit placere, eligas et in Anglorum
ecclesia, quae adhuc in fide nova est,
institutione praecipua quae de multis
ecclesiis colligere poteris, infundas.

Non enim pro locis res, sed pro rebus
loca amanda sunt. Ex singulis ergo
quibusque ecclesiis quae pia quae re-
ligiosa quae recta sunt, elige et haec
quasi in fasciculum collecta apud Anglorum mentes in consuetudinem depone.

MAGNA CHARTA LATINA

PART FIVE

TEXTS

PART FIVE

TEXTS

1. Abecedarius Mediolanensis

Hic videmus, quae res illis temporibus
civitati gloriae fuerint. Compara quas res
nostri contemporanei in libris pro viatoribus
confectis scribere soleant.

Abecedarius Rhythmus de Mediolano civitate
(written between 720 and 739   A.D.)

1. Alta urbs et spaciosa manet in Italia,
   firmiter edificata opere mirifico,
   que ab antiquitus vocatur Mediolanum civitas.

2. Bonam retinet decoris speciem et variis
   rutilat culture modis ornata perspicue;
   locus ita fructuosus constat in planiciae.

3. Celsas habet opertasque turres in circuitu,
   studio nitentes magnas scultantes forinsecus;
   que introrsus decorata manet edificiis.

4. Duodecim latitudo pedibus est moenium,
   inmensumque est deorsum quadrata ex
      ruppibus,
   perfectaque eleganter sursum ex fictilibus.

5. Erga murum pretiosas novem habet ianuas
   vinclis ferreis et claves circumspectas
      naviter,
   ante quas cataractarum sistunt propugnacula.

6. Foris valde speciosum habet edificium,
   omnem ambitum viarum firme stratum silice;
   undam capit per ductorem limphe quendam
      balastris.

7. Gloriose sacris micat ornata ecclesiis,
   ex quibus alma est Laurenti intus alavariis
   lapidibus auroque tecta, aedita in turribus.

8. Haec est urbium regina mater adque patrie,
   que precipue vocatur nomine metropolis,
   quam conlaudant universi naciones seculi.

9. Ingens permanet ipsius dignitas potencie,
   ad quam cuncti venientes presules Ausonie
   iuxta normam instruuntur sinodali canone.

10. Karitas benigna manet scilicet in populo,
    omnes sedulo ad dei properant aecclesiam,
    devota sua offerentes munera altaribus.

11. Letanter ibi quiescunt sancti circa menia:
    Victor, Nabor et Maternus, Felix et Eustorgius,
    Nazarius, Simplicianus, Celsus et Valeria.

12. Magnus presul cum duobus sociis Ambrosius
    Protasioque Gervasioque manet et Dionisius
    Calemerusque, ibi almus Benedictus recubat.

13. Nulla potest reperiri urbs in hac provincia,
    ubi tanta requiescunt sanctorum cadavera
    electorum revelata, quanta ibi excubant.

14. O quam felix et beata Mediolanum civitas,
    que habere tales sanctos defensores meruit,
    precibus invicta quorum permanet et fertilis.

15. Pollens ordo leccionum, cantilene, organum,
    modolata psalmorumque conlaudantur; regula
    artiusque adimpletur in ea cottidie.

16. Questu congrue ditantur venientes incole,
    nudi quoque vestiuntur copioso tegmine,
    pauperes et peregrini saciantur ibidem.

17. Rerum cernitur cunctarum speciebus inclita,
    generumque diversorum referta seminibus,
    vini copia et carnes adfluenter nimiae.

18. Sceptrum inde Langobardi principalem
       optinent,
    Liutprandum pium regem meritis almificum,
    cui tantam sanctitatis Christus dedit graciam.

19. Totam urbem presul magnus ornavit Theodorus
    veniens benigne, natus de regali germine,
    quem ad sedem raptum traxit pro amore populus.

20. Viribus robusti cives adstantium certamine
    nefandarum subdent colla expugnando gencium,
    palmam possident et nomen fidei amplissimum.

21. Xristum dominum precemur universi pariter,
    ut dignetur custodire hanc urbem et regere,
    adque cunctis liberare ipsam de periculis.

22. Ymnum regi modolanter cantemus altissimo,
    qui eam pulchro decoravit ornamento martyrum,
    sanctorumque confessorum ibi quiescencium.

23. Zelemus omnes Christiani salvatorem dominum,
    ut in illam nos permittat civitatem ingredi,
    in qua sancti per eterna gratulantur saecula.

from Schneider, pp. 10-12.

2. Paulinus monachus de ordine Fratrum Minorum (1344)
   De Heresia aetatis tertiae

2 pars de Almarico heresiarcha.

Tunc quidam Almalaricus de territorio Carno-
tensi, qui semper in artibus et in sacra pagina
discendi atque docendi modum et opinionem
privatam ac iudicium ab aliis separatum habuit,
ausus est constanter affirmare, quod quilibet

- 207 -

tenetur credere se membrum esse Christi, et
hoc unicum esse de articulis fidei, sine qua
nemo potest salvari. Contradixit ei Pari-
siensis universitas, unde ad summum pontificem
coactus accessit et condemnatur. Reversusque
Parisius compellitur ore profiteri, quod
predicte opinioni sentiret contrarium; unde
tedio et indignatione affectus egrotare cepit
et in brevi decessit. Post mortem vero
eius venenosa doctrina ipsius quidam infecti
surrexerunt asserentes, quod patris potestas
duravit, quamdiu viguit lex Mosayca. Christo
autem adveniente absoluta sunt omnia testamenti veteris sacramenta et viguit nova lex
usque ad tempus, quo talia predicabant. Tunc
aiunt novi testamenti sacramenta cessasse et
spiritus sancti tempus incepisse et ideo sacramenta ecclesiastica locum de cetero non habere,
sed unumquemque per gratiam spiritus sancti
tantum interius sine aliquo exteriori actu
inspiratam salvari posse. Caritatis quoque
virtutem ampliabant, ut quod alias peccatum
esset, si in caritate fieret, ratione
peccati careret et simplicibus, quos decipie-
bant, promittebant impunitatem peccati, Deum
dicentes bonum tantummodo et non iustum.
Capti sunt ergo multi secte illius clerici
et laici utriusque sexus et adducti Parisius,
ubi congregato concilio condemnantur et con-
cremantur exceptis quibusdam simplicibus ac
mulieribus seductis. Almalaricus quoque,
licet fuisset in pace sepultus, ab universo
concilio condemnatur, excommunicatur ac de
sacro cimiterio eiectus per sterquilinia proici-
tur; reprobatur quoque eius doctrina Extra:
de summa trinitate c. Damnamus.

from Holzmann, p. 8

3. <u>Patruus et Nepos</u>

Two letters written about 1120, in Northern Italy.

a.

Dulcissimo patruo suo P.C. eius unicus salutem
et obsequium.

Vestre paternitati, patruelis piissime,
innotescat me divina misericordia Papie
studio legum vel dialectice alacrem et sanum
nocte dieque adherere et incessanter utilitati
mee pro posse ingenii vacare, nisi quod vesti-
mentorum nuditas, nummorum paucitas et nimie
paupertatis sarcina me studiumque meum ultra
modum adgravat. Reverti namque propter
aliquod superveniens mihi, quod Deus avertat,
infortunium -- salva vestra loquor gratia --
non ante disposui, quam omnibus meis parentibus et amicis ingens afferam gaudium. Magis
enim cupio exul in alienis regionibus et
desolatus haberi et, ut pueriliter loquar,
mori quam ad innumeras et mordentes derisiones
sine sciencia litterarum, cuius gratia huc veni,
repatriare. Vos ergo, patruelis dulcis, ex
cuius arbitrio post Deum et sanctos eius tota
mea salus et refugium pendet, saltim amore Dei
necessaria mihi nepoti vestro et servo subdito
ministrare non differatis. Alienum panem hos-
tiatim, ut supra dixi, prius queram, quam domum
stultus redeam, quod vobis vestroque generi
contumeliam fore nemo dubitet.

b.

Precordiali nepoti suo unanimi C. salutem
et paternam dilectionem.

Magnam tue dilectionis epistola leticiam
mihi, nepos amantissime, ingessit. Quid
enim tam alacrem mentem posset redere, quam
cum tuam, de qua super omnia curo, audio

sospitatem et fortune tui studii, quam
ardenter cupio, prosperitatem, atque te
nolle redire, antequam proficias. Per quod
bone indolis ingenium tuum recognosco. Nec
mirabile, si de te audiens bona paterne
gaudeam: patruelis enim sum, non victricus.
Inter cetera tue littere mihi significavere
te paupertatem pati. Unde quia singularem
de te curam habeo, condoleo et cito tibi
secundum nostre substantie facultatem mittam.

Tu autem, fili mi, anime mee solacium et
refrigerium, sapienter expende, ne meam,
quam habes, intimam gratiam amittas.
Insuper ad cumulum nostre dilectionis et
utilitatis paternis verbis tuam sollicitu-
dinem hortari non desisto, quatinus studium
inceptum taliter exerceas, ut bonis iniciis
meliores exitus Dei favente gratia invenias.

from Erdmann, pp. 39-40.

4. De Cotidianis Operibus Monachorum Hieronymus
   (340-420) ad monachum de vivendi forma

   Nunquam de manu et oculis tuis recedat liber,
discatur Psalterium ad verbum; oratio sine
intermissione; vigil sensu, nec vanis cogitationibus patens. Corpus pariter et animus
tendatur ad Dominum. Iram vince patientia:
AMA SCIENTIAM Scripturarum, et carnis vitia
non amabis. Nec vacet mens tua variis per-
turbationibus, quae si pectori insederint
dominabuntur tui; et te deducent   ad
delictum maximum. Facito aliquid operis, ut
te semper diabolus inveniat occupatum. Si
Apostoli habentes potestatem de Evangelio vivere,   laborabant manibus suis, ne quem
gravarent; et aliis tribuebant refrigeria,
quorum pro spiritualibus debebant metere
carnalia (1. Cor. 9.11), cur tu in usus tuos
cessura non praepares? Vel fiscellam texe

junco, vel canistrum lentis plecte vimini-
bus; sarriatur humus: arcolae aequo limite
dividantur: in quibus cum olerum jacta
fuerint semina, vel plantae per ordinem
positae, aquae ducantur irriguae, ut pul-
cherrimorum versuum spectator assistas:

Ecce supercilio, clivosi tramitis undam
Elicit, illa cadens raucum per laevia murmur
Saxa ciet scatebrisque arentia temperat arva.
(Georg. 1.3)

Inserantur   infructuosae arbores, vel
gemmis, vel surculis, ut parvo post tempore,
laboris tui dulcia poma decerpas. Apum fabri-
care alvearia, ad quas te mittunt Salomonis
Proverbia (Prov. 6.8. juxta LXX); et monas-
teriorum ordinem, ac regiam disciplinam, in
parvis disce corporibus. Texantur et lina
capiendis piscibus, scribantur libri, ut
et manus operetur cibum, et animus lectione
saturetur.   In desideriis est omnis
otiosus (Prov. 13.14. juxta LXX). Aegy-
ptiorum Monasteria hunc morem tenent, ut
nullum absque operis labore suscipiant, non
tam propter victus necessitatem, quam propter
animae salutem.

Jerome, Epist., 125.11 (PL 22. 1078f)

5. Medieval Rules for the Duty and Right of Resis-
tance and Obedience

Imperatores quando pro falsitate contra
veritatem constituunt malas leges, probantur
bene credentes et coronantur perseverantes;
quando autem pro veritate contra falsitatem
constituunt bonas leges. terrentur saevientes
et corriguntur intelligentes. Quicumque
ergo legibus imperatorum quae pro Dei veritate
feruntur, obtemperare non vult, acquirit grande
supplicium. Quicumque vero legibus imperatorum,
quae contra veritatem Dei feruntur, obtemperare

non vult, acquirit grande praemium.

    <u>Corpus Iuris Canonici</u>, XII C. glossa ad I, 19
Decreti Gratiani

6. <u>Customs of Chester</u>

    Si quis liber homo regis pacem datam in-
fringens in domo hominem occidisset, terra
eius et pecunia tota regis erat, et ipse
utlagh (outlaw) fiebat. Hoc idem habebat
comes de suo tantum, homine hanc heris facturam
(forfeiture) faciente. Cuilibet autem utlagh
nullus poterat reddere pacem nisi per regem.

    End of the Investiture Struggle between
          Church and State

    Rex statuit ut ab eo tempore in reliquum,
umquam per dationem baculi pastoralis vel
annuli quisquam de episcopatu aut abbatia
per regem vel quamlibet laicam manum in
Anglia investiretur.

7. <u>Magna Charta</u>[1]

Great Charter of Liberties A.D. 1215

    Johannes Dei gratia rex Anglie, dominus
Hibernie, dux Normannie et Aquitannie, et
comes Andegavie, archiepiscopis, episcopis,
abbatibus, comitibus, baronibus, justiciariis,
forestariis, vicecomitibus, prepositis,
ministris et omnibus ballivis et fidelibus suis
salutem. Sciatis nos intuitu Dei et pro
salute anime nostre et omnium antecessorum et
heredum nostrorum, ad honorem Dei et exalta-
tionem sancte Ecclesie, et emendacionem regni

---

1. Text from McKechnie

nostri, per consilium venerabilium patrum
nostrorum, Stephani Cantuariensis archiepiscopi tocius Anglie primatis et sancte Romane
ecclesie cardinalis, Henrici Dublinensis archiepiscopi, Willelmi Londoniensis, Petri Winton-
iensis, Joscelini Bathoniensis et Glastonien-
sis, Hugonis Lincolniensis, Walteri Wygor-
niensis, Willelmi Coventriensis, et Benedicti
Roffensis episcoporum; magistri Pandulfi domini
pape subdiaconi et familiaris, fratris
Aymerici magistri milicie Templi in Anglia;
et nobilium virorum Willelmi Mariscalli comitis Penbrocie, Willelmi comitis Sarresburie,
Willelmi comitis Warennie. Willelmi comitis
Arundellie, Alani de Galeweya constabularii
Scocie, Warini filii Geroldi, Petri filii
Hereberti, Huberti de Burgo senescalli Pic-
tavie, Hugonis de Nevilla, Mathei filii
Hereberti, Thome Basset, Alani Basset,
Philippi de Albiniaco, Roberti de Roppeleia,
Johannis Mari Scalli, Johannis filii Hugonis et
aliorum fidelium nostrorum.

1. In primis concessisse Deo et hac presenti
carta nostra confirmasse, pro nobis et heredibus nostris in perpetuum, quod Anglicana
ecclesia libera sit, et habeat jura sua integra, et libertates suas illesas; et ita volumus
observari; quod apparet ex eo quod libertatem
electionum, que maxima et magis necessaria
reputatur ecclesie Anglicane, mera et spontanea
voluntate, ante discordiam inter nos et barones
nostros motam, concessimus et carta nostra confirmavimus, et eam obtinuimus a domino papa
Innocencio tercio confirmari; quam et nos
observabimus et ab heredibus nostris in perpetuum bona fide volumus observari.   Concessimus eciam omnibus liberis hominibus
regni nostri, pro nobis et heredibus nostris

in perpetuum, omnes libertates subscriptas,
habendas et tenendas eis et heredibus suis,
de nobis et heredibus nostris.

2. Si quis comitum vel baronum nostrorum, sive
aliorum tenencium de nobis in capite per
servicium militare, mortuus fuerit, et cum
decesserit heres suus plene etatis fuerit
et relevium debeat, habeat hereditatem
suam per antiquum relevium; scilicet heres
vel heredes comitis de baronia comitis integra
per centum libras; heres vel heredes baronis
de baronia integra per centum libras; heres
vel heredes militis de feodo militis integro
per centum solidos ad plus; et qui minus
debuerit minus det secundum antiquam consuetudinem feodorum.

3. Si autem heres alicujus talium fuerit infra
etatem et fuerit in custodia, cum ad etatem
pervenerit, habeat hereditatem suam sine
relevio et sine fine.

4. Custos terre hujusmodi heredis qui infra
etatem fuerit, non capiat de terra heredis
nisi racionabiles exitus, et racionabiles
consuetudines, et racionabilia servicia, et
hoc sine destructione et vasto hominum vel
rerum; et si nos commiserimus custodiam
alicujus talis terre vicecomiti vel alicui
alii qui de exitibus illius nobis respondere
debeat, et ille destructionem de custodia
fecerit vel vastum, nos ab illo capiemus
emendam, et terra committatur duobus legalibus
et discretis hominibus de feodo illo, qui
de exitibus respondeant nobis vel ei cui
eos assignaverimus; et si dederimus vel
vendiderimus alicui custodiam alicujus talis
terre, et ille destructionem inde fecerit vel
vastum, amittat ipsam custodiam, et tradatur
duobus legalibus et discretis hominibus de
feodo illo qui similiter nobis respondeant
sicut predictum est.

5. Custos autem, quamdiu custodiam terre habuerit,
   sustentet domos, parcos, vivaria, stagna,
   molendina, et cetera ad terram illam per-
   tinencia, de exitibus terre ejusdem; et
   reddat heredi, cum ad plenam etatem pervenerit,
   terram suam totam instauratam de carrucis et
   waynagiis,[1] secundum quod tempus waynagii
   exiget et exitus terre racionabiliter poterunt sustinere.

6. Heredes maritentur absque disparagacione,
   ita tamen quod, antequam contrahatur matri-
   monium, ostendatur propinquis de consan-
   guinitate ipsius heredis.

7. Vidua post mortem mariti sui statim et sine
   difficultate habeat maritagium et hereditatem
   suam, nec aliquid det pro dote sua, vel pro
   maritagio suo, vel hereditate sua quam
   hereditatem maritus suus et ipsa tenuerint
   die obitus ipsius mariti, et maneat in domo
   mariti sui per quadraginta dies post mortem
   ipsius, infra quos assignetur ei dos sua.

8. Nulla vidua distringatur ad se maritandum
   dum voluerit vivere sine marito; ita tamen
   quod securitatem faciat quod se non maritabit
   sine assensu nostro, si de nobis tenuerit,
   vel sine assensu domini sui de quo tenuerit,
   si de alio tenuerit.

9. Nec nos nec ballivi nostri seisiemus[2] terram
   aliquam nec redditum pro debito aliquo,
   quamdiu catalla[3] debitoris sufficiunt ad
   debitum reddendum; nec plegii[4] ipsius debitoris distringantur quamdiu ipse capitalis
   debitor sufficit ad solucionem debiti; et si
   capitalis debitor defecerit in solucione

---

1. waynagium ('Fr. ogagnage') = 'crops' or
   lands under cultivation' ('tillage').
2. seisio, to seize
3. catalla, chattels
4. plegii, sureties

debiti, non habens unde solvat,
plegii resondeant de debito; et, si voluerint, habeant terras et redditus debitoris,
donec sit eis satisfactum de debito quod ante
pro eo solverint, nisi capitalis debitor mon-
straverit se esse quietum inde versus eosdem
plegios.

10. Si quis mutuo ceperit aliquid a Judeis, plus
vel minus, et moriatur antequam illud solvatur, debitum non usuret quamdiu heres fuerit
infra etatem, de quocumque teneat; et si
debitum illud inciderit in manus nostras,
nos non capiemus nisi catallum contentum
in carta.

11. Et si quis moriatur, et debitum debeat Judeis,
uxor ejus habeat dotem suam, et nichil reddat
de debito illo; et si liberi ipsius defuncti
qui fuerint infra etatem remanserint, pro-
videantur eis necessaria secundum tenementum
quod fuerit defuncti, et de residuo solvatur
debitum, salvo servicio dominorum; simili modo
fiat de debitis que debentur aliis quam
Judeis.

12. Nullum scutagium[1] vel auxilium ponatur in
regno nostro, nisi per commune consilium regni
nostri, nisi ad corpus nostrum redimendum, et
primogenitum filium nostrum militem faciendum,
et ad filiam nostram primogenitam semel maritandam[2], et ad hec non fiat nisi racionabile
auxilium: simili modo fiat de auxiliis de
civitate Londonie.

13. Et civitas Londonie habeat omnes antiquas
libertates et liberas consuetudines suas, tam
per terras, quam per aquas. Preterea volumus

---

1. scutage, in lieu of military service
2. marito, to marry

et concedimus quod omnes alie civitates, et
burgi, et ville, et portus, habeant omnes
libertates et liberas consuetudines suas.

14. Et ad habendum commune consilium regni, de
auxilio assidendo aliter quam in tribus casi-
bus predictis, vel de scutagio assidendo, summoneri faciemus archiepiscopos, episcopos,
abbates, comites, et majores barones, sigilla-
tim per litteras nostras; et preterea faciemus
summoneri in generali, per vicecomites et
ballivos nostros, omnes illos qui de nobis
tenent in capite; ad certum diem, scilicet ad
terminum quadraginta dierum ad minus, et ad
certum locum; et in omnibus litteris illius
summonicionis causam summonicionis exprimemus;
et sic facta summonicione negocium ad diem
assignatum procedat secundum consilium illorum
qui presentes fuerint, quamvis non omnes summoniti venerint.

15. Nos non concedemus de cetero alicui quod
capiat auxilium de liberis hominibus suis, nisi
ad corpus suum redimendum, et ad faciendum primogenitum filium suum militem, et ad primogenitam filiam suam semel maritandam, et ad
hec non fiat nisi racionabile auxilium.

16. Nullus distringatur ad faciendum majus servicium de feodo militis, nec de alio libero
tenemento, quam inde debetur.

17. Communia placita non sequantur curiam nostram
sed teneantur in aliquo loco certo.

* *

19. Et si in die comitatus assise predicte capi
non possint, tot milites et libere tenentes
remaneant de illis qui interfuerint comitatui
die illo, per quos possint judicia sufficienter
fieri, secundum quod negocium fuerit majus vel
minus,

20. Liber homo non amercietur pro parvo delicto, nisi secundum modum delicti; et pro magno delicto amercietur secundum magnitudinem delicti, salvo contenemento suo; et mercator eodem modo, salva mercandisa[1] sua; et villanus eodem modo amercietur salvo waynagio suo, si inciderint in misericordiam nostram; et nulla predictarum misericordiarum ponatur, nisi per sacramentum proborum hominum de visneto.[2]

21. Comites et barones non amercientur[3] nisi per pares suos, et non nisi secundum modum delicti.

22. Nullus clericus amercietur de laico tenemento suo, nisi secundum modum aliorum predictorum, et non secundum quantitatem beneficii sui ecclesiastici.

23. Nec villa nec homo distringatur facere pontes ad riparias, nisi qui ab antiquo et de jure facere debent.

24. Nullus vicecomes, constabularius, coronatores[4], vel alii ballivi nostri, teneant placita corone nostre.

25. Omnes comitatus, hundrede, wapentakii,[5] et trethingie, sint ad antiquas firmas absque ullo incremento, exceptis dominicis maneriis nostris.

26. Si aliquis tenens de nobis laicum feodum moriatur, et vicecomes vel ballivus noster ostendat litteras nostras patentes de sum-

---

1. merchandise
2. neighborhood
3. see note 3, p. 223, below.
4. coronatores, coroners
5. hundredi, wapentakii, divisions of shires in south and north, respectively.

- 218 -

monicione nostra de debito quod defunctus
nobis debuit, liceat vicecomiti vel ballivo
nostro attachiare[1] et inbreviare[2] catalla
defuncti, inventa in laico feodo, ad valen-
ciam illius debiti, per visum legalium
hominum, ita tamen quod nichil inde amoveatur,
donec persolvatur nobis debitum quod clarum
fuerit; et residuum relinquatur executoribus
ad faciendum testamentum defuncti; et, si
nichil nobis debeatur ab ipso, omnia catalla
cedant defuncto, salvis uxori ipsius et
pueris racionabilibus partibus suis.

27. Si aliquis liber homo intestatus decesserit,
catalla sua per manus propinquorum parentum
et amicorum suorum, per visum ecclesie
distribuantur, salvis unicuique debitis que
defunctus ei debebat.

28. Nullus constabularius, vel alius ballivus
noster, capiat blada[3] vel alia catalla
alicujus, nisi statim inde reddat denarios,
aut respectum inde habere possit de voluntate
venditoris.

29. Nullus constabularius distringat aliquem
militem ad dandum denarios pro custodia
castri, si facere voluerit custodiam illam
in propria persona sua, vel per alium pro-
bum hominem, si ipse eam facere non possit
propter racionabilem causam; et si nos
duxerimus vel miserimus eum in exercitum,
erit quietus de custodia, secundum quantitatem temporis quo per nos fuerit in exercitu.

---

1. to attach
2. to catalogue
3. corn (grain)

30. Nullus vicecomes, vel ballivus noster,
vel aliquis alius, capiat equos vel carectas[1]
alicujus liberi hominis pro cariagio[2] faciendo,
nisi de voluntate ipsius liberi hominis.

31. Nec nos nec ballivi nostri capiemus alienum
boscum[3] ad castra, vel alia agenda nostra,
nisi per voluntatem ipsius cujus boscus
ille fuerit.

32. Nos non tenebimus terras illorum qui convicti
fuerint de felonia, nisi per unum annum et
unum diem, et tunc reddantur terre dominis
feodorum

* *

34. Breve quod vocatur <u>Precipe</u> de cetero non
fiat alicui de aliquo tenemento unde liber
homo amittere possit curiam suam.

35. Una mensura vini sit per totum regnum nostrum,
et una mensura cervisie,,[4] et una mensura
bladi, scilicet quarterium Londonie, et una
latitudo pannorum tinctorum et russetorum
et halbergectorum[5], scilicet due ulne infra
listas; de ponderibus autem sit ut de mensuris.

36. Nichil detur vel capiatur de cetero pro brevi
inquisicionis de vita vel membris, sed gratis
concedatur et non negetur.

---

1. carts
2. transport duty
3. wood
4. ale, beer
5. possibly thick cloth worn under coat of mail

37. Si aliquis teneat de nobis per feodifir-
mam, vel per sokagium, vel per burgagium, et
de alio terram teneat per servicium militare,
nos non habebimus custodiam heredis nec terre
sue que est de feodo alterius, occasione illius
feodifirme, vel sokagii, vel burgagii; nec
habebimus custodiam illius feodifirme, vel
sokagii, vel burgagii, nisi ipsa feodifirma
debeat servicium militare. Nos non habebimus
custodiam heredis vel terre alicujus, quam
tenet de alio per servicium militare, occasione
alicujus parve serjanterie quam tenet de nobis
per servicium reddendi nobis cultellos, vel
sagittas, vel hujusmodi.

38. Nullus ballivus ponat de cetero aliquem ad
legem simplici loquela[1] sua, sine testibus
fidelibus ad hoc inductis.

39. Nullus liber homo capiatur, vel imprisonetur,
aut disseisiatur[2], aut utlagetur[3], aut exule-
tur, aut aliquo modo destruatur, nec super
eum ibimus, nec super eum mittemus, nisi
per legale judicium parium suorum vel per
legem terre.

40. Nulli vendemus, nulli negabimus, aut differemus,
rectum aut justiciam.

41. Omnes mercatores habeant salvum et securum
exire de Anglia, et venire in Angliam, et
morari et ire per Angliam, tam per terram
quam per aquam, ad emendum et vendendum,
sine omnibus malis toltis[4], per antiquas et

---

1. complaint
2. disseised, interruption of possession of
   land, violently ejected.
3. exiled, outlawed
4. tells

rectas$_1$consuetudines, preterquam in tempore
gwerre^1, et si sint de terra contra nos
gwerrina; et si tales inveniantur in terra
nostra in principio gwerre, attachientur
sine dampno corporum et rerum, donec sciatur
a nobis vel capitali justiciario nostro quomodo
mercatores terre nostre tractentur, qui tunc
invenientur in terra contra nos gwerrina; et
si nostri salvi sint ibi, alii salvi sint
in terra nostra.

42. Liceat unicuique de cetero exire de regno
nostro, et redire, salvo et secure, per
terram et per aquam, salva fide nostra, nisi
tempore gwerre per aliquod breve tempus,
propter communem utilitatem regni, exceptis
imprisonatis et utlagatis secundum legem
regni, et gente de terra contra nos gwerrina,
et mercatoribus de quibus fiat sicut predictum
est.

* *

44. Homines qui manent extra forestam non veniant
de cetero coram justiciariis nostris de
foresta per communes summoniciones, nisi sint
in placito, vel plegii alicujus vel aliquorum,
qui attachiati sint pro foresta.

45. Nos non faciemus justiciarios, constabularios,
vicecomites vel ballivos, nisi de talibus qui
sciant legem regni et eam bene velint observare.

46. Omnes barones qui fundaverunt abbatias, unde
habent cartas regum Anglie, vel antiquam
tenuram, habeant earum custodiam cum vaca-
verint, sicut habere debent.

---

1. war

47. Omnes foreste que afforestate[1] sunt tempore
    nostro, statim deafforestentur[2] ; et ita fiat
    de ripariis que per nos tempore nostro posite
    sunt in defenso.

48. Omnes male consuetudines de forestis et
    warennis[3], et de forestariis et warennariis,
    vicecomitibus et eorum ministris, ripariis et
    earum custodibus, statim inquirantur in quoli-
    bet comitatu per duodecim milites juratos de
    eodem comitatu, qui debent eligi per probos
    homines ejusdem comitatus, et infra quadra-
    ginta dies post inquisicionem factam, penitus,
    ita quod numquam revocentur, deleantur per
    eosdem, ita quod nos hoc sciamus prius,
    vel justiciarius noster, si in Anglia non
    fuerimus.

49. Omnes obsides et cartas statim reddemus que
    liberate fuerunt nobis ab Anglicis in securi-
    tatem pacis vel fidelis servicii.

    *

51. Et statim post pacis reformacionem amovebimus
    de regno omnes alienigenas milites, balistarios,
    servientes, stipendiarios, qui venerint cum
    equis et armis ad nocumentum regni.

52. Si qui fuerit disseisitus vel elongatus per
    nos sine legali judicio parium suorum, de
    terris, castellis, libertatibus, vel jure
    suo, statim ea ei restituemus et si contencio
    super hoc orta fuerit, tunc inde fiat per
    judicium viginti quinque baronum, de quibus

---

1. to make into forest
2. to deafforest
3. fish ponds

fit mencio inferius in securitate pacis: de
omnibus autem illis de quibus aliquis disseisitus fuerit vel elongatus sine legali judicio
parium suorum, per Henricum regem patrem nostrum vel per Ricardum regem fratrem nostrum,
que in manu nostra habemus, vel que alii
tenent que nos oporteat warantizare[1], respectum habebimus usque ad communem terminum
crucesignatorum[2], exceptis illis de quibus
placitum motum fuit vel inquisicio facta per
preceptum nostrum, ante suscepcionem crucis
nostre: cum autem redierimus de peregrinacione
nostra, vel si forte remanserimus a peregrinacione nostra, statim inde plenam justiciam exhibebimus.

53. Eundem autem respectum habebimus, et eodem
modo, de justicia exhibenda de forestis
deafforestandis vel remansuris forestis quas
Henricus pater noster vel Ricardus frater
noster afforestaverunt, et de custodiis
terrarum que sunt de alieno feodo, cujusmodi
custodias hucusque habuimus occasione feodi
quod aliquis de nobis tenuit per servicium
militare, et de abbaciis que fundate fuerint
in feodo alterius quam nostro, in quibus dominus feodi dixerit se jus habere; et cum redierimus, vel si remanserimus a peregrinacione
nostra, super hiis conquerentibus plenam
justiciam statim exhibebimus.

54. Nullus capiatur nec imprisonetur propter
appellum femine de morte alterius quam viri
sui.

55. Omnes fines qui injuste et contra legem terre
facti sunt nobiscum, et omnia amerciamenta[3]

---

1. to warrant
2. crusaders
3. amercements, money payments of a wrongdoer
   to the crown, for pardon.

facta injuste et contra legem terre, omnino
condonentur, vel fiat inde per judicium viginti
quinque baronum de quibus fit mencio inferius
in securitate pacis, vel per judicium majoris
partis eorundem, una cum predicto Stephano
Cantuariensi archiepiscopo, si interesse
poterit, et aliis quos secum ad hoc vocare
voluerit: et si interesse non poterit,
nichilominus procedat negocium sine eo, ita
quod, si aliquis vel aliqui de predictis
viginti quinque baronibus fuerint in simili
querela, amoveantur quantum ad hoc judicium,
et alii loco eorum per residuos de eisdem
viginti quinque, tantum ad hoc faciendum
electi et jurati substituantur.

56. Si nos disseisivimus vel elongavimus Walenses
de terris vel libertatibus vel rebus aliis,
sine legali judicio parium suorum, in Anglia
vel in Wallia, eis statim reddantur; et si
contencio super hoc orta fuerit, tunc inde
fiat in marchia per judicium parium suorum,
de tenementis Anglie secundum legem Anglie,
de tenementis Wallie secundum legem Wallie,
de tenementis marchie secundum legem marchie.
Idem facient Walenses nobis et nostris.

57. De omnibus autem illis de quibus aliquis
Walensium disseisitus fuerit vel elongatus
sine legali judicio parium suorum per Henricum
regem patrem nostrum vel Ricardum regem fratrem
nostrum, que nos in manu nostra habemus, vel
que alii tenent que nos oporteat warantizare,
respectum habebimus usque ad communem terminum
crucesignatorum, illis exceptis de quibus
placitum motum fuit vel inquisicio facta per
preceptum nostrum ante suscepcionem crucis
nostre: cum autem redierimus, vel si forte
remanserimus a peregrinacione nostra, statim

eis inde plenam justiciam exhibebimus, secundum leges Walensium et partes predictas.

* *

59. Nos faciemus Alexandro regi Scottorum de sororibus suis, et obsidibus reddendis, et libertatibus suis, et jure suo, secundum formam in qua faciemus aliis baronibus nostris Anglie, nisi aliter esse debeat per cartas quas habemus de Willelmo patre ipsius, quondam rege Scottorum; et hoc erit per judicium parium suorum in curia nostra.

60. Omnes autem istas consuetudines predictas et libertates quas nos concessimus in regno nostro tenendas quantum ad nos pertinet erga nostros, omnes de regno nostro, tam clerici quam laici, observent quantum ad se pertinet erga suos.

61. Cum autem pro Deo, et ad emendacionem regni nostri, et ad melius sopiendam discordiam inter nos et barones nostros ortam, hec omnia predicta concesserimus, volentes ea integra et firma stabilitate in perpetuum gaudere, facimus et concedimus eis securitatem subscriptam; videlicet quod barones eligant viginti quinque barones de regno quos voluerint, qui debeant pro totis viribus suis observare, tenere, et facere observari, pacem et libertates quas eis concessimus, et hac presenti carta nostra confirmavimus, ita scilicet quod, si nos, vel justiciarius noster, vel ballivi nostri, vel aliquis de ministris nostris, in aliquo erga aliquem deliquerimus, vel aliquem articulorum pacis aut securitatis transgressi fuerimus, et delictum ostensum fuerit quatuor baronibus de predictis viginti quinque baronibus, illi quatuor barones accedant ad nos vel ad justiciarum nostrum, si fuerimus extra regnum, pro-

ponentes nobis excessum, petent ut excessum
illum sine dilacione faciamus emendari. Et
si nos excessum non emendaverimus, vel, si
fuerimus extra regnum justiciarius noster non
emendaverit, infra tempus quadraginta dierum
computandum a tempore quo monstratum fuerit
nobis vel justiciario nostro si extra regnum
fuerimus, predicti quatuor barones referant
causam illam ad residuos de viginti quinque
baronibus, et illi viginti quinque barones
cum communa tocius terre distringent et grava-
bunt nos modis omnibus quibus poterunt,
scilicet per capcionem castrorum, terrarum,
possessionum, et aliis modis quibus poterunt,
donec fuerit emendatum secundum arbitrium
eorum, salva persona nostra et regine nostre
et liberorum nostrorum; et cum fuerit emendatum intendent nobis sicut prius fecerunt. Et
quicumque voluerit de terra juret quod ad predicta omnia exequenda parebit mandatis predictorum viginti quinque baronum, et quod
gravabit nos pro posse suo cum ipsis, et nos
publice et libere damus licenciam jurandi
cuilibet qui jurare voluerit, et nulli umquam jurare prohibebimus. Omnes autem illos
de terra qui per se et sponte sua noluerint
jurare viginti quinque baronibus, de dis-
tringendo et gravando nos cum eis, faciemus
jurare eosdem de mandato nostro, sicut predictum est. Et si aliquis de viginti quinque
baronibus decesserit, vel a terra recesserit,
vel aliquo alio modo impeditus fuerit, quominus ista predicta possent exequi, qui
residui fuerint de predictis viginti quinque
baronibus eligant alium loco ipsius, pro
arbitrio suo, qui simili modo erit juratus
quo et ceteri. In omnibus autem que istis
viginti quinque baronibus committuntur exequenda, si forte ipsi viginti quinque presentes
fuerint, et inter se super re aliqua discorda-
verint, vel aliqui ex eis summoniti nolint vel

nequeant interesse, ratum habeatur et firmum
quod major pars eorum qui presentes fuerint
providerit, vel preceperit, ac si omnes
viginti quinque in hoc consensissent; et
predicti viginti quinque jurent quod omnia
antedicta fideliter observabunt, et pro toto
posse suo facient observari. Et nos nichil
impetrabimus ab aliquo, per nos nec per alium,
per quod aliqua istarum concessionum et liber-
tatum revocetur vel minuatur; et, si aliquid
tale impetratum fuerit, irritum sit et inane
et numquam eo utemur per nos nec per alium.

62. Et omnes malas voluntates, indignaciones,
et rancores ortos inter nos et homines
nostros, clericos et laicos, a tempore discordie, plene omnibus remisimus et condonavimus. Preterea omnes transgressiones factas
occasione ejusdem discordie, a Pascha anno
regni nostri sextodecimo usque ad pacem re-
formatam, plene remisimus omnibus, clericis
et laicis, et quantum ad nos pertinet plene
condonavimus. Et insuper fecimus eis fieri
litteras testimoniales patentes domini Stephani
Cantuariensis archiepiscopi, domini Henrici
Dublinensis archiepiscopi, et episcoporum
predictorum, et magistra Pandulfi, super securitate ista et concessionibus prefatis.

63. Quare volumus et firmiter precipimus quod
Anglicana ecclesia libera sit et quod homines
in regno nostro habeant et teneant omnes pre-
fatas libertates, jura, et concessiones, bene
et in pace, libere et quiete, plene et integre
sibi et heredibus suis, de nobis et heredibus
nostris, in omnibus rebus et locis, in perpetuum, sicut predictum est. Juratum est autem
tam ex parte nostra quam ex parte baronum, quod
hec omnia supradicta bona fide et sine malo ingenio observabuntur. Testibus supradictis et

multis aliis. Data per manum nostram in prato
quod vocatur Ronimede, inter Windlesoram et
Stanes, quinto decimo die Junii, anno regni
nostri decimo septimo.

8. <u>Writ of Summons for Two Knights of the Shire
to Grant an Aid</u>

Forma directa magnatibus et vicecomitibus
Angliae.

Rex Vicecomiti Bedeford. et Bukingeham.,
salutem. Cum comites et barones et ceteri
magnates regni nostri nobis firmiter pro-
miserint, quod erunt Londoniis a die Paschae
proximo futuro in tres septimanas cum equis
et armis parati et bene muniti ad tendendum
sine ulla dilatione versus Portesmuth, ad
transfretandum ad nos in Vasconiam contra
regem Castellae qui terram nostram Vasconiae
in manu forti in aestate proximo futura hos-
tiliter est ingressurus, et tibi mandaverimus
quod omnes illos de ballia tua qui tenent xx.
libratas terrae de nobis in capite, vel de
aliis quo sunt infra aetatem et in custodia
nostra, ad idem distringues; tibi districte
praecipimus, quod praeter omnes praedictos
venire facias coram consilio nostro apud Westmonasterium in quindena Paschae proximo futuro,
quattuor legales et discretos milites de comitatibus praedictis quos iidem comitatus ad
hoc elegerint, vice omnium et singulorum
eorundem comitatuum, videlicet duos de uno
comitatu et duos de alio, ad providendum,
una cum militibus aliorum comitatuum quos
ad eundem diem vocari fecimus, quale auxilium,
nobis in tanta necessitate impendere voluerint.
Et ipse militibus et aliis de comitatibus
praedictis necessitatem nostram et tam urgens
negotium nostrum diligenter exponas, et eos

ad competens auxilium nobis ad praesens im-
pendendum efficaciter inducas; ita quod
praedicti quattuor milities praefato consilio
nostro ad praedictum terminum praecise respondere possint super praedicto auxilio
pro singulis comitatuum praedictorum. Firmiter etiam tibi praecipimus quod omnis debita
quae nobis a retro sunt in baillia tua et
solvi debuerunt ad scaccarium nostrum ante
Pascha iam instans, vel solvi debent ad
scaccarium eiusdem Paschae, habeas ad idem
scaccarium in quindena praedicti Paschae,
sciturus quod nisi praedicta debita tunc
ibidem habueris non solum corpus tuum ar-
restari faciemus, sed debita illa de terris
et tenementis tuis levari faciemus ad damnum
tuum non modicum. T. A. Regina et R. comite
Cornubiae apud Windlesoram xi. die Februarii.

9. The Fiction of English Particularity: Henricus de Bracton

Cum autem fere in omnibus regionibus utantur
legibus et jure scripto, sola Anglia usa est
in suis finibus jure non scripto et consue-
tudine. In ea quidem ex non scripto jus
venit, quod usus comprobavit.

10. On Justice (De Justitia)

Est autem justitia constans et perpetua
voluntas jus suum cuique tribuens. Et si
justitia intelligatur prout est in Deo, plana
sunt omnia cum justitia sit Dei dispositio.
Ipse enim Deus tribuit unicuique secundum
opera sua. Ipse non est variabilis nec
temporabilis in dispositionibus et voluntati-
bus suis. Eius voluntas est constans et
perpetua. Ipse enim non habuit principium
nec habet nec habebit finem.

11. Dialogus de Scaccario (AD 1177)

Liber Primus.

I. Quid sit Scaccarium, et quae ratio hujus nominis.

Discipulus. Quid est scaccarium[1]?

Magister. Scaccarium tabula est quadrangula quae longitudinis quasi decem pedum, latitudinis quinque, ad modum mensae circumsedentibus apposita, undique habet limbum altitudinis quasi quatuor digitorum, ne quid appositum excidat. Superponitur autem scaccario pannus in termino Paschae emptus, non quilibet, sed niger virgis distinctus, distantibus a se virgis vel pedis vel palmae extentae spatio. In spatiis autem calculi sunt juxta ordines suos de quibus alias dicetur. Licet autem tabula talis scaccarium dicatur, transumitur tamen hoc nomen, ut ipsa quoque curia quae consedente scaccario est scaccarium dicatur; adeo ut si quis per sententiam aliquid obtinuerit, vel aliquid de communi consilio fuerit constitutum, dicatur factum ad scaccarium illius vel illius anni. Quod autem hodie dicitur ad scaccarium, olim dicebatur ad taleas...

XII. Quid Regis Foresta, et quae ratio hujus nominis.

M. Foresta regis est tuta ferarum mansio; non quarumlibet sed sylvestrium; non quibuslibet in locis sed certis et ad hoc idoneis; unde foresta dicitur, e mutata in o,

---

1. scaccarium, exchequer

quasi feresta, hoc est ferarum statio[1].

D. Numquid in singulis comitatibus foresta
regis est?

M. Non; sed in nemorosis, ubi et ferarum lati-
bula sint et uberrima pascua; nec interest
cujus sint nemora; sive enim sint regis,
sive regni procerum, liberos tamen et in-
dempnes habent ferae circumquaque discursus.

XV.   Qui sit usus Sigilli Regii quod est in
      Thesauro.

   Usus sigilli regii qualis esse debeat ex
praemissis constare potest: hoc enim factae
summonitiones et alia pertinentia dumtaxat ad
scaccarium regis mandata signantur. Nec
effertur alias; sed sicut supra dictum est,
a cancellario custoditur per vicarium. Ex-
pressam autem habet imaginem et inscriptionem
cum deambulatorio curiae sigillo, ut par
cognoscatur utrobique jubentis auctoritas,
et reus similiter judicetur pro hoc ut pro
illo, qui secus egerit. Porro liber ille de
quo quaeris sigilli regii comes est individuus
in thesauro. Hujus institutionis causam ab
Henrico quondam Wintoniensi episcopo sic
accepi.

XVI. Quid Liber Judiciarius, et ad quid
      compositus.

   Cum insignis ille subactor Angliae rex
Willelmus, ejusdem pontificis sanguine pro-
pinquus, ulteriores insulae fines suo sub-
jugasset imperio, et rebellium mentes terri-
bilibus perdomuisset exemplis; ne libera de

1, Re vera, foresta derivatur a 'foris,'
    outside.

cetero daretur erroris facultas, decrevit
subjectum sibi populum juri scripto legi-
busque subjicere. Propositis igitur legibus
Anglicanis secundum tripartitam earum dis-
tinctionem, hoc est Merchenelage, Denelage,
Westsexenelage, quasdam reprobavit, quasdam
autem approbans, illis transmarinas Neustriae
leges, quae ad regni pacem tuendam efficacis-
simae videbantur, adjecit. Demum ne quid
deesse videretur ad omnem totius providentiae
summam, communicato consilio, discretissimos
a latere suo destinavit viros per regnum in
circuitu. Ab hiis itaque totius terrae descriptio diligens facta est, tam in nemoribus,
quam in pascuis et pratis, nec non et agri-
culturis, et verbis communibus annotata in
librum redacta est; ut videlicet quilibet jure
suo contentus, alienum non usurpet impune.
Fit autem descriptio per comitatus, per
centuriatas, et per hidas, praenotato in ipso
capite regis nomine, ac deinde seriatim aliorum
procerum nominibus appositis secundum status
sui dignitatem, qui videlicet de rege tenent
in capite. Apponuntur autem singulis numeri
secundum ordinem sic dispositis, per quos
inferius in ipsa libri serie, quae ad eos
pertinent, facilius occurrunt. Hic liber ab
indigenis Domesdei nuncupatur, id est, dies
judicii per metaphoram; sicut enim districti
et terribilis examinis illius novissimi sententia nulla tergiversationis arte valet
eludi, sic cum orta fuerit in regno contentio
de hiis rebus quae illic annotantur, cum
ventum fuerit ad librum, sententia ejus
infatuari non potest vel impune declinari.
Ob hoc nos eundem librum judiciarium nominavi-
mus; non quod in eo de propositis aliquibus
dubiis feratur sententia; sed quod ab eo
sicut a praedicto judicio non licet ulla ratione
discedere.

D. Quid comitatus, quid centuriata, vel
quid sit hida, si placet edissere; alioquin
plana non erunt quae praemissa sunt.

from Stubbs, Select Charters, pp. 201, 222-224.

12. Res Gestae Divi Augusti[1]

Rerum gestarum divi Augusti quibus orbem
terrarum imperio populi Romani subiecit, et
inpensarum quas in rem publicam populumque
Romanum fecit, incisarum in duabus aheneis
pilis quae sunt Romae positae, exemplar
subiectum.

CAP. I

I. 1-3. Annos undeviginti natus exercitum
privato consilio et privata impensa comparavi
per quem rem publicam dominatione factionis
oppressam in libertatem vindicavi.

I. 3-5. Ob quae senatus decretis honorificis
in ordinem suum me adlegit C. Pansa L. Hirtio
consulibus[2], consularem locum simul dans sen-
tentiae ferendae, et imperium mihi dedit.

I. 6-7. Res publica ne quid detrimenti
caperet me pro praetore simul cum consulibus
providere iussit.

I. 7-9. Populus autem eodem anno me consu-
lem, cum consul uterque bello cecidisset, et
trium virum rei publicae constituendae creavit.

---

1. From stones found in Ankara, the capital
    of modern Turkey; hence this inscription
    is known as the Monumentum Ancyranum.
    Text is taken from the edition of Rogers,
    Scott, and Ward (1935).
2. 43 B.C.

CAP. II

I. 10-12. Qui parentem meum interfecerunt,
eos in exilium expuli, iudiciis legitimis ultus
eorum facinus, et postea bellum inferentis
rei publicae vici bis acie.

CAP. III

I. 13-15. Bella terra et mari civilia exter-
naque toto in orbe terrarum suscepi, vic-
torque omnibus superstitibus civibus peperci.
Externas gentes quibus tuto ignosci potuit,
conservare quam excidere malui.

I. 16-19. Millia civium Romanorum adacta
sacramento meo fuerunt circiter quingenta.
Ex quibus deduxi in colonias aut remisi in
municipia sua stipendis emeritis millia
aliquantum plura quam trecenta et iis omnibus
agros a me emptos aut pecuniam pro praediis
a me dedi.

I. 19-20. Naves cepi sescentas praeter eas,
si quae minores quam triremes fuerunt.

CAP. IV

I. 21. Bis ovans triumphavi, tris egi curulis
triumphos.

I. 21-22. Et appellatus sum viciens semel
imperator.

I. 22-24. Cum deinde pluris triumphos mihi
senatus decrevisset, eis supersedi. Item saepe
laurus deposui, in Capitolio votis quae quoque
bello nuncupaveram solutis.

I. 24-27. Ob res a me aut per legatos meos
auspicis meis terra marique prospere gestas

quinquagiens et quinquiens decrevit senatus
supplicandum esse dis immortalibus. Dies
autem, per quos ex senatus consulto supplica-
tum est fuere DCCCLXXXX.

I. 27-28. In triumphis meis ducti sunt ante
currum meum reges aut regum liberi novem.

I. 28-30. Consul fueram terdeciens, cum
scribebam haec, et agebam septimum et tri-
gesimum annum tribuniciae potestatis.

CAP. V

I. 21-32. Dictaturam et apsenti et prae-
senti mihi datam...a populo et senatu M.
Marcello et L. Arruntio consulibus non accepi.

I. 32-35. Non recusavi in summa frumenti
penuria curationem annonae, quam ita adminis-
travi, ut...paucis diebus metu et periculo
quo erat populum universum meis impensis
liberarem.

I. 35-36. Consulatum tum datum annuum et
perpetuum non accepi.

CAP. VI

I. 37-39. Consulibus M. Vinucio et Q_2
Lucretio[1] et postea P. et Cn. Lentulis[2] et[3]
tertium Paullo Fabio Maximo et Q. Tuberone[3]
senatu populoque Romano consentientibus,..
ut curator legum morumque cum maxima potestate solus crearer, magistratum nullum praeter
majorum exempla datum accepi.

---

1. 19 B.C.
2. 18 B.C.
3. 13 B.C.

I. 39. Quae tum per me senatus fieri voluit
per tuibuniciam potestatem perfeci. Cuius
potestatis collegam et ipse ultro quinquiens
mihi a senatu depoposci et accepi.[1]

CAP. VII

I. 42-43. Triumviratum rei publicae constituendae fui per continuous annos decem.[2]

I. 44-45. Princeps senatus fui usque ad
eum diem, quo scripseram haec, per annos
quadraginta.

I. 45, 46. Pontifex, augur, quindecimvirum
sacris faciundis, septemvirum epulonum,
frater arvalis, soladis Titius, fetialis fui.

CAP. VIII

II. 1. Patriciorum numerum auxi consul quintum iussu populi et senatus.

II. 1-11. Senatum ter legi. In consulatu
sexto censum populi conlega M. Agrippa egi.
Lustrum post annum alterum et quadragensimum
feci. Quo lustro civium Romanorum censa sunt
capita quadragiens centum millia et sexa-
ginta tria millia. Iterum consulari cum
imperio lustrum solus feci C. Censorino et
C. Asinio cos. Quo lustro censa sunt civium
Romanorum capita quadragiens centum millia et
ducenta triginta tria millia. Tertium consulari cum imperio lustrum conlega Tib.
Caesare filio meo feci Sex. Pompeio et Sex.
Appuleio cos. Quo lustro censa sunt civium
Romanorum capita quadragiens centum millia
et nongenta triginta et septem millia.

---

1. Supplemented from the Greek text of the
inscription.
2. Supplemented from the Greek.

II. 12-14. Legibus novis latis complura
exempla maiorum exolescentia iam ex nostro
usu reduxi, et ipse multarum rerum exempla
imitanda posteris tradidi.

CAP. IX

II. 15-18. Vota pro valetudine mea suscipi
per consules et sacerdotes quinto quoque anno
senatus decrevit. Ex iis votis saepe fecerunt vivo me ludos aliquotiens sacerdotum
quattuor amplissima collegia, aliquotiens
consules.

II. 18-20. Privatim etiam et municipatim
universi cives sacrificaverunt semper apud
omnia pulvinaria pro valetudine mea.

CAP. X

II. 21. Nomen meum senatus consulto inclusum
est in Saliare carmen.

II. 21-23. Et sacrosanctus ut essem...et ut
quoad viverem, tribunicia potestas mihi esset,
lege sanctum est.

II. 23-28. Pontifex maximus ne fierem in
vivi conlegae locum, populo id sacerdotium
deferente mihi quod pater meus habuerat,
recusavi. Cepi id sacerdotium aliquod post
annos eo mortuo qui civilis motus occasione
occupaverat, cuncta ex Italia ad comitia
mea...tanta multitudine quanta Romae nunquam antea fuisse fertur coeunte P. Sulpicio
C. Valgio consulibus.

CAP. XI

II. 29-33. Aram Fortunae reduci iuxta [?]
aedes Honoris et Virtutis ad portam Capenam
pro reditu meo senatus consacravit, in qua

pontifices et virgines Vestales anniversarium sacrificium facere iussit eo die quo
consulibus Q. Lucretio et M. Vinucio in urbem ex Syria redi, et diem Augustalia ex
cognomine nostro appellavit.

CAP. XII

II.   34-37.   Senatus consulto eodem tempore
pars praetorum et tribunorum plebi cum con-
sule Q. Lucretio et principibus viris ob-
viam mihi missa est in Campaniam, qui honos
ad hoc tempus nemini praeter me est decretus.

II.   37-41.   Cum ex Hispania Galliaque,
rebus in his provinciis prospere gestis,
Romam redi Ti. Nerone P. Quintilio consulibus, aram Pacis Augustae senatus pro reditu
meo consacrari censuit ad campum Martium,
in qua magistratus et sacerdotes et virgines
Vestales anniversarium sacrificium facere
iussit.

CAP. XIII

II.   42-45.   Ianum Quirinum quem claussum
esse maiores nostri voluerunt, cum per totum
imperium populi Romani terra marique esset
parta victoriis pax, cum prius, quam nascerer,
a condita urbe bis omnino clausum fuisse pro-
datur memoriae, ter me principe senatus
claudendum esse censuit.

CAP. XIV

II.   46--III. 1-6.   Filios meos, quos iuvenes
mihi eripuit fortuna, Gaium et Lucium Caesares
honoris mei caussa senatus populusque Romanus
annum quintum et decimum agentis consules desig-
navit, ut eum magistratum inirent post quin-
quennium.   Et ex co die, quo deducti sunt

in forum, ut interessent consiliis publicis
decrevit senatus. Equites autem Romani universi principem inventutis utrumque eorum
parmis et hastis argenteis donatum ap-
pellaverunt.

CAP. XV

[The gifts and congiaria which follow, ranging
from 44 to 2 B.C., are numbered for the sake
of distinction.]

(1) III. 7-8. Plebei Romanae viritim $\overline{\text{HS}}$.
trecenos numeravi ex testamento patris mei;

(2) III. 8-9. et nomine meo $\overline{\text{HS}}$. quadringenos
ex bellorum manibiis consul quintum dedi;

(3) III. 9-11. iterum autem in consulatu
decimo ex patrimonio meo $\overline{\text{HS}}$. quadringenos
congiari viritim pernumeravi;

(4) III. 11-12. et consul undecimum duodecim
frumentationes frumento privatim coempto
emensus sum:

(5) III. 12-15. et tribunicia potestate
duodecimum quadringenos nummos tertium viritim
dedi. Quae mea congiaria pervenerunt ad
hominum millia nunquam minus quinquaginta et
ducenta.

(6) III. 15-17. Tribuniciae potestatis duo-
devicensimum consul XII trecentis et viginti
millibus plebis urbanae sexagenos denarios
viritim dedi.

(7) III. 17-19. In colonis militum meorum
consul quintum ex manibiis viritim millia
nummum singula dedi; acceperunt id triumphale
congiarium in colonis hominum circiter centum
et viginti millia.

(8) III. 19-21. Consul tertium decimum sexagenos denarios plebei, quae tum frumentum
publicum accipiebat, dedi; ea millia hominum
paullo plura quam ducenta fuerunt.

CAP. XVI

III. 22-28. Pecuniam pro agris, quos in consulatu meo quarto et postea consulibus M.
Crasso et Cn. Lentullo augure adsignavi militibus, solvi municipis. Ea summa sestertium
circiter sexsiens milliens fuit, quam pro
Italicis praedis numeravi, et circiter bis
milliens et sescentiens, quod pro agris pro-
vincialibus solvi. Id primus et solus omnium,
qui deduxerunt colonias militum in Italia aut
in provincis, ad memoriam aetatis meae feci.

III. 28-33. Et postea Ti. Nerone et Cn.
Pisone consulibus, itemque C. Antistio et
D. Laelio cos. et C. Calvisio et L. Pasieno
consulibus, et L. Lentulo et M. Messalla consulibus, et L. Caninio et Q. Fabricio cos.
militibus, quos emeriteis stipendis in sua
municipia remisi, praemia numerato persolvi,
quam in rem sestertium quater milliens libenter impendi.

CAP. XVII

III. 34-35. Quater pecunia mea iuvi aerarium,
ita ut sestertium milliens et quingentiens ad
eos qui praeerant aerario detulerim.

III. 35-39. Et M. Lepido et L. Arruntio
consulibus in aerarium militare quod ex consilio meo constitutum est, ex quo praemia
darentur militibus, qui vicena aut plura
stipendia emeruissent, $\overline{HS}$. milliens et septin-
gentiens ex patrimonio meo detuli.

CAP. XVIII

III. 40-43. Inde ab eo anno, quo Cn. et
P. Lentuli consules fuerunt, cum deficerent
vectigalia, tum centum millibus hominum tum
pluribus inlato frumento vel ad nummarios
tributus ex agro et patrimonio meo opem tuli.

CAP. XIX

IV. 1-8. Curiam et continens ei Chalcidicum,
templumque Apollinis in Palatio cum portici-
bus, aedem divi Iuli, Lupercal, porticum ad
circum Flaminium, quam sum appellari passus
ex nomine eius, qui priorem eodem in solo
fecerat Octaviam, pulvinar ad circum maximum,
aedes in Capitolio Iovis Feretri et Iovis
Tonantis, aedem Quirini, aedes Minervae et
Iunonis Reginae et Iovis Libertatis in
Aventino, aedem Larum in summa sacra via,
aedem deum Penatium in Velia, aedem Iuventa-
tis, aedem Matris Magnae in Palatio feci.

CAP. XX

IV. 9-10. Capitolium et Pompeium theatrum
utrumque opus impensa grandi refeci sine ulla
inscriptione nominis mei.

IV. 10-11. Rivos aquarum compluribus locis
vetustate labentes refeci.

IV. 11-12. Et aquam, quae Marcia appellatur
duplicavi fonte novo in rivum eius immisso.

IV. 12-16. Forum Iulium, et basilicam quae
fuit inter aedem Castoris et aedem Saturni,
coepta profligataque opera a patre meo perfeci et eandem basilicam consumptam incendio
ampliato eius solo sub titulo nominis filiorum
meorum incohavi et, si vivus non perfecissem,
perfici ab heredibus iussi.

IV. 17-18. Duo et octoginta templa deum in urbe
consul sextum ex decreto senatus refeci, nullo
praetermisso quod eo tempore refici debebat.

IV. 19-20. Consul septimum viam Flaminiam
ab urbe Ariminum feci et pontes omnes praeter
Mulvium et Minucium.

CAP. XXI

IV. 21-22. In privato solo Martis Vltoris
templum forumque Augustum ex manibiis feci.

IV. 22-23. Theatrum ad aede Apollinis in solo
magna ex parte a privatis empto feci, quod sub
nomine M. Marcelli generi mei esset.

IV. 23-26. Dona ex manibiis in Capitolio et
in aede divi Iuli et in aede Apollinis et in
aede Vestae et in templo Martis Vltoris con-
sacravi, quae mihi constiterunt H̄S̄. circiter
milliens.

IV. 26-30. Auri coronari pondo triginta et
quinque millia municipiis et colonis Italiae
conferentibus ad triumphos meos quintum consul remisi, et postea, quotienscumque imperator appellatus sum, aurum coronarium non accepi
decernentibus municipiis et colonis aeque benigne adque antea decreverant.

CAP. XXII

IV. 31-33. Ter munus gladiatorium dedi meo
nomine et quinquens filiorum meorum aut
nepotum nomine; quibus muneribus depugna-
verunt hominum circiter decem millia.

IV. 33-35. Bis athletarum undique accitorum
spectaclum populo praebui meo nomine et tertium nepotis mei nomine.

IV. 35-36. Ludos feci meo nomine quater,
aliorum autem magistratuum vicem ter et viciens.

IV. 36-37. Pro conlegio quin decimvirorum
magister conlegii collega M. Agrippa Ludos
saeclares C. Furnio C. Silano cos. feci.

IV.   38-39.   Consul XIII ludos Martiales
primus feci, quos post id tempus deinceps
insequentibus annis . . . fecerunt consules.

IV.   39-42.   Venationes bestiarum Africanarum
meo nomine aut filiorum meorum et nepotum in
circo aut in foro aut in amphitheatris populo
dedi sexiens et viciens.

CAP. XXIII

IV.   43-48.   Navalis proeli spectaclum populo
dedi trans Tiberim, in quo loco nunc nemus
est Caesarum, cavato solo in longitudinem
mille et octingentos pedes, in latitudinem
mille et ducenti.   In quo triginta rostratae
naves, triremes aut biremes, plures autem
minores inter se conflixerunt.   Quibus in
classibus pugnaverunt praeter remiges millia
hominum tria circiter.

CAP. XXIV

IV.   49-51.   In templis omnium civitatium
provinciae Asiae victor ornamenta reposui,
quae spoliatis templis is cum quo bellum
gesseram privatim possederat.

IV.   51-54.   Statuae meae pedestres et
equestres et in quadrigeis argenteae steter-
unt in urbe XXC circiter, quas ipse sustuli
exque ea pecunia dona aurea in aede Apollinis
meo nomine et illorum, qui mihi statuarum
honorem habuerunt, posui.

CAP. XXV

V.   1-3.   Mare pacavi a praedonibus.   Eo
bello servorum, qui fugerant a dominis suis
et arma contra rem publicam ceperant, triginta
fere millia capta dominis ad supplicium sumen-
dum tradidi.

V. 3-6. Iuravit in mea verba tota Italia
sponte sua et me belli, quo vici ad Actium,
ducem depoposcit. Iuraverunt in eadem verba
provinciae Galliae, Hispaniae, Africa, Sicilia,
Sardinia.

V. 6-9. Qui sub signis meis tum milita-
verint, fuerunt senatores plures quam DCC,
in iis qui vel antea vel postea consules
facti sunt ad eum diem quo scripta sunt haec,
LXXXIII, sacerdotes circiter CLXX.

CAP. XXVI

V. 9-10. Omnium provinciarum populi Romani,
quibus finitimae fuerunt gentes quae non
parerent imperio nostro, fines auxi.

V. 10-12. Gallias et Hispanias provincias
et Germaniam qua includit Oceanus a Gadibus
ad ostium Albis fluminis pacavi.

V. 12-14. Alpes a regione ea quae proxima
est Hadriano mari, ad Tuscum pacari feci
nulli genti bello per iniuriam inlato.

V. 14-18. Classis mea per Oceanum ab ostio
Rheni ad solis orientis regionem usque ad
fines Cimbrorum navigavit, quo neque terra
neque mari quisquam Romanus ante id tempus
adit, Cimbrique et Charydes et Semnones et
eiusdem tractus alii Germanorum populi per
legatos amicitiam meam et populi Romani
petierunt.

V. 18-23. Meo iussu et auspicio ducti sunt
duo exercitus eodem fere tempore in Aethiopiam
et in Arabiam, quae appellatur eudaemon,[1] maxi-
maeque hostium gentis utriusque copiae caesae
sunt in acie et complura oppida capta. In
Aethiopiam usque ad oppidum Nabata perventum
est, cui proxima est Meroë. In Arabiam usque

---

1. felix

in fines Sabaeorum processit exercitus ad
oppidum Mariba.

CAP. XXVII

V. 24. Aegyptum imperio populi Romani adieci.

V. 24-31. Armeniam maiorem interfecto rege
eius Artaxe cum possem facere provinciam,
malui maiorum nostrorum exemplo regnum id
Tigrani regis Artavasdis filio, nepoti autem
Tigranis regis, per Ti. Neronem tradere, qui
tum mihi privignus erat. Et eandem gentem
postea desciscentem et rebellantem domitam per
Gaium filium meum regi Ariobarzani regis Medorum Artabazi filio regendam tradidi et post
eius mortem filio eius Artavasdi. Quo interfecto Tigrane(m), qui erat ex regio genere
Armeniorum oriundus, in id regnum misi.

V. 31-34. Provincias omnis quae trans Had-
rianum mare vergunt ad orientem, Cyrenasque,
iam ex parte magna regibus eas possidentibus,
et antea Siciliam et Sardiniam occupatas bello
servili reciperavi.

CAP. XXVIII

V. 35-36. Colonias in Africa Sicilia Mace-
donia utraque Hispania Achaia Asia Syria
Gallia Narbonensi Pisidia militum deduxi.

V. 36-38. Italia autem XXVIII colonias, quae
vivo me celeberrimae et frequentissimae fuerunt,
meis auspicis deductas habet.

CAP. XXIX

V. 39-40. Signa militaria complura per alios
duces amissa devictis hostibus reciperavi ex
Hispania et Gallia et a Dalmateis.

V. 40-43. Parthos trium exercitum Romanorum
spolia et signa reddere mihi supplicesque
amicitiam populi Romani petere coegi. Ea
autem signa in penetrali, quod est in templo
Martis Vltoris, reposui.

CAP. XXX

V. 44-49. Pannoniorum gentes quas ante me
principem populi Romani exercitus nunquam adit,
devictas per Ti. Neronem, qui tum erat privignus et legatus meus, imperio populi Romani
subieci protulique fines Illyrici ad ripam
fluminis Danui. Citra quod Dacorum transgressus exercitus meis auspicis victus pro-
fligatusque est, et postea trans Danuvium
ductus exercitus meus Dacorum gentes imperia
populi Romani perferre coegit.

CAP. XXXI

V. 50-51. Ad me ex India regum legationes
saepe missae sunt, nunquam antea visae apud
quemquam Romanorum ducem.

V. 51-53. Nostram amicitiam petierunt per
legatos Bastarnae Scythaeque et Sarmatarum
qui sunt citra flumen Tanaim et ultra reges,
Albanorumque rex et Hiberorum et Medorum.

CAP. XXXII

V. 54 -- VI. 1-3. Ad me supplices confuger-
unt reges Parthorum Tiridates et postea Phrates
regis Phratis filius; Medorum Artavasdes;
Adiabenorum Artaxares; Britannorum Dumnobellau-
nus et Tim...; Sugambrorum Maclo; Marcomanorum
Sueborum......rus.

VI. 3-6. Ad me rex Parthorum Phrates Orodis
filius filios suos nepotesque omnes misit
in Italiam, non bello superatus, sed amicitiam

nostram per liberorum suorum pignora petens.

VI. 6-8. Plurimaeque aliae gentes expertae
sunt populi Romani fidem me principe, quibus
antea cum populo Romano nullum extiterat
legationum et amicitiae commercium.

CAP. XXXIII

VI. 9-12. A me gentes Parthorum et Medorum
per legatos principes earum gentium reges peti-
tos acceperunt Parthi Vonenem regis Phratis
filium, regis Orodis nepotem; Medi Ariobar-
zanem regis Artavazdis filium, regis Ariobar-
zanis nepotem.

CAP. XXXIV

VI. 13-16. In consulatu sexto[1] et septimo,
bella ubi civilia exstinxeram per consensum
universorum potitus rerum omnium, rem publicam ex mea potestate in senatus populique
Romani arbitrium transtuli.

VI. 16-21. Quo pro merito meo senatus consulto Aug. appellatus sum et laureis postes
aedium mearum vestiti publice coronaque civica
super ianuam meam fixa est clupensque aureus
in curia Iulia positus, quem mihi senatum
populumque Romanum dare virtutis clementiae
iustitiae pietatis caussa testatum est per
eius clupei inscriptionem.

VI. 21-23. Post id tempus praestiti omnibus
dignitate, potestatis autem nihilo amplius
habui quam qui fuerunt mihi quoque in magis-
tratu conlegae.

---

1. 28 B.C.

CAP. XXXV

VI. 24-27. Tertium decimum consultatum[1] cum gerebam, senatus et equester ordo populusque Romanus universus appellavit me patrem patriae, idque in vestibulo aedium mearum inscribendum esse et in curia et in foro A ug sub quadrigis, quae mihi ex s.c. positae sunt, decrevit.

VI. 27-28. Cum scripsi haec, annum agebam septuagensumum sextum.[2]

APP. I

VI. 29-30. Summa pecuniae, quam dedit in aerarium vel plebei Romanae vel dimissis militibus: denarium sexiens milliens.[3]

13. <u>The Germ of American Liberty</u>

Johannes Calvin on the duty of preferring exile to religious tyranny. His letter, in 1553, perhaps was sent to an Italian lady living in England. Thus the letter well shows the international usefulness of Latin, besides its general plea for religious emigration, later practiced by the Pilgrim Fathers and other Calvinist groups, but raised here for the first time in the history of Christendom. But cf. <u>Petit traicte monstrant que deit faire un homme fidele entre les papistes</u> (CR6.573ff.). [1543].

1890

CALVINUS AGNETI ANGLAE (AD 1553)

Mulierem piam in sua patria evangelium profiteri vetitam ad constantiam hortatur, et exsilium potius subendum docet quam fidem renunciandam.

---

1. 2 B.C.
2. 13 A.D.
3. Centena millia

(**Manuscripta non exstat.** Edidit Beza Genev.
p. 130, Laus. p. 283, Hanov. p. 317, Chouet
p. 175, Amst. p. 80. Gallice versa legitur
in edit. Berol. p. 171)

Quanquam sciebam opus fore interprete,
generosa Domina, ut literas meas intelligeres,
scribendi tamen fiduciam mihi dederunt quidam amici: imo ad hoc officium tibi praestan-
dum vehementer hortati sunt. Linguam vero
latinam potius elegi, quia sperabam tibi
multos fore ad manum, qui Italice exponerent,
quum linguae Gallicae nulla fere vel rara
sit apud vos cognitio. Principio autem ne
fructu careant meae literae, mihi roganda
es ut eas comiter excipere ne graveris. Quod
facile abs te impetrabo, si consilii mei finem
spectes. Quin etiam quod postulo sponte et
libenter facturam promittunt, quorum hortatu
scribo. Nec vero pietati tuae consentaneum
esset, quem unum agnoscis ex servis Christi
spernere, praesertim salutis tuae, studio
loquentem. Ac iusta quidem causa est, ut a
gratulatione incipiam. Nam evangelii fidem
sic te amplexam esse audio, ut nihil tibi potius
sit sincero Dei cultu: cuius singulare studium
in eorum omnium animis vigere debet, qui suavi-
tatem illam gratiae, quae nobis in Christo
offertur, vere gustarunt. Ideo enim apparuit
filius Dei, et quotidie suos thesauros nobis
proponit, ut mundi illecebris renunciantes
coelestem vitam meditemur. Ideo etiam semine
incorruptibili suae doctrinae nos Deus rege-
nerat, ut iustitiae fructus proferat tota
vita nostra, qui sacrae eius adoptioni respondeant. Multi quidem impie hodie illudunt
Christo, praetextum licentiae quaerentes ex
eius doctrina: sed videmus quam horrendis
modis haec sacrilegia Deus vindicet. Te vero
in hoc totam esse, ut sancta vita evangelium
ornes, magnopere gaudeo. Atque hinc apparet
evangelium in te vivas egisse radices. Cae-
terum, quia innumeris hodie corruptelis refer-

tus est mundus, non modo recte animatam te
esse convenit ad pergendum in hoc cursu, sed
invicta quoque fortitudine esse armatam necesse
est, ut sub Christo coelesti duce milites.
Nam sic hodie invaluit impietas, ac praesertim
apud vos sic grassatur tyrannis Antichristi,
ut non possis sine magnis periculis, et certam-
inibus integrum Deo cultum praestare. Cuius
rei tu optima testis es: atque in eo maxime
refulget pietatis tuae vigor, quod non solum
tibi non indulges in vitiis communibus, sicuti
multi solent: sed quia pro tua prudentia
vides quam misera sit istic tua servitus,
voluntarium exsilium subire mavis, quam in
illis sordibus, quae te contaminant, manere
defixa. Porro quando huc usque te Deus
spiritu suo expergefecit, mearum partium esse
duxi, currenti addere stimulos, et sanctum
hoc consilium adiuvare. Si tibi istic esset
integrum, Deum non fraudare debito obsequio:
manere potius suaderem, quam relicta patria,
longo itinere, magno sumptu, et ingenti
molestia longinquam et incognitam regionem
petere. Nunc vero quum minae et terrores
hostium Christi tibi fidem tuam, ut decebat,
profiteri non permittant, te etiam impediat
carnis infirmitás, ut ab his laqueis exitiali-
bus quamprimum evoles, consulere et hortari
non dubito: adeoque me tacente fieri non
potest, quin te conscientiae inquietudo ad
quaerendum remedium assidue sollicitet. Interim cavendum tibi est, ne longa deliberatione
frustra tempus terendo, exitum tibi praecludas.
Fateor sane in tam arduo negotio temere nihil
esse tentandum: verum si tibi obscura non
est Dei voluntas, non potes sine gravi eius
iniuria, perplexo animo hoc et illud diu
agitare. Serio igitur statue, quod Deus
praecipit statim esse exsequendum, et simul
te absque mora accinge. Nec te retineant
vanae et fallaces blanditiae, quibus sibi
plerique adulantur: sed in mentem subinde

tibi recurrat, fidei confessionem Deo magis
esse pretiosam, quam ut leve delictum sit,
impuris superstitionibus se polluere. Huc
etiam accedit, quod istic tanquam ovis famelica
extra ovile et pascua Christi in sterili deser-
to vagaris. Nec me latet, quam tibi difficile
ac molestum sit, ex patria migrare, ut in
alieno solo procul a cognatis habites, ac
iam provectae aetatis matrona non modo mutes
domicilium, sed etiam commoditatibus te exuas,
quibus in flore aetatis carere durum et
acerbum foret. Ad haec omnia quid obiiciam
non habeo, praeter hoc unum, quod tamen, ut
spero, abunde tibi sufficiet: si sapiat
nobis coelestis vita, nihil in terra esse
tanti quod ab illius studio nos retardet:
deinde, filium Dei non solum quia de nobis
ita meritus est, sed quia summo imperio
potitur, dignum esse cuius honorem omnibus
mundi honoribus, delitiis, opibus et commodis
praeferamus. Quod si nobis locum incolere
liceat ubi pure colitur et invocatur Deus,
longe praestat illic exsulare, quam in
patria quiescere, unde Christus rex coeli
et terrae exsulat. Si nulla te necessitas
a nido discedere cogeret, filia tamen Dei
non esses, nisi tibi peregrinatio esset
terrena vita. Nunc quum te illinc violenter
expellat sacrilega tyrannis Antichristi, et
Dominus clara voce te exire iubeat, ne tibi
adeo molesta sit peregrinandi conditio, donec
in aeternam haereditatem nos simul Deus col-
ligat. Vale, nobilis et eximia Domina, mihi-
que ex animo colenda. Dominus te spiritu
prudentiae regat, fortitudinem et constantiam
tibi augeat, suoque praesidio tueatur.

14. Theophrastus von Hohenheim, called Paracelsus
     (1493-1541)[1]

     1. His motto, the motto of a self-made man:
         Alterius non sit qui suus esse possit.

---

1. See Robert Browning's poem, _Paracelsus_

2. The impression which he made on his contemporaries (from Pierre Ramus):

Nemo nescit Theophrastum ingenio acutissimo, ac fere divino fuisse praeditum, et in universa Philosophia tam ardua tam arcana et abdita eruisse mortalium neminem; et cotidie per duas horas Basileae tum activam[1] tum speculativam Philosophiam summa diligentia magnoque auditorum fructu lingua vernacula esse interpretatum, doctrina quam non ex libris sed ex experientia assecutus est. In intima naturae viscera sic penitus introiit, metallorum stirpiumque vires et facultates tam incredibili ingenii acumine exploravit et pervidit ad morbos omnes vel desperatos vel hominum opinione insanabiles percurandum, ut primo eum ipse medicina nata videatur.

3. Some of his rules:

Nunquam enim hoc ita persuasum sit medico quasi unus morbus unam saltem naturam ac conditionem habeat. Quod ex scholis ipsorum[2] non prodii et ad praescriptum eorum non loquor, id mihi crimini dant. Nihil enim numquam citra[3] experientiam quicquam scripsi.

15. Letters of the Famous English Philosopher and Physician John Locke to his French Friends
    1. 1698 to Thoynard

[43]   Oates 25 Mars 98.

Multa sunt quae me festinantem hactenus impediunt quominus voluntati ad scribendum pronae non obtemperaverit manus. Valetudo hac hieme ad fauces orci redacta, serus librorum quibus

---

1. activam, "practical"
2. the academic professional teachers
3. citra, this side of, outside of, apart from

me cumulasti adventus et irrita istius paquet-
boat expectatio, Mr. Nelson[1] rediens pene
naufragus, in mare arca illius aqua salsa
perfusa quam degustarunt libri in ea inclusi,
in terra aegrotus, ego rure absens, inde
libri quos ad me tam benigne miseras non
nisi incurrente jam mense martio ad me pervenerunt humidi sane et ignis indigi.

Itinerarium amici tui cum voluptate perlegi,
multa si coram adessem rogarem praecipue de
insula Cayenne ubi diutissime commoratus est
e.g.: Si observaverint longitudinem penduli
ea in insula quae liniae aequinoctiali tam
vicina est, Si Indi in vicinio deum praeter
astra vel colunt vel agnoscunt et quo cultu.
Quot annos communiter vivunt; quae herba sit
illa Pite[2] de qua loquitur et si altitudine
canabim aequet et si agris sponte nascitur,
si vanilla quae illic producuntur aeque grati
sunt odoris ac illae quae nobis ex nova Hispania asportantur; et multa alia. Sed haec
hactenus nolo enim te quaestionibus ultra
flagitare.

Gaudeo tam commodum nuntium meas tibi attu-
lisse literas, aveo multum illum videre ut
multa de te sciscitarem, pauca enim sitienti
animo non satisfaciunt quanquam magna per-
fusus fuerim laetitia ex literis tuis quibus
de sanitate tua adhuc integra me certiorem
facis, precor Deum optimum maximum ut te
salvum validumque diutissime conservet.

Illum Watsonum quem tibi nominavit non novi
nec credo in mathematicis esse eximium. Forsan in horologiis construendis aliquid enixus

---

1. Mr. Nelson, the carrier of the letter, Fellow
   of Trinity College, 1656-1715.
2. Pite = Agave (Olion, p. 125, n. 1)

est, sed ea ipsa in arte Tompiono nostro aequa-
lem esse multum dubito. De vitri usu in for-
mandis horologiis cum Tompiono sermones olim
habui, unde didici inutile esse commentum.

Laetor maxime opus tandem perfectum im-
pressumque esse [paginis 136]. Quando possim
ego promittere amicis meis hisce in regionibus qui impatienter expectant quanto citius
tanto melius.

Ego etiam ex quo te vidi nescio quo fato aliquorum
librorum auctor factus, omnia ad te transmitterem
nisi quod vernacula usus, tibi Barbarus sum. Hol-
landiae cum essem vacuas aliquas horas impendi
literis ad amicum in Anglia de ratione instituendi,
quem tum parvulum habebat, filii....Cupio tuum de
eo judicium si probas quartam brevi habebit edi-
tionem cum auctario. Ante octo annos etiam pub-
lici juris feci Tentamen de Intellectu humano opus
in folio quod brevi credo prodibit in lingua tibi
notiore quam qua scriptum est. Versionem eo
studiosius maturandam cupio ut si possit me
vivo ad te pervenire possit, quem novi aequum
juxta et perspicacem fore judicem nec favore
nec ira utram in partem inclinatum.

Quod dicis de Arithmetica Africanorum et
Brasiliensium: maxime placet. Nescio an
olim te rogaverim ut mihi indicares si quos
noveris populos qui numerationis nodum alicubi[1] quam in denario locaverint; si quos
noveris rogo denuo ut me certiorem facias, id
enim aveo scire et jam diu quaesivi. De moribus incolarum ad flumen Senegal sitatum si quid
novisti, id mihi scire pergratum esset.

---

1. alicubi = elsewhere

Roganti quorsum methodus edulcorandi aquas[1]
non reducatur ad praxin, respondeo: nescio
plane.

Si Londinum iterum liceat reverti de his te
certiorem faciam. Ad me enim quod attinet
gratularis mihi in tam prospero statu res meas
esse.[2] Agnosco negotium salario satis locu-
ples mihi non quaerenti oblatum[3]; sed sero
tamen cum jam ingravescit senectus et valetudo
satis incommoda, receptui aliquando cavendum
est ut mihi intra limites meos reducto vacet
quod reliquum est vitae otio literario placide
impendere; id ego jamdudum fecissem nisi invi-
tum me et secessum quaerentem amici aliquot
non [I mot]detinuissent. Sed haec inter nos.

Si quem habes Caleti[4] vel Dieppae cui res
tibi destinatas mittere possem facilius esset
librorum commercium. Londino enim plurimum
absum et hujusmodi res aliorum diligentiae
commissae negligentius plerumque curantur;
sed te nimium fatigo. Vale vir optime et
me ut facis ama

                        Tui amantissimum
                        J.L.

Inscriptio literarum 6ªDec. datarum recte
se habet; eadem semper servanda ubicumque
fuero

          [Adres. à Paris. -- De la main de
          Thoyn:] mars 25, 98.

---

1. aquas (maris)
2. "Locke was not only 'commissioner of appeals,'
    but also member of the 'Council of Trade
    and Plantations' from 1696, at $5,000 a
    year." (Olion, p. 127, n. 1).
3. oblatum (esse)
4. Caleti = Calais

2. 1688 To Philippe de Limborch On Convales-
    cence and Diet

[31]   [15 --] 25 Nov. 1688.

VIR AMPLISSIME

Magna me cura et sollicitudine liberarunt
gratissimae tuae mihi heri redditae literae;
ex tuo silentio si non male ominabar metuebam
certe et ut amantium mos est, quia quae opta-
veram non audivi, quae timebam finxi. Sed
gaudeo jam omnia in tuto esse et periculosum
filii tui) morbum ita praeteriisse ut nihil
restet jam ad perfectam sanitatem nisi quod
diaetae regimine perfici posse existimatur.
Quandoquidem prior illa mea de morbo illius
monitio tibi adeo grata fuit, liceat mihi et
alteram addere. Non quod credam meo tibi opus
posse esse consilio ubi doctissimus et longo
usu prudentissimus Veenius[1] adsit, sed ut
persuasum tibi sit me tibi fidem habere cum
testeris tibi acceptum esse quod cum re non
possim voluntate tamen et studio adjuvem.
Post hujusmodi morbum solent nostri medici
semel atque iterum purgare, et praecavenda
mala, quae ex reliquiis miasmatis variolosi[2]
in corpore haerentibus oriri possint, mihi
etiam et alia causa hujusmodi iteratam purga-
tionem requiere vide[n]tur.   Nempe[3] quod
solent convalescentes ex hoc morbo magno
appetitu laborare, unde si non caute et moder-
ate alantur metus est, ne eduliorum nimio
onere nondum penitus defaecatus[4] oppressus
sanguis succrescenti alicui morbo materiam

---

1. Veenius, a Dutch doctor.
2. Smallpox
3. nempe = namely
4. defaecatus (et)

praebeat.

Sed qui tuto convalescere volunt cavere
debent ne nimis propere convalescant et in
eo ut plurimum peccant mulierculae praesertim
clinicae, quod nihil credant ad vires restauran-
das tantum conferre quantum nutrimenti copiam,
cum assumendorum vis et quantitas sensim tantum augenda sit prout augentur vires.   Quod enim
bene subigit ventriculus, bene digerit sanguis,
id solum robur addit corpori, vigoremque spir-
itibus impertit; quicquid justam illam mensuram superat non solum inutile onus est sed
in humores noxios et morborum causas degenerat.
Haec ego fusius hic mihi dicenda existimavi
quia nostrates[1] in hac re plerumque peccant;
apud vos forsan hoc, uti[2] caetera, prudentius
et moderatius.

Vale cum filio totaque familia et me ut
facis ama

                    Tui amantissimum
                         J.L.

Uxorem tuam dilectissimam et universam fami-
liam Veenii et Guenellonis nostri collegasque
omnes meo nomine officiosissime salutes.

Filium tuum plurimum salvere jubeo.

3.   On the Glorious Revolution to Philippe
     de Limborch

[35]   London 12[--22] Apr. [16]89.

         VIR AMPLISSIME

Heri Regis et Reginae inauguratio sive ut
dicunt coronatio summo cum splendore et maxi-

---

1.   nostrates = nostri
2.   uti = ut

mo concursu plausuque populi celebrata est,
eodem die utrumque in Scotia istius regni
regem et reginam solenni modo promulgatum
sive uti nos loqui amamus proclamatum credimus; nam nostro Gulielmo et Mariae solium
istud ante aliquot dies ab ordinibus istius
regni designatum et decretum fuisse expeditis
nuntiis constat. Burnetus jam Episcopus
Salisburiensis in hesterna solennitate suas
habuit partes. Concionatus est coram rege
et regina et ita concionatus est...ut omnes
laudent.

De toleranti apud nos stabilienda non
prorsus despero etiamsi lente admodum procedat.

An Burnettus tuus eodem uti tibi persuades
animo futurus sit Salisburi quo fuit Amstelo-
dami nonnulli dubitare incipiunt, interim
dicam tibi quid accidit: cum primum post
consecrationem suam Episcopalem ad regem
accessit Burnetus, observavit rex quod galerus[1]
illius solito amplior erat rogavitque, quid
sibi vellit ista fimbriae ampliatio, respondit Episcopus convenire istam formam ordini
suo, cui Rex 'Galerus spero non immutabit caput
tuum."

Sed meus famulus adhuc, credo, Roterodami
est, ille navem quibus[2] libri mei vehuntur
conscendit ante meum decessum, sed nautae
negligentia qui otiose Roterodami haesit,
amisit navigandi nobiscum occasionem, ante
aliquot dies cum praesidio bellicarum navium
solvit et ad Litus Angliae accessit tam prope
ut pene[3] manu tangi potuisset, sed vi tempe-
statis ab ancoris avulsus et fluctibus diu
jactatus tandem summo cum periculo Mosam
repetivit. Quando iterum navigaturus, nescio.
Vale et me ut facis ama tui amantissimum.

J. Locke

---

1. Galerus = cap   2. quibus = qua   3. pene = paene

4. 1691 Disappointment over a Bad Latin
Translation of his Essay on Human Understanding. To Philippe de Limborch.

[45]   Oates 13 [--23] Mar.[16]9$\frac{0}{1}$

VIR ERUDITISSIME

Has ego chartas tibi in manus tradendas cura-
vi, ut iis si libet perlectis Interpreti[1] reddas et simul gratias agas, quod tantum labor-
em meis scriptis impendere dignatus sit. Op-
tassem sane[2], ut initio operis sui, antequam tam longe esset progressus, mihi unam[3]
vel alteram paginam sua Latinitate donatam
misisset. Tunc forte liberius de versione
ejus judicium meum interposuissem. Tu ex
iis quae tribus primis capitibus manu mea ad-
scripsi (ubi tamen multa emendanda non attigi)
facile judicabis quod minus laboriosum mihi
foret novam instituere versionem quam hanc
corrigere. Interpres non mihi videtur ubique
satis callere[4] linguam Anglicanam. Inde for-
sant (sic)[5] evenit, ut, dum verbum verbo
fidus nimis reddit et voces sequatur, sensum
meum aliquando non ita assequatur et Latine
exprimat, ut facile capiant lectores. Hoc
tibi legenti abunde constabit nec dubito,
quin in Latina hac versione Latinitatem subinde
desiderabis. Ego nihilominus docti et amici
Interpretis laudo industriam, an vero hoc in
opere eum habuerit successum, ut erudito hoc
saeculo commendari et cum laude scriptoris in
publicum prodire possit, penes te amicosque
ejus sit judicium. Ego verborum plane negli-
gentissimus et forsan plusquam par est elegan-
tiarum contemptor, si modo lectoribus stilus

---

1. Verrijn = interprete
2. sane = however
3. donatam = redditam
4. callere = to know
5. forsan

non fastiditus sensum meum clare et perspicue
exhibeat nec res per se satis obscuras magis
involvat, caetera non curo.

Incoatas hasce nondum finiveram literas cum
tuae 16° Martij datae mihi redditae sunt tanto
acceptiores quod post diuturnum et inusitatum
silentium male ominantem animi aegritudinem
mihi levarent. Versio de qua agitur sero admodum mihi hic rure reddita est nullis adjunctis
nec a te nec a Verrino[1] literis quod miratus
sum. Postquam hic aliquamdiu commoratus essem,
monuit me per epistolam Hospes meus Londinensis
se accepisse fasciculum chartarum ex altera
parte urbis ad me domum suam missum per baju-
lum, quid vero essent vel a quo venerint se
plane nescire.

Suspicatus quid esse possit rescripsi ut
fasciculum aperiret et in eo si reperiret
aliquam partem libri mei Latine versam complicaret[2] rursum et, quam primum daretur occasio,
fidi internuncii ad me mitteret, si aliud quid
contineat mihi indicaret quid esset, et apud
se retineret; res accidit ut conjeceram et
aliquanto post famulus hujus in qua versor
familia, Londinum petens mihi versionem asportavit.[3] Literae ubi interciderint[4] plane
nescio, sed cum diu expectatus de his chartis
per epistolam ne verbum acceperim, credidi fido
alicui amico huc proficiscenti festinato sine
literis commissas[5] ab eo Verrinum de iis[6] certiorem factum quievisse.

---

1.   Verrino = interprete
2.   complicaret = fold
3.   asportavit = adportavit
4.   interciderint = fallen away
5.   commissas (eas)
6,   iis (chartis)

Quid de ipsa versione sentiendum sit, vobis
prorsus relinquo. Multum me Eruditi Verrini
studio benevolentiae humanitati, imo et labori
debere libens agnosco, nec tantum mihi arrogo
ut de alieno$_1$opere multis lucubrationibus jam
ad umbelicum^1 perducto aliquid statuem. Hoc
vobis integrum sit, vos amici ingenuo et indus-
trio juveni consulite; operam quam meis cogi-
tatis^2 impenderit, ego semper agnoscam, quid
alii in erudito et critico hoc saeculo facturi
sint, vos videte. Hoc eo libentius dico quia
non mea res agitur. De meo opere jam factum
est judicium et cum jam prodiit, non amplius
mei juris est. Quicquid de verisione judices,
rogo ut authorem quam officiosissime salutes
meo nomine, eique promittas meo nomine, omnem
meam operam studium industriam si qua in re
ipsi utilis esse potuerim; interim aestimo
maxime et amplector una cum fratre cujus humanitati multum debeo.

Vale Vir Amplissime, et, ut facis, me ama

Tui Amantissimum

J. Locke,

5. On the Same Subject Four Years Later. To
   Philippe de Limborch

[60]   Oates 10[--20] Maij.[16]95.

Nuper a Dno Verrijn^3 literas accepi quibus
testatur se adhuc cupere versionem suam libri
mei de intellectu recensere et ita parare ut
in lucem prodeat.

---

1. umbelicum = umbilicum
2. cogitatis = cogitationibus
3. Verrijn = interprete

Quid de hac re olim dixerim, tu meministi,
cui hoc jam adjiciendum est quod vir apud nos
doctissimus eam curam in se suscepit ut in
linguam Latinam summo studio et nitore verta-
tur, et id opus jam aliquamdiu inchoatum.
Huic Editioni Latinae ego novas aliquas dis-
sertationes et additamenta... inseram. Hanc
inclusam ad eum epistolam per tuas manus ideo
tradendam misi, quia locum ubi sit, domumve
non indicavit. Illum quaeso...salutes persuas-
umque reddas illius in me voluntatem et benevo-
lentiam acceptissimam esse semperque futuram
meque dolere Idioma nostrum adeo perplexum
sensumque meum phrasibus nostris[1] ita involu-
tum ut saepe eum capere nisi in lingua nostra
versatissimo difficillimum sit. Saluta reli-
quos nostros.....

16   EXTRACTS FROM THE BOOK OF JOB

Vir erat in terra Hus nomine Iob, et
erat vir ille simplex et rectus ac timens
Deum et recedens a malo. [2]Natique sunt ei
septem filii et tres filiae. [3]Et fuit possessio
eius septem milia ovium et tria milia camelorum,
quingenta quoque iuga boum et quingentae
asinae ac familia multa nimis: eratque vir
ille magnus inter omnes orientales. [4]Et ibant
filii eius et faciebant convivium per domos
unusquisque in die suo. Et mittentes vocabant
tres sorores suas, ut comederent et biberent
cum eis. [5]Cumque in orbem transissent dies
convivii, mittebat ad eos Iob et sanctifica-
bat illos consurgensque diluculo offerebat
holocausta pro singulis; dicebat enim: Ne
forte peccaverint filii mei et benedixerint
Deo in cordibus suis.

---

1.   nostris = Anglicis

Sic faciebat Iob cunctis diebus.

[6]Quadam autem die, cum venissent filii Dei
ut adsisterent coram Domino, adfuit inter
eos etiam Satan. Cui dixit Dominus: Unde
venis? Qui respondens ait: Circuivi terram
et perambulavi eam. [8]Dixitque Dominus ad eum:
Nunquid considerasti servum meum Iob, quod
non sit ei similis in terra, homo simplex et
rectus ac timens Deum et recedens a malo?
[9]Cui respondens Satan ait: Nunquid Iob frustra
timet Deum? [10]Nonne tu vallasti eum ac domum
eius universamque substantiam per circuitum:
operibus manuum eius benedixisti, et possessio
eius crevit in terra? [11]Sed extende paulu-
lum manum tuam et tange cuncta quae possidet,
nisi in faciem benedixerit tibi. [12]Dixit ergo
Dominus ad Satan: Ecce universa, quae habet,
in manu tua sunt; tantum in eum ne extendas
manum tuam. Egressusque est Satan a facie
Domini.

[13]Cum autem quadam die filii et filiae eius
comederent et biberent vinum in domo fratris
sui primogeniti, [14]nuntius venit ad Iob, qui
diceret: Boves arabant et asinae pascebantur
iuxta eos, [15]et irruerunt Sabaei tuleruntque
omnia et pueros percusserunt gladio, et evasi
ego solus ut nuntiarem tibi.

[16]Cumque adhuc ille loqueretur, venit alter
et dixit: Ignis Dei cecidit e caelo et
tactas oves puerosque consumpsit, et effugi
ego solus ut nuntiarem tibi.

[17]Sed, et illo adhuc loquente, venit alius et
dixit: Chaldaei fecerunt tres turmas et in-
vaserunt camelos et tulerunt eos, necnon et
pueros percusserunt gladio, et ego fugi
solus ut nuntiarem tibi.

[18]Adhuc loquebatur ille, et ecce alius intravit et dixit: Filiis tuis et filiabus ves-

centibus et bibentibus vinum in domo fratris
sui primogeniti, [19] repente ventus vehemens
irruit a regione deserti et concussit quattuor angulos domus, quae corruens oppressit
liberos tuos, et mortui sunt, et effugi ego
solus ut nuntiarem tibi.

[20]Tunc surrexit Iob et scidit vestimenta
sua et, tonso capite, corruens in terram
adoravit [21]et dixit: Nudus egressus sum
de utero matris meae et nudus reverta illuc.
Dominus dedit, Dominus abstulit; sicut Domino
placuit, ita factum est: sit nomen Domini
benedictum. [22]In omnibus his non peccavit
Iob labiis suis neque stultum quid contra Deum
locutus est.

A Letter of Dante from Exile about His Return
to Florence (perhaps composed by Boccaccio)

EPISTOLA IX.

Amico Florentino

1. In litteris vestris, et reverentia debita
et affectione receptis, quam repatriatio mea
curae sit vobis ex animo, grata mente ac
diligenti animadversione concepi; et inde
tanto me districtius obligastis, quanto rarius
exules invenire amicos contingit. Ad illarum
vero significata respondeo; et si responsio
non erit qualiter forsan pusillanimitas appe-
teret aliquorum, ut sub examine vestri consilii
ante iudicium ventiletur, affectuose deposco.
2. Ecce igitur quod per litteras vestri mei-
que nepotis, nec non aliorum quamplurium
amicorum, significatum est mihi per ordina-
mentum nuper factum Florentiae super absolu-
tione bannitorum: quod si solvere vellem cer-
tam pecuniae quantitatem, vellemque pati notam
oblationis, et absolvi possem et redire ad
praesens. In quo quidem duo ridenda et male

praeconsiliata sunt, Pater; dico male praeconsiliata per illos qui talia expresserunt,
nam vestrae litterae discretius et consultius
clausulatae nihil de talibus continebant.
3. Estne ista revocatio gloriosa, qua Dantes
Aligherius revocatur ad patriam, per trilus-
trium fere perpessus exilium? Hocne meruit
innocentia manifesta quibuslibet? Hoc sudor
et labor continuatus in studio? Absit a viro
philosophiae domestico temeraria terreni
cordis humilitas, ut more cuiusdam Cioli et
aliorum infamium quasi victus, ipse se
patiatur offerri! Absit a viro praedicante
iustitiam ut perpessus iniurias, iniuriam
inferentibus, velut benemerentibus, pecuniam
suam solvat!
4. Non est haec via redeundi ad patriam,
Pater mi; sed si alia per vos aut deinde per
alios invenietur, quae famae Dantis atque
honori non deroget, illam non lentis passibus
acceptabo. Quod si per nullam talem Florentia
introitur, numquam Florentiam introibo. Quidni?
nonne solis astrorumque specula ubique con-
spiciam? Nonne dulcissimas veritates potero
speculari ubique sub coelo, ni priús inglorium,
immo ignominiosum, populo Florentinaeque
civitati me reddam? Quippe nec panis deficiet.

Moore, pp. 413f.

Dante on Language

Vulgarem locutionem appellamus, quam sine
omni regula nutricem imitantes accipimus. Haec
prima fuit humano generi usitata; hac totus
orbis ipsa perfruitur, licet in diversas
prolationes et vocabula sit divisa; Soli
homini datum fuisse loqui cum solum sibi
necessarium fuit. Non angelis, non inferi-
oribus animalibus necessarium fuit loqui....

Quod autem prius vox primi loquentis sonaver-
it, viro sanae mentis in promptu esse non titu-
bo, ipsum fuisse quod Deus est, scilicet El,...
Absurdum videtur ante Deum ab homine quicquam
nominatum fuisse, cum ab ipso et in ipsum factus fuisset homo. Nam sicut, post lapsum
humani generis, quilibet exordium suae locu-
tionis incipit ab heu; rationabile est quod
ante qui fuit inciperet a gaudio: et quod
nullum gaudium sit extra Deum sed totum in
Deo, et ipse Deus totus sit gaudium, conse-
quens est quod primus loquens primo et ante
omnia dixisset, Deus.

Opinamur autem ad ipsum Deum primitus
primum hominem direxisse locutionem,.... Si
quis vero obiicit quod non oportebat illum
loqui cum solus adhuc homo existeret, et
Deus omnia sine verbis arcana nostra discernat,
etiam ante quam nos; cum illa reverentia
dicimus qua uti oportet cum de aeterna voluntate aliquid iudicamus, quod licet Deus sciret,
imo praesciret (quod idem est quantum ad Deum),
absque locutione conceptum primi loquentis,
Voluit tamen et ipsum loqui; ut in explicatione
tantae dotis gloriaretur ipse qui gratis
dotaverat.

Moore, 379-381
De Vulg. Elog. 1:2,4,5.

18. Cassiodorus on the Praise of Reason

(PL 70. 1285B)

Rationis itaque largitate dotata, quot bona
munere Divinitatis invenit! Litterarum for-
mas reperit, diversarum artium utilitates
disciplinasque protulit, civitates defensibili
muro cinxit, varii generis amictus [Iur.,
armenta] ejecit, meliores fructus per industriam exegit, terras transcurrit, abyssos

alato [ms., Aud., apto] navigio, vastos montes
in usum viantium, perforavit, portus ad
utilitatem navigantium lunari dispositione
conclusit, ornavit pulcherrima fabricarum
dispositione tellurem. Quis jam de ejus
ratione dubitet, quando ab auctore suo illu-
minata facit arte conspici, quod debeat sub
omni celebritate laudari? Convenit nunc de
ejus immortalitate disserere.

19. Ex Novo Organo Baconis de Verulam Aphorismus
XXXIX et qui sequuntur de Idolis.

XXXIX

Quatuor sunt genera Idolorum quae mentes
humanas obsident. Iis (docendi gratia) nomina
imposuimus; ut primum genus, Idola Tribus;
secundum, Idola Specus; tertium, Idola Fori;
quartum, Idola Theatri vocentur.

XLI

Idola Tribus sunt fundata in ipsa natura
humana, atque in ipsa tribu seu gente hominum.
Falso enim asseritur, sensum humanum esse
mensuram rerum; quin contra, omnes percep-
tiones tam sensus quam mentis sunt ex analogia
hominis, non ex analogia universi. Estque
intellectus humanus instar speculi inaequalis
ad radios rerum, qui suam naturam naturae rerum immiscet, eamque distorquet et inficit.

XLII

Idola Specus sunt idola hominis individui.
Habet enim unusquisque (praeter aberrationes
naturae humanae in genere) specum sive caver-
nam quandam individuam, quae lumen naturae
frangit et corrumpit; vel propter naturam
cujusque propriam et singularem; vel propter
educationem et conversationem cum aliis;

vel propter lectionem librorum, et authoritates
eorum quos quisque colit et miratur; vel propter differentias impressionum, prout occurrunt
in animo praeoccupato et praedisposito aut
in animo aequo et sedato, vel ejusmodi; ut
plane spiritus humanus (prout disponitur in
hominibus singulis) sit res varia, et omnino
perturbata, et quasi fortuita: unde bene Hera-
clitus, homines scientias quaerere in minori-
bus mundis, et non in majore sive communi.

XLIII

 Sunt etiam Idola tanquam ex contractu et
societate humani generis ad invicem, quae Idola
Fori, propter hominum commercium et consortium,
appellamus. Homines enim per sermones socian-
tur; at verba ex captu vulgi imponuntur. Itaque mala et inepta verborum impositio miris
modis intellectum obsidet. Neque definitiones
aut explicationes, quibus homines docti se
munire et vindicare in nonnullis consueverunt,
rem ullo modo restituunt. Sed verba plane
vim faciunt intellectui, et omnia turbant;
et homines ad inanes et innumeras controversias
et commenta deducunt.

XLIV

 Sunt denique Idola quae immigrarunt in
animos hominum ex diversis dogmatibus philoso-
phiarum, ac etiam ex perversis legibus demon-
strationum; quae Idola Theatri nominamus;
quia quot philosophiae receptae aut inventae
sunt, tot fabulas productas et actas censemus,
quae mundos effecerunt fictitios et scenicos.
Neque de his quae jam habentur, aut etiam de
veteribus philosophiis et sectis, tantum loqui-
mur; cum complures aliae ejusmodi fabulae
componi et concinnari possint; quandoquidem

errorum prorsus diversorum causae sint nihilominus fere communes. Neque rursus de philosophiis universalibus tantum hoc intelligimus,
sed etiam de principiis et axiomatibus compluribus scientiarum, quae ex traditione et
fide et neglectu invaluerunt. Verum de singulis istis generibus idolorum fusius et distinc-
tius dicendum est, ut intellectui humano cau-
tum sit.

20.   Sancti Thomae à Becket, Archiepiscopi Cantuariensis Epistulae duae, altera ad Papam
Romanum Alexandrum Tertium, cum Thomas exul
in Gallia moram faceret, altera eodem tempore
ad regem Angliae Henricum Secundum (abbreviated).

1.   Ad Papam Alexandrum

Abutitur ecclesiae patientia rex Angliae et
tanta immanitate in sponsam Christi iugiter
saevit, ut Petrus, cuius fidei et zelo illa
commissa est, gladium cogatur educere, et
persecutorum Christi in virtute sancti spiritus malitiam cohibere. Iterato enim rapitur
Christus et ad crucem trahitur, discipuli
disperguntur, qui...non omnino abiecerunt
fidem; alii iterum machinantur, quomodo
Filium Dei prodant in osculo pacis....

Quia nos, memores officii nostri et judicium
Dei, in quo nulli parcetur culpae, formidantes,
pro iustitia mutire ausi sumus,...expositi
sumus pro Christo periculis omnibus, tanquam
signum ad sagittam. Tandem addiciti exilio
cum omnibus nostris, clericis et laicis,
mulieribus et parvulis, pusillis et majoribus,
ut nec reverentia ordinis, nec conditio sexus,
nec aetatis miseratio quidquam irae detraheret
aut furori. Multi eorum iam in exilio mortui
sunt: quos, quoniam innocenter pro iustitia
patiebantur, confidimus ad requiem convolasse,

et cum electis laborum suorum recepisse merce-
dem. Plurimi vero adhuc exspectant misericordiam Dei, in fame et siti, in frigore et
nuditate. Alii tenentur in vinculis; inter
quos capellanus noster, ...qui de...consensu
regis remanserat in Anglia,...tenetur in
carcere.

Haec omnia sustinuimus, tentantes, an per
patientiam mansuetudinis nostrae possemus
aliquo modo mitigare saevitiam eius. Sed
quanto plura patimur, tanto magis crudescit
immanitas, ut publice fateatur se nullo modo
posse placari, nisi ei ad nutum exponatur
ecclesia....Quia ergo non acquiescimus, et
praedicamus Deo potius oboediendum quam homini,
quaerit animam nostram, ut cum ea auferat
ecclesiae libertatem....

Miseremini si placet, nostri, immo totius
ecclesiae Dei.

2. Thomas Cantuariensis Archiepiscopus
   Henrico Regi Angliae....

Desiderio desideravi videre faciem vestram,
et loqui vobiscum. Multum quidem propter me,
sed maxime propter vos.

Propter me, ut visa facie mea reduceretis
ad memoriam servitia quae, dum agerem in obsequio vestro, exhibui vobis devote et fideliter
juxta animi mei conscientiam. Sic deus me
adjuvet in examine ultimo, quando omnes ad-
stabimus ante tribunal ipsius, recepturi quout
gesserimus in corpore, sive bonum sive malum.
Et ut moveremini pietate super me, quem oportet
mendicando vivere inter alienos, licet tamen
Dei gratia cum abundantia victualia ad suf-
ficientiam habeamus,

Propter vos ex tribus causis: tum quia-
dominus meus estis, tum quia rex meus, tum
quia filius meus spiritualis.

Eo quod rex, teneor ad reverentiam vobis et
commonitionem. Eo quod filius, officii ratione
ad castigationem teneor et coercitionem. Cor-
ripit enim pater filium, nunc blandis, nunc
asperis, ut vel sic revocet eum ad benefacien-
dum.

Nosse debetis vos dei gratia regem esse....
Potestatis auctoritatem ab ecclesia accepistis
...sacramento unctionis. Inunguntur enim
reges tribus in locis: in capite, in pectore,
in brachiis. Quod significat: gloriam, scientiam, fortitudinem.

Christus fundavit ecclesiam, eiusque com-
paravit libertatem sanguine proprio, sustin-
endo flagella, sputa, clavos, mortis angus-
tias, nobis relinquens exemplum ut sequamur
ejus vestigia.... Ecclesia...Dei in duobus
constat ordinibus: clero et populo. In
clero sunt apostoli, apostolici viri, episcopi, et caeteri doctores ecclesiae.... In
populo sunt reges, principes, duces, comites,
et aliae potestates.,... Et quia certum est
reges potestatem suam accipere ab ecclesia,
non ipsam ab illis sed a Christo,... non habe-
tis episcopis praecipere.

Audiat itaque dominus meus, si placet, consilium fidelis sui, commonitionem episcopi
sui, et castigationem sui patris.... Per-
mittatis etiam nobis, si placet, libere et
in pace et cum omni securitate redire in
sedem nostram officioque nostro libere uti,
sicut debemus....

3. Epistula regis Henrici
    (an amnesty)

Pro amore Dei et domini papae, pro salute
nostra et heredum nostrorum, remitto Cantuari-
enso archiepiscopo et suis, qui cum eo et pro
eo exulant, iram meam et offensam, et eidem
remitto omnes querelas praecedentes, si quas
habebam adversus eum et concedo ei et suis
veram pacem et firmam securitatem de me et
meis, et reddo ei ecclesiam Cantuariensem in
ea plenitudine, in qua eam habuit cum factus
est archiepiscopus, et omnes possessiones,
quas habuit cum factus est archiepiscopus,
et omnes possessiones, quas habuit ecclesia
et ipse, ad habendum ita libere et honori-
fice, sicut melius et honorificentius eas
habuerunt et tenuerunt et sui, salvo honore
regni mei.

21. De Lingua et Grammatica

From Ben Jonson, (1573-1637) The English
Grammar: Consuetudo certissima loquendi
magistra.

Grammaticae unus finis est recte loqui.
Neque necesse habet scribere. Accidit enim
scriptura voci, neque aliter scribere debemus
quam loquamur.

Grammatica est ars bene loquendi.

Articulata vox dicitur, qua genus humanum
utitur, distinctim a ceteris animalibus,
quae muta vocantur; non quod sonum non edant;
sed quia soni eorum nullis exprimantur proprie
litterarum notis. (The true difference is
not in this, as we have shown in Sect.1, above.
But the naive statement shows how it takes
thousands of years fully to become conscious
of the process flourishing all these thousands
of years; articulated speech.)

Litterae pars minima vocis articulatae.

Litterae quae per seipsas possint pronunti-
ari, vocales sunt; quae non, nisi cum aliis,
consonantes sunt.

Vocalium nomina simplici sono, nec differ-
ente a potestate, proferuntur. Consonantes
additis vocalibus egent, quibusdam praeposi-
tis, aliis postpositis. (Confer Scauri
grammatici Latini animadversiones in litteras
k, c, q, supra, Sect. 143.)

Omnes vocales ancipites sunt, id est, modo
longae; modo breves; eodem tamen modo semper
depictae (nam scriptura est imitatio sermonis,
ut pictura corporis; [nec mirandum quod pictura minus perfecta sit quam exemplar], et eodem
sono pronuntiatae. Nisi quod vocalis longa bis
tantum temporis in proferendo retinet quam
brevis. Ut recte cecinit ille poeta de vocalibus:

Temporis unius brevis est, ut longa duorum.

From Ben Jonson, Grammatica Anglicana,
Works, ed. Oxford 1947, VIII.463,
466-469.

22. Gabriele d'Annunzio (1863-1938): Inscription
in his Garden, written by himself

Ego sum Gabriel qui adsto ante deos alitibus de fratribus unus oculeus [unoculus][1] Postvortae alumnus arcani divini minister humanae
dementiae sequester volucer demissus ab alto
princeps et praeco.

_____

1. The suggested emendation, unoculus, makes
the word an allusion to d'Annunzio's loss
of an eye, mentioned above.

Translation

I am Gabriele who stands before the Gods,
the one with one eye among my winged brothers,
nourished by the Goddess of the Future [?][1]
ministering the divine secret, and following
human folly, air pilot sent down from the
heights, a prince and a herald.

Commentary

The Italian poet in 1919 took Fiume, lost
one eye in the attack, and was made Prince of
Monte Nevoso; the word princeps is an allusion
to this.

This is an imitation of the words of the
Archangel Gabriel in Luke 1:19: "Ego sum
Gabriel qui adsto ante Deum." Gabriel is
one of the four archangels standing before
God, i.e., Rafael, Uriel, and Michael. Gabriel
is the "annuntiator salvationis" so that Gabriele d'Annunzio really is fraught by the comparison by his two names. It is amusing to
find the greatest authority on d'Annunzio's
life, his secretary and biographer, Tom
Antongini, stumbling over this inscription.
Since he does not recognize the pun of the
poet with his angel-namesake, Antongini trans-
lates the inscription as follows:
Ego sum Gabriel qui adsto ante deos
I am Gabriel who presents himself before the
Gods (as an offering)
alitibus de Fratribus unus oculeus
among the winged brothers the most perspicacious
Arcani divini minister
Priest of the arcane and of the divine
humanae dementiae sequester
Interpreter of human dementia
Postvortae alumnus

---

1. We have chosen this as the more likely of
   the two meanings of Postvorta.

The underlined terms used by Antongini
are wrong, and change the meaning completely.
Perhaps there is something in the saying that
nobody is a hero with his servant: The
greatest stylist is no stylist before his
secretary. And at the only place where we
depend wholly on Antongini's inside knowledge, he fails us; the word "Postvortae"
is found in Varro and Macrobius and means
either the goddess of the future or the goddess of breech-birth (as opposed to the goddess
of normal birth, Antevorta). This is a rare
word, here perhaps containing some obscure
word-play which we are unable to recover. But
Antongini possibly misread the monument in the
Vittoriale.

23. From the "Songs" of St. Augustine's <u>Confessions</u>

Domine deus
pacem da nobis --
omnia enim praestitisti nobis --
pacem quietis, pacem sabbati,
pacem sine vespera.
Omnis quippe iste ordo pulcherrimus
rerum valde bonarum
modis suis peractis transiturus est:
et mane quippe in eis factum est et vespera.

Dies autem septimus
sine vespera est nec habet occasum,
quia sanctificasti eum ad permansionem sempiternam,
ut id, quod tu post opera tua bona valde,
quamvis ea quietus feceris,
requievisti septimo die,
hoc praeloquatur nobis vox libri tui,
quod et nos post opera nostra ideo bona valde,
quia tu nobis ea donasti, sabbato vitae aeternae
requiescamus in te.   [13.35.50-36.51]

SOME BOOKS USED IN THE PREPARATION OF THIS BOOK

A. INDIVIDUAL AUTHORS

Augustine

St. Augustine, The Philosophy of Teaching, by Francis E. Tourcher, O.S.A. Villanova College, Pa., 1924.

Bible

Stier, E. R. & Theile K.G.W. Polyglottenbibel zum praktische Handgerauch
Bielefeld, 1863-64   RCBAA   1863
Original texts + LXX, Vulg. Luther tr.

Breviary

Breviarium Romanum Romae, Typis Polyglottis Vaticanis
Missale Romanum

Clemens Scotus (c. 825)

Tolkiehn, Johannes, Clementis Ars Grammatica Leipzig, Dieterich, 1928.

Dante

Dante, Works in Moore, E., Tutte le Opere di Dante Alighieri, Oxford, U. P. 1904.
Latham, C. S., A Translation of Dante's Eleven Letters, Boston 1891.

Ennius

Ennianae Poesis Reliquiae, ed. Johannes Vahlen, Leipzig, Teubner, 1903.

Francis of Assisi

Legenda S. Francisci ad Quaracchos
Analecta Franciscana, t10

Sextus Julius Frontinus

Frontinus, The Stratagems, and the Aqueducts of Rome, ed. C. E. Bennett: The Loeb Classical Library, London: Heinemann, 1925.

Hugo Primas

Hugo primas, Derselbe Die Oxforder Gedichte des Primas, Nachrichten der Goettinger Gessellschaft der Wissenschaften, Philil. historische Klasse 1907, p. 75, ff., 113 ff., 231 ff.

Joannes Secundus

Ioannis Nicolaii Secundi Hagani Opera Omnia edd. Peter Burmann II and Peter Bosscha Leyden, 1821

Wright, F. A., The Love Poems of Joannes Secundus New York, Dutton, 1930.

Ben Jonson

Jonson, Ben, Works, vol: VIII, ed. by C. H. Herford, Percy and Evelyn Simpson, Oxford, Clarendon, 1947.

John Locke

Locke, John, Lettres Inedites de John Locke à ses amis Nicolas Thoynard, Philippe van Limborch et Edward Clarke, ed. Henry Ollion, The Hague, 1912.

Magna Charta

McKechnie, W. S., Magna Charta, Glasgow, Maclehc 1905.

Martianus Capella

Martianus Capella, ed. A. Dick, Leipzig, Teubner, 1925.

Monumentum Ancyranum

Caesaris Augusti Res Gestae et Fragmenta by R. S Rogers, K. Scott, M. M. Ward, D. C. Heath, 1935

Res Gestae Divi Augusti ed. Th. Mommsen, Berlin, Weidmann, 1883.

Monumentum Antiochenum, Klio Beiheft 19 (the new text of the Res Gestae as edited by W. M. Ramsay und Anton von Premerstein) Leipzig, Dieterich, 1927. The Monumentum Ancyranum ed by E. G. Hardy, Oxford, 1923.

New Testament

Novum Testamentum, Graece et Latine, ed. Eberhard Nestle, Stuttgart, 1914.

Novum Testamentum interprete Th. Beza, New York, 1899.

Paulinus of Venice (d. 1345)

Holzmann, Walther
Bruchstücke aus der Weltchronik des Minoriten Paulinus von Venedig
Heft 1
Rome: Rogensberg, 1927

Pomponius Mela

omponius Mela, De Chronographia, ed. C. Frick,
Leipzig, Teubner, 1880.

Rodolfus Tertarius

odolfi Tertarii Carmina edited by M. B. Ogle
and D. M. Sullivan American Academy in
Rome, 1933.

ANTHOLOGIES, AND COLLECTIONS OF TEXTS, ETC.

llen, P. S., Medieval Latin Lyrics, Chicago,
U.P., 1931.

rpus Inscriptionum Christianarum

rpus Scriptorum Ecclesiasticorum Latinorum,
Vienna & Leipzig.

agg, Florence Alden, Latin Writings of the
Italian Humanists, New York. Scribner, 1927.

onke, Peter, Medieval Latin and the Rise of
European Love-Lyric, 2 vols. Oxford, Clarendon,
1965-66.

dmann, Carl, ed. Ausgewählte Briefe aus der
alierzeit, Rome, Regenberg, 1933.

e Oxford Book of Medieval Latin Verse, Oxford,
928.

rrington, Karl Pomeroy, Mediaeval Latin,
Boston, 1925] Chicago: U.P., 1963.

criptiones Latinae Selectae, ed. H. Dessau
rlin, Weidmann, 1892ff.

l, Heinrich, Grammatici Latini, I-VI, Leipzig,
eubner, 1857ff.

nmuench, Otto J., Early Christian Latin Poets
rom the Fourth to the Sixth Century, Chicago,
oyola University Press, 1929.

cucchi, Orazio, Christian Epigraphy, tr.
A. Willis, Cambridge, U. P., 1912.

gne, J. P., Patrologia Latina

umenta Germaniae Historica, Poetae Carolini
-IV

ratori Scriptores Rerum Italicarum

onicles and Memorials of Great Britain and
eland during the Middles Ages, published
der the direction of the Master of the Rolls

Salonius, A. H., Vitae Patrum; Kritische
Untersuchungen, Lund, Gleerup, 1920.

Schneider, Fedor, Fünfundzwanzig lateinische
weltliche Rhythmen aus der Frühzeit (VI bis
XI Jahrhundert), Rome: Regenberg, 1925.

Stubbs, Wm., Select Charters (9th. ed.).
Oxford, Clarendon, 1913.

Ulrich, Jakob, Proben der lateinischen
Novellistik des Mittelalters, Leipzig, Renger,
1906.

Waddell, Helen Jane, Medieval Latin Lyrics,
New York, R. R. Smith, 1930.
_____, The Wandering Scholar,
Boston, Houghton Mifflin, 1927.
_____, A Book of Medieval Latin
for Schools, London, Constable, 1931.

Wright, Thomas, Early Mysteries and other Latin
Poems of the 12th and 13th Centuries, London,
John R. Smith, 1844.

C. GRAMMARS, DICTIONARIES, WORKS ON LINGUISTICS AND
ON THE LATIN LANGUAGE

Baxter, J. H. and Johnson, Charles, Medieval Latin
Word List from British and Irish Sources, London,
Oxford U.P., 1934.

Bartsch, Karl, Die lateinischen Sequenzen des
Mittelalters, Rostock, Stiller, 1868.

Beeson, Charles Henry, A Primer of Medieval
Latin, Chicago, Scott Foresman, 1925.

Bennett, Charles E., Syntax of Early Latin
(Two Volumes) Boston, Allyn and Bacon; and
Leipsic 1910 and 1917.

Bennett, C. E., and Bristol, G. P., The Teaching of Latin and Greek, New York, Longmans,
Green, 1901.

Brugmann, Karl, Die Syntax des einfachen
Satzes im Indogermanischen, Berlin and
Leipzig, de Gruyter, 1925.

Brugmann, K. N., Verschiedenheiten der
Satzgestaltung nach Massgabe der selischen
Grundfunktionen in den indogermanischen
Sprachen - Berichte der Saessischen Ges.
der Wissenschaften zu Leipzig phili.
Historische - Klasse 70. Band 1918 1-93.

Conway, R. S., The Making of Latin 2nd ed.
London, Murray, 1928.

Doherty, Ella Tormey and Cooper, Elsie E.,
Word Heritage, Chicago, and Philadelphia,
Lippincott, 1929.

Ernout, A. et Meillet A., Dictionnaire Etymologique de la Langue Latine, Historie des Mots, Paris, Klincksieck, 1939.

Ernout, A., Morphologie Historique du Latin, 2nd edition, Paris, Klincksieck, 1927.

Faral, Edmond, Les Arts Poétiques du XII et XIII siècle. Recherches et Documents sur la Technique Littéraire du Moyen Âge, Paris, Champion, 1924.

Gardiner, Alan H., The Theory of Speech and Language, Oxford, Clarendon, 1932.

Gautier, Léon, Histoire de la Poésie Liturgique au Moyen Âge, Paris, Pal me 1886.

Gibson, Charles, Hepworth, Limen Latinum, A Latin Book for Beginners, London, Rolfe, 1907.

de Gourmont, Rémy, Le Latin Mystique, Paris, Cres, 1913.

Grandgent, Charles Hall, An Introduction to Vulgar Latin, Boston, Heath, 1907.

Habel, E., Mittellateinisches Glossar, Paderborn, 1931.

Hettich, E. L. and Maitland, A. G. C., Latin Fundamentals, New York, Prentice-Hall, 1934.

Hilka, Alfons, Beiträge zur lateinischen Erzählungsliteratur des Mittelalters Akademie der wissenschaften, Göttingen, Berlin, 1935.

Hofmann, Johann Baptist, Lateinische Umgangssprache, Heidelberg, Winter, 1935.

Hussey, George B., A Handbook of Latin Homonyms, Boston, Sanborn, 1905.

Koch, Carl, Der Römische Juppiter, Frankfurt, Klostermann, 1937.

Magnussen, Peter Magnus, Some Applications of Logical and Psychological Principles in Grammar, Ph.D. Thesis, Minneapolis, 1893.

Manitius, Masimilianus, Geschichte der Christlich-Lateinischen Poesie, bis 3 auf Mitte des VIII Jahrhunderts, Stuttgart, 1891 Geschichte der Lateinischen Literatur des Mittelalters, Munich, Beck, 1911-31.

Meillet, Antoine, Esquisse d'une Histoire de la Langue Latine, Paris, Hachette, 1928.

_____, Linguistique Historique et Linguistique Générale, Paris, Champion, 1921-38.

du Meril, E. P. Poésies inedites du Moyen Âge... Paris, 1854.

Morris, Edward Parmelee, On Principles and Methods in Latin Syntax, New York, Scribner, 1901.

Nunn, H. P. V., An Introduction to Ecclesiastical Latin, Cambridge, U. P., 1927.

Paulhan, Frédéric, La Double Fonction du Langage Paris, Alcan, 1929.

Plater, Wm. Edward and White, H. J.; A Grammar of the Vulgate, Oxford, Clarendon, 1926.

Raby, F. J. E., A History of Christian-Latin Poetry from the Beginnings to the Close of the Middle Ages, Oxford, Clarendon, 1927.

Raby, F. J. E., A History of Secular Latin Poetry in the Middle Ages, 2 Vols., Oxford, Clarendon, 1934.

Schulze, Wilhelm, Zur Geschichte lateinischer Eigennamen, Berlin, Weidmann, 1933.

Sleumer, Albert, Kirchenlateinisches Woerterbuch Limburg an der Lahn, Steffen, 1925.

Sommer, Ferdinand, Handbuch der lateinischen Laut – und Formenlehre, Heidelberg, Winter, 1902.

Sommerfelt, Alf., La Langue et La Société, Caractères sociaux d'une Langue de Type archaïque, Oslo, Aschehoug, 1938.

Spitzer, Leo, ed. Hugo Schurchardt-Brevier, Ein Vademekum der allgemeinen Sprachwissenschaft, Halle, 1922.

Steinthal, H., Einleitung in die Psychologie und Sprachwissenschaft, Berlin, 1881.

Stand und Aufgaben der Sprachwissenschaft, Festschrift fuer Wilhelm Streitberg, ed. J. Friedrich, et. al., Heidelberg, Winter, 1924.

Stoltz, F., Schmalz, J. H., Leumann, M., Hofmann, J. R., Lateinische Grammatik, Muenchen, 1928.

Strecker, Karl, Introduction to Medieval Latin, Eng. tr., R. B. Palmer [Berlin, 1957] 3rd. ed. Zürich, Wiedemann, 1965.

Sturtevant, E. H., The Pronunciation of Greek and Latin, 2nd ed., Philadelphia, Linguistic Society of America, 1940.

WORD LIST

The Latin words in the vocabularies, readings, exercises and grammatical notes of Chapters I-XIX have been gathered together here for the convenience of the beginner. For the remainder of Magna Charta Latina the student is encouraged to use a good Latin dictionary such as that of Lewis and Short, reprinted by Oxford University Press. The Section number indicates where first used or discussed.

-A-

ā, ab (prep./abl.   59
  from, by

abbās, -ātis (m)   82
  abbot

aberrō, -āre, -ārī, -ātus   71
  to wander, go astray

absque (prep./abl.)   59
  without

accurrō, -ere, -currī, cursus   109
  to run to, hasten to

acer, acris, acre (adj.)   48
  sharp

actiō, -iōnis (f)   54
  action
  verbum actiōnis: verb

acūtus, -a, -um (adj.)   31
  sharp, pointed

ad (prep./acc.)   4,40
  to, toward; for (expressing purpose)

adaptō, āre, -āvī, -ātus   77
  to fit, adjust, adapt, make fit

adhuc (adv.)   93
  hitherto, thus far, until now

adiectīvus, -a, -um (adj.)   105
  adjective

adiūtor, -ōris (m)   35
  helper, assistant

admīrābilis, -e, (adj.)   50
  admirable, wonderful

adōrō, -āre, āvī, -ātus   19
  to reverence, worship, adore

adscendō, -ere, -scendī, -scensus   94
  to go up, rise, ascend

adstō, -āre, -stitī   86
  to stand at or near, assist

adveniō, -īre, -vēnī, -ventus   104
  to come, arrive

adverbium, ī (n)   105
  adverb

aedificō, -āre, -āvī, -ātus   41
  to build, establish, edify

aeger, -gra, -grum (adj.)   90
  ill, sick

aequus, -a, -um (adj.)   93
  equal

āēr, āeris (m)   47
  air

aetās, -ātis (f)   86
  age, time of life

aeternus, -a, -um (adj.)   33
  eternal

afficiō, -ere, -fēcī, -fectus   43
  to affect

afflīgō, -ere, -ixī, -ictus   43
  to weaken, afflict

agricola, -ae (m)   14
  farmer

āiō (vb. irr.)   86
  to say

alācer, -cris, -cre (adj.)   48
  excited, quick

albeō, -ēre, -uī   109
  to be white

albus, -a, -um (adj.)   37,55
  white

aliēnigena, -ae (m)   86
  foreigner, stranger

aliquandō (adv.)   58
  at some time, once, at any time, ever

aliquis, -qua, -quid   101
  somebody, a certain

alius, -a, -ud (adj.)   47,96
  other

allocūtiō, iōnis (f)   54
  address, exhortation

alter, altera, alterum (adj.)   50
  another

altus, -a, -um (adj.)   31
  high

ambulō, -āre, -āvī, -ātus   14,65
  to walk

amīcus, ī (m)   19
  friend

amitto, -ere, -mīsī, missus   94
  to lose

amor, -ōris (m)   50
  love

amplus, -a, -um (adj.)   53
  full, ample

ancilla, -ae (f.)   14,65
  maid, female servant

angelus, ī (m.)   19
  angel, messenger

Anglia, -ae (f.)   40
  England

Anglicus, -a, -um (adj.)   32
  English

anima, -ae (f.)   14
  soul
animal, -alis (n.)   8
  a living being, animal
animus, -ī (m.)   59
  mind, heart
annus, -ī (m.)   19
  year
ante (prep./acc.)   40
  before
anteā (adv.)   87
  before, previously
antīquus, -a, -um (adj.)   24,37
  old, ancient

appāreð, -ēre, -uī, -itus   103
  to appear
appello, -āre, -avi, -atus   96
  to call
apud (prep./acc.)   40
  among, with, at, by, near; at the house of
aqua, -ae (f.)   14
  water
arābilis, -e (adj.)   48,54
  ploughable, arable
arātor, -ōris (m)   54
  plowman
aratrum, -ī (n.)   54
  plow
arbor, -ōris (f.)   31
  tree
archiepiscopus, -ī (m.)   82
  archbishop
arēna, -ae (f.) [harēna]   35
  sand, place of combat in the amphitheater
argūmentum, -ī (n.)   59
  argument, proof
arō, -āre, -āvī, -ātus   19,54
  to plow, till
ars, artis (f.)   37
  art
articulo, -āre, -āvī, -ātus   90
  to articulate
artifex, -ficis (m.)   89
  maker, artist, artificer
arx, arcis (f.)   37
  citadel, stronghold
asper, aspera, asperum (adj.)   41
  harsh, severe
assedeō, -ēre, -sēdī, -sessus   86
  to sit
athlēta, -ae (m.)   94
  athlete
attendō, -ere, -tendī, -tentus   109
  to attend to, consider

audeō, -ēre, ausus sum   106
  to dare
audiō, -īre, -īvī, -ītus   8,62
  to hear
audītor, -ōris (m.)   103
  hearer

augeō, -ēre, auxī, auctus   109
  to increase
auris, -is (f.)   36
  ear
aurum, -ī (n.)   33
  gold
auxilium, -ī (n.)   24
  help, assistance
avārus, -a, -um (adj.)   106
  greedy
avārus, -i (m)   106
  miser
avē!   50
  hail!

-B-

beātus, -a, -um (adj.)   33,35
  blessed
bellum, -ī (n.)   24
  war
bene (adv.)   56
  well
benedīcō, -ere, -dīxī, -dīctus   57
  to bless
benevolus, -a, -um (adj.)   53
  benevolent, kindly, friendly, favorable
bonum, -ī (n.)   46
  the good
bonus, -a, -um (adj.)   19,27,53
  good
bracchium, -ī (n.)   24
  forearm
brevis, -e (adj.)   46,77
  short, little, small, narrow

Britannia, -ae   14
  Britain

-C-

cadō, -ere, cecidī, casūs   86
  to fall down
Caesar, -aris (m.)   31
  Caesar
calamitās, -tātis (f.)   86
  loss, misfortune, calamity, disaster, ruin
camera, -ae (f.)   32
  arch, arched roof, chamber
campāna, -ae (f.)   89
  bell
candidus, -a, -um (adj.)   55
  shining, white
canis, -is (comm.)   83
  dog
canonicus, -a, -um (adj.)   50
  according to rule or measure, canonical
cantātor, -ōris (m.)   54
  singer

cantātrix, -trīcis (f.) 54
singer (woman), chantress
cantō, -āre, -āvī, -ātus 14
to sing
caper, caprī (m.) 90
he-goat
capiō, -ere, cēpī, captus 46,109
to take, occupy, seize, capture
caput, capitis (n.) 96
head
careō, -ēre, -uī, -itum 90
to lack, be without
caritās, -tātis (f.) 55
love, charity, affection
carō, carnis (f.) 59
flesh
carta, -ae (f.) 8
map, charter

cārus, -a, -um (adj.) 73
dear, precious, valued, esteemed
casa, -ae (f.) 65
hut, cottage
casus, -ūs (m.) 90
fall, case
catēna, -ae (f.) 73
chain
caupo, -ōnis (m.) 90
tradesman, huckster
causa, -ae (f.) 55
cause, reason
cēdō, -ere, cessī, cessus 46,47,109
to yield, grant, retreat
celebrō, -āre, -āvī, ātus 57
to frequent, celebrate, honor, praise
celer, -eris, -ere (adj.) 48
swift, quick
celeriter (adv.) 4,56
swiftly, quickly
Cerēs, -evis (f.) 31
Ceres, goddess of agriculture
certāmen, -inis (n.) 106
contest, struggle
certus, -a, -um (adj.) 27
sure, certain
cessō, -āre, -āvī, -ātus
to yield, be inactive, idle
chorus, ī (m.) 19
dance, chorus
Cinderella, -ae (f.) 32
Cinderella (=the girl of ashes)
cinis, cineris (m.) 31,45
ashes
citrā (prep./acc.) 93,94
on this side, apart from, except
cīvīlis, -e (adj.) 50
civil
cīvis, -is (m.) 87
citizen
cīvitās, -ātis (f.) 41,54
city

clamō, -āre, -āvī, -ātus 14,78

clārē (adv.) 59
clearly
clārus, -a, -um (adj.) 29
clear, bright, famous
clēricus, -ī (m.) 106
clerk, clergyman
cochleāre, -āris (n.) 37
spoon
coelum, -ī (n: sing.; m: plur.) 24
heaven, sky
cōgitō, -āre, -āvī, -ātus 64
to think, ponder, consider
cognoscō, -ere, cognōvī, cognītus 109
to examine, recognize, know
colligō, -ere, -lēgī, lectus 50
to gather, collect
collis, -is (m.) 37
hill
comes, -itis (comm.) 83
companion
commiserātio, -iōnis (f.) 57
compassion
compleō, -ēre, -ēvī, ētus 61
to fill
computō, -āre, āvī, ātus 89
to reckon, compute
concordō, -āre, āvī, -ātus 35
to agree, harmonize, to unite
concors, concordis (adj.) 48
united, agreeing, concordant, harmonious
concurrō, -ere, -currī, cursus 109
to run together, meet, happen
conductiō, -iōnis (f.) 54,75
a bringing together, uniting
conductor, -ōris (m.) 75
leader
confessiō, -iōnis (f.) 85
confession

confortātus, -a, -um (adj.) 33,35
strengthened, comforted
congregō, -āre, -āvī, -ātus 19,41
to gather, flock, assemble
coniugātiō, -iōnis (f.) 105
conjugation
conscientia, -ae (f.) 28
conscience
conservō, -āre, -āvī, -ātus 32
to save, keep, conserve
consōlātrix, -tricis 50
woman who consoles (=Virgin Mary)
constō, -āre, consteti, constatus 93
to agree with, be in accord or agreement,
correspond (See also Section 96.)
constat
it is settled, established, certain
construō, -ere, -strūxī, -strūctus 84,86
to construct, build
consul, consulis (m.) 94
consul

consummō, -āre, -āvī, -ātus   93
   to bring about, perfect, complete,(cf 96)
   finish, consummate
consumō, -āre, -sumpsī, -sumptus
   to consume
consurgō, -ere, -surrēxī, -surrectus
   to rise up
contendō, -ere, -tendī, .tentus   109
   to strive, contend
contrā (prep./ acc.)   24,40
   against, opposite to
contrārius, -a, -um (adj.)   59
   opposite, contrary
conveniō, -īre, -vēnī, -ventus   50
   to come together, meet together, join,
   combine, couple
convertō, -ere, -tī, -sus   94
   to turn, change, transform
cor, cordis (n.)   33
   heart

cōram (prep./abl.)   59
   before, in the presence of
corōna, -ae (f.)   32
   crown
corporālis, -e (adj.)   85
   physical, bodily
corpus, corporis (n.)   50
   body
corrumpō, -ere, -rūpī, -ruptus   33
   to destroy, ruin, corrupt
cotidiānus, -a, -um (adj.)   104
   daily
crās (adv.)   55
   tomorrow
crēdō, -ere, credidī, creditus   87
   to believe (See Section 90a, above)
crescō, -ere, crēvī, crētus   109
   to grow, come forth
crīmen, -inis (n.)   90
   accusation, crime
crux, crucis   85
   cross
cubō, -ere, -uī, -itum   109
   to recline, sleep
cum (conj.)   24
   with indic.: when, after, etc.
   with subjunc.: since, although, seeing
     that, etc.
cum (prep./abl.)   14,59
   with
cunctus, -a, -um (adj.)   55
   all, the whole, all together
cupidus, -a, -um (adj.)   24,87
   desiring, eager, fond, passionate
cūr (interr. adv.)   88
   why
cūria, -ac (f.)   86
   court
currō, -ere, cucurrī, cursus   109
   to run
custodiō, -īre, -īvī, -ītus   62
   to guard

D

dē (prep./alb.)   59
   from, about, concerning
dēbellō, -āre, -àvī, -ātus   70
   to conquer, vanquish, subdue
dēbeō, -ēre, -uī, -itus
   to owe; ought
dēbitor, -ōris (m.)   104
   debtor
debitum,-Ī (n.)   104
   debt
dēcīdō, -ere, -cīdī, -cīsus   93
   to cut down, reduce, diminish
dedicātiō, -ātiōnis (f.)   86
   dedication, consecration
dedīcō, -āre, -āvī, -ātus   86
   to dedicate, consecrate
deficiō, -ere, -fēcī, -fectus   106
   to fail, be lacking
dēgener, -eris (adj.)   90
   degenerate
dēlectō, -āre, -āvī, -ātus   14
   to delight, please
demon, -onis (m.)   **86**
   demon
dēliquō, -ere, -līquī, -lictus   94
   to transgress, offend, fail
dēmonstrō, -āre, -āvī, -ātus   78
   to point out, indicate, show, prove,
   demonstrate
dens, dentis (m.)   37
   tooth
dēpereō, īre, -iī   90
   to perish, die, be lost
dēputō, -āre, -āvī, -ātus   71
   to destine, allot, give to
desertum, -Ī (n.)   78
   desert, waste
dēsīderō, -āre, -āvī, -ātus   73
   to long for, desire

Deus, -Ī (m.)   19
   God   See Section 19a, above.)
dexter, -tra, -trum (adj.)   27
   right
diabolus, -Ī (m.)   86
   devil
dīco, -ere, dīxī, dictus   55
   to say, tell, speak
diēs, diēī (m./f.)   3,79
   day
difficilis, -e (adj.)   53
   difficult
dīgerō, -ere, -gessī, gestus   93
   to separate, divide, distribute
dīligō, -ere, dīlēxī, dīlectus   64
   to love
dīmittō, -ere, -mīsī, -missus   94
   to discharge, dismiss, release,
   forgive

discipulus, -i (m.)   109
  pupil
discō, discere, didicī   109
  to learn
discrīmen, -inis (n.)   93
  distinction, difference
disputō, -āre, -avī, -ātus   57
  to discuss, dispute, contend
dissimilis, -e (adj.)   53
  unlike
dīvès, dīvitis (adj.)   48
  rich
dīvidō, -ere, dīvīsī, dīvīsus   93,109
  to divide, separate
dīvīnus, -a, -um (adj.)   73
  divine
dō, dare, dedī, datus   14
  to give
doceō, -ēre, -uī, doctus   61,109
  to teach
doctē (adv.)   57
  learnedly

docīlis, -e (adj.)   54
  teachable
doctor, -ōris (m.)   50,75
  teacher
doctrīna, -ae (f.)   40
  teaching, instruction, doctrine
dogma, -atis (n.)   103
  dogma, doctrine
domina, -ae (f.)   55
  mistress
dominica, -ae (f.)   95
  Sunday
dominus, -ī (m.)   19
  Lord
domus, -ūs/-ī (f.)   32
  home
dōnō, -āre, -āvī, -ātus   14
  to present, bestow
dōnum, -ī (n.)   55
  gift
dormiō, -īre, īvī (īī), ītus   65
  to sleep
dubitō, -āre, -āvī, -ātus   70
  to doubt
dūcō, -ere, dūxī, ductus   96,109
  to lead
dulcis, -e (adj.)   53
  sweet, gentle
duplex, -cis (adj.)   48
  double
duplicātiō, ionis (f.)   93
  doubling, duplication. X 2
dūrō, -āre, -āvī, -ātus   87
  to harden
dūrus, -a, -um (adj.)   73
  hard
dux, ducis (m.)   67
  leader

-E-

ē, ex (prep./abl.)   59
  from
eburneus, -a, -um (adj.)   30
  ivory
ecclēsia, -ae (f.)   14
  church
edō, edere*, ēdī, ēsus   109
  to each
  * or: ēsse
ēdō, -ere, -didī, -ditus   109
  to give out, put forth, bring forth
ēducō, -āre, -āvī, ātus   61
  to educate
ēducātor, -ōris (m.)   61
  educator
efficiō, -ere, -fēcī, -fectus   43,93
  to accomplish, bring about, yield
egeō, -ēre, -uī   64
  to be needy, to lack
ego, meī (pron.)   102
  I
electiō, -iōnis (f.)   50
  choice, election
ēlegantia, -ae (f.)   85
  exquisitenness, fastidiousness,
  elegance
emendō, -āre, -āvī, ātus   14
  to mend, correct, improve
emō, -ere, ēmī, emptus   109
  to buy
enarrō, -āre, -āvī, -ātus   19
  to expound, interpret
eō, īre, īvī, (īī)   4,7
  to go
episcopus, -ī (m.)   82
  bishop
epistula [epistola], -ae (f.)   46
  letter, epistle

ergā (prep./acc.)   40
  over against, toward (on behalf of)
ergō (adv.)   58
  therefore
ērogō, -āre, -āvī, -ātus
  to pay out, expend
errō, -āre, -āvī, -ātus   78
  to wander, err
et (conj.)   14
  and
Eucharistia, -ae (f.)   57
  Lord's Supper, communion
exanimis, -e (adj.)   86
  lifeless
excavō, -āre, -āvī, -ātus   96
  to hollow out, excavate
excellens, entis (adj.)   55
  distinguished, superior, excellent
exclāmō, -āre, -āvī, -ātus   35
  to cry out, exclaim

exemplar, -āris (n.)   37
   pattern, exemplar, model
exeō, -īre, -iī   7
   to go out, forth or away
exilium, -ī (n.)   90
   banishment, exile
existō, -ere, -stitī, -stitus   43
   to come forth, exist
exitus, -ūs (m.)   7
   departure, end, issue, result, death
expectō, -āre, -āvī, -ātus   77
   to await, expect, wait for
explicō, -āre, -āvī, -ātus   73
   to set forth, explain
expugnō, -āre, -āvī, -ātus   89
   to conquer, subdue, overcome
extrā (prep./acc; abl.)   40
   outside of, without, beyond;
   beyond, apart; except, besides
extrahō, -ere, xī, -ctum   86
   to drag out, extricate release

-F-

facile (adv.)   48,56
   easily
facilis, -e (adj.)   46,53
   easy
faciō, -ere, fēcī, factus   8,109
   to do, make
factum, -ī (n.)   94
   deed, act
facultās, -ātis (f.)   86
   skill, ability, efficacy; goods,
   riches
famēs, -is   33,35
   hunger
familiāris, -e (adj.)   48
   familiar, intimate, friendly,
   customary, habitual
fēbris, -is (f.)   95
   fever
   quintana f.: fever recurring every
     fifth day (like malaria)
fēcundus, -a, -um (adj.)   27
   fruitful, fertile, rich, abundant
fēlīx, -īcis (adj.)   55
   lucky, happy, fortunate
fēmina, -ae (f.)   14
   woman
ferē (adv.)   94
   almost, nearly
   (with negatives: scarcely, hardly)
fēria, -ae (f.)   95
   f. secunda: Monday
   f. tertia: Tuesday
   f. quarta: Wednesday
   f. quinta: Thursday
   f. sexta: Friday
festīvitās, -ātis (f.)   57
   festival, feast; festive
   gaiety, mirth, merriment, joy
fictilis, -e (adj.)   48,54
   made of clay, earthen, fictile

fidēlis, -e (adj.)   48
   faithful
fidēs, -eī (f.)   33,35
   faith, belief
fidus, -a, -um (adj.)   15
   faithful, steadfast
fīlia, -ae (f.)   14
   daughter
fīlius, -iī (m.)   19
   son, child
fīniō, -īre, -īvī (-iī), -ītus   62
   to determine, fix, appoint, end,
   cease
fīnis, -is (m.)   62
   end
fīō, fierī, factus sum   93
   [pass. of faciō] See Section 122c.
   to be made, become
firmāmentum, -ī (n.)   24
   support, prop; firmament
firmiter (av.)   57
   firmly
firmus, -a, -um (adj.)   37
   steadfast, stable, firm
floreō, ēre, -uī   68,109
   to bloom, flower
flectō, -ere, flēxī, flexus   109
   to bend, bow, curve, turn
flōs, flōris (m.)   31,45
   flower
fons, fontis (m.)   50
   source, fountainhead
forma, -ae (f.)   32
   form, shape, appearance; beauty
formīdō, -āre, -āvī, -ātus   106
   to fear, dread
formō, -āre, -āvī, -ātus   8
   to shape, fashion, form
forsitan (adv.)   58
   perhaps, peradventure

fortassē (adv.)   58
   perhaps, probably, possibly
forte (adv.)   58
   by chance, by accident, casually,
   accidentally
fortis, -e (adj.)   48
   strong, powerful
fortiter (adv.)   56
   strongly, powerfully
fortitūdō, -inis (f.)   64
   strength
fortūna, -ae (f.)   35
   chance, luck, fate, fortune
frangō, -ere, frēgī, fractus   109
   to break
frāter, frātris (m.)   45
   brother
fraus, fraudis (f.)   90
   deceit, imposition, fraud
frustrā (adv.)   58
   in vain
fugō, -āre, āvī, ātus   106
   to put to flight

illinc (adv.)   98
   thence
illuc (adv.)   58,98
   thither
illūsiō, -iōnis (f.)   86
   illusion
imāgo, -inis   45
   image
imperātor, -tōris   54
   commander-in-chief, general,
   emperor
imperātrīx, -trīcis   54
   empress
imperium, -ī (n.)   70
   command, authority, rule, sway,
   dominion
imperō, -āre, -āvī, -ātus   95
   to command, rule **(with dative)**
impleō, -ēre, -ēvī, -ētus   61
   to fill up, make full, complete,
   finish, end
implōrō, -āre, -āvī, -ātus   73
   to call upon, invoke, implore

impōnō, -ere, imposuī, impositus   70
   to put or lay upon, impose
impossibilis, -e (adj.)   50
   impossible
in (prep./acc.)   14,41
   to, into
   (prep./abl.)   59
   in
incola, -ae (comm.)   24
   inhabitant
indignus, -a, -um (adj.)   86,87
   unworthy
indulgeō, -ēre, -dulsī, -dultus   109
   to be kind, tender, indulgent to;
   to pardon
infirmitās, -ātis (f.)   86
   weakness, infirmity, feebleness
inflexiō, -ōnis (f.)   90
   inflection
inimicus, -ī (m.)   86
   enemy
initium, -ī (n.)   7
   beginning
innocens, -entis (adj.)   55
   innocent
innumerābilis, -e   101
   innumerable
inops, -opis (adj.)
   destitute, helpless, indigent
instō, -āre, -stetī, stātus   106
   to press forward, approach
insuper (adv.)   58
   above, overhead; moreover, besides
integer, -gra, -grum (adj.)   27
   whole, upright
intendō, -ere, -tendī, tentus/tensus   109
   to stretch out, extend, direct, turn.
   turn, bend
inter (prep./acc.)   40
   between, among, amid

interficiō, -ere, -fēcī, -fectum   33
   to kill, sly, murder
interpretōr, -ārī, -ātus sum   73
   to explain, translate
intrā (prep./acc.)   40
   within
intrō, -āre, -āvī, -ātus   87
   to enter
intus (adv.)   58
   within, inside
   ab intus: from within
invādō, -ere, -vāsī, -vasus   109
   to assail, attack, invade
invāsiō, -ōnis (f.)   75
   invasion
invāsor, -ōris (m.)   75
   invader
invehō, -ere, -vexī, vectus   106
   to attack, assail, inveigh against
invocō, -āre, -āvī, -ātus   102
   to invoke, call upon
ipse, -a, -um (pron.)   99
   -self
īra, -ae (f.)   27
   anger, wrath
ironicē (adv.)   83
   ironically
is, ea, id (pron.)   99
   this, that
iste, ista, istud (demon. pron.)   97,99
   this, that
istinc (adv.)   98
   thence
istuc (adv.)   98
   thither
ita (adv.)   58
   thus, so
itaque (adv.)   94
   therefore
iter, itineris (n.)   65
   a journey. way, path, road

itinerārium, -ī (n.)   7
   itinerary
iubeō, -ēre, iussī, iussus   64,109
   to order, bid, command
iubilō, -āre, -āvī, -ātus   24
   to shout, to shout for joy
iucundus, -a, -um (adj.)   55
   pleasant, agreeable, delightful
iūdex, iūdicis (m.)   45
   judge
iudicium, -ī (n.)   28
   judgment
iurō, -āre, -āvī, -ātus   96
   to swear, take an oath
iūs, iūris (n.)   50
   right, law, justice, duty
iustitia, -ae   28
   righteousness, justice
iustus, -a, -um (adj.)   27,28
   lawful, right, true, just
iuvenis, -is   85
   a youth

iuventūs, -tūtis (f.)   54
  youth (time of)
iuxtā (prep./acc.)   40
  close to, near to, together with,
  according to

-L-

labor, -ī, lapsus sum   109
  to fall down, slip
labōrō, -āre, -āvī, -ātus   14,86
  to labor, strive; to be oppressed,
  afflicted, troubled; to work out,
  elaborate, form, make
laedō, -ere, laesī, laesus   109
  to wound, injure, damage
langueō, -ēre   73
  to be faint, weary

lascīvus, -a, -um (adj.)   86
  wanton, licentious
lateō, -ēre, -uī   81,106,109
  to lie hidden
Latīnus, -a, -um (adj.)   32
  Latin
lātitūdō, -lātitūdinis (f.)   96
  breadth, width
lātrō, -inis (m.)   101
  thief, robber
laudabilis, -e (adj.)   50
  praiseworthy, laudable
laudō, -āre, -āvī, -ātus   104
  to praise
lavātor, -ōris (m.)   54
  launderer
lavātrix, tricis (f.)   54
  laundress
lēctor, -ōris (m.)   81
  reader
legātus, -ī (m.)   46,47
  ambassador, legate, provincial,
  governor
legō, -ere, lēgī, lēctus   46,47,109
  to gather, choose, read
leo, -ōnis (m.)   90
  lion
lepus, -ōris (m.)   90
  hare, rabbit
lēx, lēgis (f.)   31,45
  law
līber, lībera, līberum (adj.)   94
  free
līber, lībrī (m.)   89
  book
līberālis, -e (adj.)   85
  generous
līberātiō, -ōnis (f.)   85
  freeing, liberation
līberō, -āre, -āvī, -ātus   73
  to free, liberate, deliver

lībertās, -tātis (f.)   54
  freedom, liberty
libet, -ēre, -uit   64,128
  it pleases, is agreeable
licet, -ēre, -uit, -itum est   64,128
  it is lawful, allowed, permitted;
  one may, can, is at liberty,
  be free to
licet (conj.)   128
  although
lignum, -ī   (n.)   24
  wood
ligō, -āre, -āvī, -ātus   65
  to tie, bind
lilium, -ī (n.)   55
  lily
līmen, līminis (n.)   65
  threshold, lintel, sill
līnea, -ae (f.)   100
  line
linquō -ere, līquī, lictus   109
  to leave, give up
locūtor, -ōris (m.)   103
  speaker
longē (adv.)   56
  far
longitūdō, -inis (f.)   96
  length
longus, -a, -um (adj.)   37
  long
loquor, -ī, locūtus sum   103
  to speak
lūcidus, -a, -um (adj.)   27
  light, clear, bright, **lucid, radiant**
lucrātīvus, -a, -um (adj.)   27
  gainful, profitable, lucrative
lūdus, -ī (m.)   96
  game, play, show; a school
luō, -ere, luī, luitūrus   109
  to release from debt, let go, set
  free

lupus, -ī (m.)   90
  wolf
lūx, lūcis (m., **later f.**)   45
  light

-M-

maereō, -ēre, -uī   106,109
  to sorrow, grieve, lament
magis (adv.)   53
  more, rather
magister, -trī (m.)   19
  masterchief, head; dictator;
  teacher, instructor
magnificus, -a, -um (adj.)   53
  splendid, grand, rich, fine, costly,
  sumptuous
magnōpere (adv.)   56
  greatly, exceedingly, **very much**

magnus, -a, -um (adj.)   4,14,53
    great, large
maledicus, -a, -um (adj.)   53
    abusive, scurrilous, slanderous
malevolus, -a, -um (adj.)   53
    ill-disposed, envious, spiteful,
    malevolent
malum, -ī (n.)   104
    evil
malus, -ī (m.)   104
    evil one (=devil)
malus, -a, -um (adj.)   53
    evil, bad, wicked
mānē (adv.)   85
    in the morning
maneō, -ēre, mānsī, mānsus   61,109
    to remain, stay
mansuētūdō, -inis (f.)   50
    mildness, gentleness, clemency
manus, -ūs (f.)   65
    hand

Maria, -ae (f.)   28
    Mary
Martyr, -yris (comm.)   55
    witness, martyr
māter, -tris (f.)   50
    mother
medicus, -ī (m.)   50,64
    physician, surgeon
meminī, -isse   70,105
    to remember
memor, -ōris (adj.)   48
    mindful of, remembering
mendācium, -ī (n.)   50
    falsehood, lie
mendīcō, -āre, -āvī, -ātus   90
    to beg, ask for alms
mēnsa, -ae (f.)   86
    table
mēnsis, -is (m.)   37
    month
mensūra, -ae (f.)   101
    measure
mensūrō, -āre, -āvī, -ātus   50
    to measure
mercātor, -ōris (m.)   54
    trader, merchant
meridiēs, -eī (m.)   79
    midday, noon
meus, -a, -um (poss. adj.)   86
    my, mine
migrō, -āre, -āvī, -ātus   90
    to depart, migrate
mīles, mīlitis (m.)   45
    soldier
mīlitāris, -e (adj.)   85
    military
mīlitō, -āre, -āvī, -ātus   33,35
    to make way, wage war
minimum cochlear, -āris   37
    a teaspoon
minister, -trī (m.)   82
    minister

minuō, -ere, -uī, -ūtus   109
    to lessen
mīrābilis, -e (adj.)   50
    wonderful, marvellous, admirable
miser, -era, -erum   73
    wretched, unfortunate, miserable
miseria, -ae (f.)   86
    misfortune, misery
misericordia, -ae (f.)   28
    mercy, pity
missiō, -iōnis (f.)   54
    a sending, mission
mītis, -e (adj.)   48
    mild, gentle
mittō, -ere, mīsī, missus   8,46
    to send
modus, -ī (m.)   24
    bound, limit, manner, way
moneō, -ēre, uī, -itus   61,109
    to advise, warn
monitor, -ōris (m.)   54
    admonisher, monitor, warner
mons, montis (m.)   37
    mountain
monumentum, -ī (n.)   94
    memorial, monument
mordeō, -ēre, momordi, morsus   109
    to bite
morior, morī, mortuus sum   70
    to die
mors, mortis (f.)   33,37,45
    death
mōs, mōris (m.)   45
    custom, manner, way, usage
mōtiō, -ōnis (f.)   75
    motion
mōtor, -ōris (m.)   75
    mover
moveō, -ēre, mōvī, mōtus   65,109
    to move
mox (adv.)   86
    soon
multiplex, -plicis (adj.)   50
    manifold, many
multiplicātiō, -ōnis (f.)   93
    multiplication
multitūdō, -inis (f.)   93
    multitude (See also Section 96.)
multum (adv.)   56
    much
multus, -a, -um (adj.)   9,14,53
    many
mundus, -ī (m.)   19
    world
mundus, -a, -um (adj.)   35
    clean, neat, elegant
mūnificentia, -ae (f.)   24
    munificence, liberality,
    generosity
mūrus, -ī (m.)   87
    wall
mūtātiō, -ōnis (f.)   54,75
    change, alteration
mūtātor, -ōris (m.)   75
    changer

mysterium, -ī (n.)   33,35
  mystery

-N-

narrō, -āre, -āvī, -ātus   64
  to tell, narrate
nāta, -ae (f.)   90
  daughter, offspring
nascor, -ī, nātus sum   67
  to be born
nātālis, -is (m.)   82
  birthday

navis, -is (f.)   35
  ship
nē (adv. conj.)   58
  lest, that not
necessārius, -a, -um (adj.)   105,132
  necessary
necesse (n. adj.)   132
  necessary
necessitās, -ātis (f.)   8,73
  necessity, need
negō, -āre, -āvī, -ātus   77
  to deny, refuse, negate
negōtium, -ī (n.)   86,140
  business
nēmō, nēminis (m./f.)   94
  no one
nequeō, -īre, īvī (-iī), -ītum   90
  to be unable
nesciō, -īre, -īvī (-iī), -ītum   70
  not to know, be ignorant of
neuter, -tra, -trum (pron.)   50,100
  neither (one)
niger, -gra, -grum (adj.)   32
  black
nimis (adv.)   58
  too much
nimirum (adv.)   94
  without doubt, doubtless
Ninivīta, ae (f.)   86
  Nineveh (capital of ancient Assyria)
nisi (conj.)   83
  if not, unless
niteō, -ēre, -uī   109
  to shine
nōbilis, -e (adj.)   55
  noble, high-born
nocēns, -entis   90
  bad, wicked, criminal
nōmen, nōminis (n.)   50
  name

nōn (adv.)   14,58
  not
nonne (adv.)   102
  [introduces a question for which an
  affirmative answer is expected.]
nōnnisi (adv.)   103
  only

nōs, nōstrī (pron.)   102
  we
noscō, -ere, nōvī, nōtus   109
  to know, become acquainted with
noster, -tra, -trum (poss. adj.)   27
  our, ours
nōtitia, -ae (f.)   86
  knowledge, idea, fame
novus, -a, -um (adj.)   89
  new
nox, noctis (f.)   33,45
  night
nūbō, -ere, nūpsī, nūptus   102
  to marry
nullus, -a, -um (adj.)   100
  not any, none, no
num (adv.)   102
  [introduces a question for which
  a negative answer is expected.]
numerō, -āre, -āvī, -ātus   94
  to count, reckon, number
numerus, -ī (m.)   24,26
  number
numquam (adv.)   103
  never
nunc (adv.)   27,56
  now
nuntiō, -āre, -āvī, -ātus   19
  to announce

-O-

ob (prep./acc. + abl.)   40
  on account of, because of, by reason of
obdormiscō, -ere -dormīvī*   109
  to fall asleep
  [*obdormiō]
obiectum, -ī (n.)   103
  object
obtemperō, -āre, -āvī, ātus   19
  to obey
obviō, -āre, -āvī, -ātus   86
  to withstand, resist, oppose,
  prevent, hinder, obviate; to meet
occupō, -āre, -āvī, -ātus   87
  to occupy
occurrō, -ere, -currī, -cursus   109
  to run up to, meet, come to,
  fall in with, appear, occur
ocellus, -ī (m.)   25,128
  little eye
oculus, -ī (m.)   25
  eye
offendō, -ere, -dī, -sus   86
  to offend, commit an offense
olim (adv.)   56,58
  once, in time past, formerly
omnis, -e (adj.)   48
  all
optō, -āre, -āvī, -ātus   67
  to wish, desire
opus, operis (n.)   50
  work; need, necessity

ōrātiō -ōnis (f.)   54,75
    prayer
orbis, -is   55
    ring, circle, world, universe
ordō, inis (m.)   105
    order

ornō, -āre, -āvī, -ātus   14
    to furnish, equip, adorn, embellish
ōrō, -āre, -āvī, -ātus   14
    to pray
ōs, ōris (n.)   86
    mouth
os, ossis (n.)   59
    bone
ostium, -ī (n.)   65
    door, entrance
ovis, -is (f.)   46
    sheep

-P-

pācō, -āre, -āvī, -ātus   96
    to quiet, pacify
paenitet, -ēre, -uit   64,109,128
    to repent, be sorry, be irked
pagīna, -ae (f.)   86
    page
    sacra pagīna: Holy Writ, Bible
palātium, -ī (n.)   24
    palace
pallidus, -a, -um (adj.)   37
    pale, pallid
panis, -is (m.)   83
    bread
papa, -ae (m.)   47
    pope
pār, paris (adj.)   93
    equal
parcō, -ere, pepercit, parsus   70
    to spare (with dative)
pars, partis (f.)   93
    part
parvulus, -a, -um (adj.)   55
    very small

parvus, -a, -um (adj.)   24,36,37
    small
Pascha, ae (f.); -atis (n.)   82
    passover, Easter
paschālis, -e (adj.)   83
    of or belonging to Easter
pateō, -ēre, -uī   109
    to lie open, be open, extend
pater, patris (m.)   45
    father
patria, -ae (f.)   14,104
    fatherland
paulō minus (adv.)   58
    a little less

paulus, -a, -um (adj.)
    little, small
pauper, -eris (adj.)   33,35,48
    poor
pavīmentum, -ī (n.)   86
    pavement
pāx, pācis (f.)   44,45
    peace
peccātor, -ōris (m.)   50,54
    sinner
peccātrīx, trīcis (f.)   54
    a woman sinner
peccātum, ī (n.)   24
    sin
peccō, -āre, -āvī, -ātus   41
    to sin
pecūnia, -ae (f.)   67
    property, wealth, money
pellō, -ere, pepulī, pulsus   109
    to beat, strike, knock
pentēcostē, -ēs (f.)   82
    pentecost, whitsunday
per (prep./acc.)   14,40
    through
percolō, -āre, -āvī, -ātus   14
    to sift, filter

pereō, -īre, -īvī (-iī), -ītus   89
    to perish, waste away, come to naught
perīculum, -ī (n.)   104
    peril, danger
perītus, -a, -um   19
    skilled, expert
permittō, -ere, -misī, -missus   83
    to permit
persōna, -ae (f.)   27
    person
pertineō, -ēre, -uī, -tentus   103
    to extend, tend, pertain to, concern
perturbō, -āre, -āvī, -ātus   86
    to confuse, disturb
pervagor, -ārī, -ātus sum   86
    to wander abroad
pēs, pedis (m.)   45
    foot
petō, -ere, -īvī (-iī), -ītum   70
    to seek
petra, -ae (f.)   35
    rock
Petrus, -ī (m.)   4
    Peter
phantasticus, -a, -um (adj.)   86
    imaginary
pietās, -tātis (f.)   90
    piety, godliness
pincerna, -ae (m.)   86
    cupbearer
piscis, -is (m.)   37
    fish
pius, -a, -um (adj.)   50
    pious, godly
placō, -āre, -āvī, -ātus   35
    to appease, placate

plangō, -ere, planxī, planctus 109
  to beat the breast or head, bewail
plēnitūdō, -inis (f.) 104
  fulness

plēnus, -a, -um (adj.) 27
  full
pluit, -ere 67
  to rain
poena, -ae (f.) 73
  punishment, penalty
poenitentia, -ae (f.) 14
  penance, repentance
poeta, -ae (m.) 14
  poet
pons, pontis (m.) 37
  bridge
populus, -ī (m.) 19
  people
portō, -āre, -āvī, -ātus 82
  to carry
poscō, -ere, poposcī 109
  to demand
possessīvus, -a, -um (adj.) 103
  possessive
possibilis, -e (adj.) 48
  possible
possum, posse, potuī
  to be able; can
post (prep./acc.) 40
  behind, after
postrēmō (adv.) 56
  at last, finally
potēns, potentis (adj.) 48
  able, mighty, powerful
potenter (adv.) 56
  strongly, mightily, powerfully
pōtō, -āre, āvī, -ātus [potus] 106
  to drink
prae (prep./abl.) 59
  before, in front of
praeceptum, -ī (n.) 28
  command, precept
praeda, -ae (f.) 90
  booty, spoils

praedicātor, -ōris (m.) 61
  preacher
praedīcō, -āre, -āvī, -ātus 61
  to publish, proclaim, preach
praesēns, praesentis (adj.) 33,49
  present
praesidium, -ī (n.) 86
  defense, protection, garrison,
  fortification, camp
praeses, praesides (comm.) 90
  defender, president
praesum, -esse 100
  to be set over, preside, be in
  charge or command
praeter (prep./acc.) 40
  past, by, before, in front of,
  along; besides, except, contrary to

praeterita, -ōrum (n.) 7
  the past
prandeō, -ēre, -dī, -sum 106
  to breakfast, lunch
pretiōsus, -a, -um (adj.) 27
  costly, dear, expensive
prīmō (adv.) 56
  first
prīmum (adv.) 56
  first
princeps, -cipis (m.) 86
  prince, leader
prior, prius (adj.) 33
  former, previous, prior
prīvātim (adv.) 56
  privately
prō (prep./abl.) 14,59
  for, on behalf of
probō, -āre, -āvī, -ātus 90
  to prove
procēdō, -ere, -cessī, -cessus 94
  to proceed
prōdigus, -a, -um (adj.) 106
  wasteful, lavish, prodigal
  prodigus, -ī (m.): spendthrift
proelium, -ī (n.) 87
  battle
profundus, -a, -um 84
  deep
profundē (adv.) 84
  deeply
promittō, -ere, -mīsī, missus 43
  to promise
prōnōmen, -inis (n.) 103,105
  pronoun
prope (adv.) 40,53,56
  near
prope (prep/acc.) 40
  nearly
proprietārius, -iī (m.) 102
  owner, proprietor
proprius, -a, -um (adj.) 96
  one's own, particular, special
propter (prep./acc.) 40
  because, on account of, by reason of
proptereā (adv.) 56
  therefore
prōtinus (adv.) 93
  immediately, straightway
prōvidus, -a, -um (adj.) 35
  provident, prudent
prōvincia, -ae (f.) 87
  province
proximus, -a, -um (adj.) 85
  next nearest
pudet, -ēre, -uit, pūditum 64,128
  to be ashamed
pudor, -ōris (m.) 90
  shame
puella, -ae (f.) 14
  girl
puer, puerī (m.) 19
  boy

pugno, -āre, -āvī, -ātus   24
    to fight

pulcher, -chra, -chrum (adj.)   26,53
    pulcer   105
    beautiful
pulchrē (adv.)   56
    beautifully
puppis, -is (f.)   31
    stern (of a ship)
pulvis, -eris (m.)   87
    dust
putō, -āre, -āvī, -ātus   26
    to think, consider, hold

-Q-

quadrivium, -ī (n.)   83
    crossroads
quaerō, -ere, quaesīvī (-iī), -ītus   106
    to seek, ask
quālis (interr. adj.)   88
    of what sort
quam (interr, adv.)   88
    how much?
----- (adv. conj.)   58
    than
quandō (interr. adv.)   88
    when?
quantus, -a, -um (interr. adj.)   88
    how much
quasi (adv. conj.)   65,86
    as if; almost
quemadmodum (adv., conj.)   56
    in what manner, how
quī, quae quod (rel. pro.)   87
    who; what
quia (conj.)   86
    because, that
quidem (adv.)   58
    even, indeed
    he...quidem: not even
quiētus, -a, -um (adj.)   35
    quiet

quīn (conj.)   93
    but that, without (+participial clause)
quis, quid (interr. pro.)   87
    who? what?
quomodō (adv.)   56
    how, as
quoque (adv.)   105
    also
quot (interr. adv.)   88
    how many?
quotannīs (adv.)   82
    yearly
quotidiē (adv.)   56
    daily
quousque (interr. adv.)   88
    how long?

-R-

rādix, rādīcis   45
    root
rapīna, -ae (f.)   90
    robbery, plundering, pillage:
    prey, plunder, booty
rapiō, ere, -uī, raptus   109
    to seize
rārō (adv.)   56
    far apart, thinly, sparsely,
    here and there
rārus, -a, -um   56
    far apart, scattered, thin, few, rare
ratiō, -ōnis (f.)   90,103
    reckoning, account, method, system,
    way, means, plan, reason, consideration
recens, -entis (adj.)   73
    recent
recīdo, -ere,-dī,-sum   93
    to reduce, diminish

rēctus, -a, -um (adj.)   27
    straight, upright, right
recuperō, -āre, -āvī, -ātus   77
    to regain, recover, recuperate,
    reclaim
recurrō, -ere, -currī   109
    to return, revert, recur
redemptor, -ōris (m.)   50
    redeemer
redeō, -īre, -iī, ītum   7
    to go or come back, return
redimō, -ere, -ēmī, -emptum   33
    to buy back, repurchase, redeem
refugium, -ī (n.)   28
    refuge
rēgīna, -ae (f.)   14
    queen
regnō, -āre, -āvī, -ātus   14
    to reign, rule
regnum, -ī (n.)   24,100
    royal authority, kingship, dominion,
    rule, authority; kingdom
regō, -ere, -ēxī, rēctus   109
    to rule, direct
relinquō, -ere, -līquī -lictum   109
    to leave behind, abandon, bequeath
remaneō, -ēre, -mansī, mansūrus   103
    to remain
remissiō, -ōnis (f.)   86
    remission, forgiveness (of sins)
repleō, -ēre, -ēvī, -ētus   61
    to refill
replicātiō, -ōnis (f.)   93
    repetition, reduction (of a number)
replicō, -āre, -āvī, -ātus   93
    to fold, turn or bend back;
    to reduce (of a number)
requiēs, -eī (f.)   59
    rest, repose

sententia, -ae (f.)   59
   opinion, judgment, purpose; decision,
   sentence; meaning, idea, notion
sentiō, -īre, sēnsī, sēnsus   109
   to perceive, feel, realize
sēparātim (adv.)   56
   separately
sepeliō, -īre, -pelīvī (-iī), -pultum   83
   to bury
septimana, ae (f.)   95
   week
   septimana sancta: Holy Week [Easter]

sermō, -ōnis (m.)   31
   talk, discourse, word
serviō, -īre, -īvī, (iī), -ītus   62
   to serve
servitium, -ī (n.)   24
   service
servus, -ī (m.)   19
   servant, slave
sīc (adv.)   58
   thus, so
sīgnificō, -āre, -āvī, -ātus   50
   to signify
signō, -āre, -āvī, -ātus   71
   to sign, mark
signum, -ī (n.)   24
   mark, token, sign
similis, -e (adj.)   53,93
   like, similar
simplex, -icis   50
   simple
sine (prep./abl.)   59
   without
singulāritās, -ātis (f.)   93
   singleness, unity (See Section 96.)
sinister, -tra, -trum (adj.)   32
   left, awkward, improper, unlucky
sitiō, -īre, -īvī (-iī), -itue   106
   to thirst
solidus, -ī (m.)   33,35
   a shilling
solidus, -a, um (adj.)   27
   firm, compact, solid
sōlum (adv.)   56
   only
sōlus, -a, -um (adj.)   32,100
   sole, alone, only
sonō, -āre, -uī, -itus   89
   to sound, resound
spectāculum, -ī (n.)   94
   show, sight, spectacle, stage-play

sperō, -āre, -āvī, -ātus   73
   to hope
spiritus, -ūs (m.)   33
   spirit
spondeō, -ēre, spopondī, sponsus   109
   to bind, pledge, engage
statuō, -ere, -uī, -ūtus   109
   to place, station, set up, establish;
   take action, determine
stella, -ae (f.)   14
   star

stīpendium, -ī (n.)   33,35
   pay, expense (usually in plural)
stō, stare, stetī, status   109
   to stand
stupor, -ōris   59
   numbness, dullness, insensibility
sub (prep./acc. + abl.)   41,59
   under, about
subiectus, -a, -um (adj.)   70
   adjacent, subject (to)
substantia, -ae (f.)   73
   substance
succurrō, -ere, -currī, -cursus   109
   to help, aid, assist, be useful for,
   occur, come to mind
suffocō, -āre, -āvī, -ātus   83
   to strangle, throttle, suffocate
sum, esse, fuī, futūrus   14,76
   to be
summātim (adv.)   56
   summarily, cursorily, briefly
sūmō, -ere, sūmpsī, sūmptus   87,109
   to bake, assume, spend, put on
super (prep./acc. + abl.)   41,59
   above, over, on top of, on, about
superbus, -a, -um (adj.)   70
   proud, haughty
superō, -āre, āvī, -ātus   19
   to conquer, overcome
supplicō, -āre, -āvī, -ātus   96
   to humble, to beseech, beg humbly
suprā (prep./acc.)   40
   above, over beyond, upon;
   before [time]
surgō, -ere, surrēxī, surrectus   106
   to raise, arise
suspiciō, -ere, spexī, -spectus   86
   to suspect
suspīrō, -āre, -āvī, -ātus   86
   to sigh

-T-

taceō, -ēre, tacuī, tacitus   33,35,90
   to be silent
taedet, -ēre, -uit, taesum   64,128
   to be disgusted, offended, tired,
   weary
tam (adv.)   58
   so, so much as
tangibilis, -e (adj.)   103
   touchable, tangible
tangō, -ere, tetigī, tactus   109
   to touch
tantum (adv.)   56
   so much, so greatly, to such
   a degree, so
taxō, -āre, -āvī, -ātus   87
   to reckon, compute, tax, estimate
tegō, -ere, tēxī, tectus   109
   to cover
tellūs, tellūris (f.)   31
   earth

templum, -ī (n.) 28
  temple
temptātiō, -ōnis (f.) 87
  temptation, test, trial
tempus, ōris (n.) 33,35
  time
tendō, -ere, tetendī, tentus 109
  to stretch, extend
teneō, -ēre, tenuī, tentus 8
  to hold, keep, have, grasp, seize
tener, -era, -erum (adj.) 53
  soft, delicate, tender
tenor, -ōris (m.) 90
  uninterrupted course, career, tenor
terra, -ae (f.) 14
  earth, land, ground, soil
terminō, -āre, -āvī, -ātus 86
  to end, terminate
terreō, -ēre, -uī, -itus 109
  to frighten, terrify
terribilis, -e (adj.) 109
  frightful, dreadful, terrible
testis, -is (comm.) 33
  witness
thematicus, -a, -um 103
  thematic
Tiber, -eris (-eridis) (m.) 40
  Tiber (river)
timeō, ēre, -uī 67
  to fear
timidus, -a, -um (adj.) 35
  fearful, timid
timor, -ōris (m.) 31
  fear, dread
titulus, -ī (m.) 50
  title, lable
tōtus, -a, -um 100
  all, whole, entire
tractō, -āre, -āvī, -ātus 103
  to handle, manage, treat
trāditor, -ōris (m.) 86
  betrayer, traitor
trādō, -ere, trādidī, trāditus 109
  to hand over, give up, entrust, yield
trahō, -ere, trāxī, trāctus 109
  to drag, draw
trans (prep./acc.) 40
  across, over, beyond
tribūnicius, -a, -um (adj.) 96
  pertaining to the tribune's office
tribus, -ūs (f.) 79
  tribe
trinitās, -ātis (f.) 103
  Trinity
tristis, -e (adj.) 48
  sad, sorrowful
triumphō, -āre, -āvī, -ātus 96
  to triumph
triumphus, -ī (m.) 94
  triumph
tū, tuī (pron.) 102
  thou, you (sing.)
tum (adv.) 58
  then
tunc (adv.) 56
  then
turris, -is (f.) 30
  tower

-U-

ubı (adv.) 57,58
  where; when
ubīque (adv.)
  wherever, everywhere
ullus, -a, -um (adj.) 100
  any, any one
ultrā (prep./acc.) 40
  beyond, on the farther side
umquam (adv.) 103
  ever
unde (adv.) 58
  whence
universus, -a, -um (adj.) 50
  all, whole, entire, general,
  universal
urbs, urbis (f.) 4
  town, city
ūrō, -ere, ussī, ustus 35,109
  to burn
usque (adv.) 85
  as long as, as far as, even to
ut (conj.)
  as
ut (conj. with subjunctive)
  that [esp. with clauses of purpose
  and result]
uter, utra, utrum 50,100,101
  which of two, each, either, each
  one, one and the other, both
uterque, etc (pron.) 52,101
  both, each of both

-V-

valdē (adv.) 58
  very
valeō, -ēre, uī 105
  to be strong, be worth, have power
  valē, valēte: farewell
vānus, -a, -um (adj.) 27
  empty, vain
vastō, -āre, -āvī, -ātus 24
  to lay waste, ravage, devastate
Vāticānus, -a, -um 37
  Vatican (a hill in Rome)
veniō, -īre, vēnī, ventus 62,109
  to come
ventus, -ī (m.) 8,35
  wind
verāx, -ācis (adj.) 83
  truthful
verbum, -ī (n.) 28
  word
vēritās, -ātis (f.) 50
  truth
vertō, -ere, vertī, versus 109
  to turn
vērus, -a, -um (adj.) 27
  true
vestis, -is (f.) 37
  clothes, clothing
vetō, -āre, -uī, -ītus 90

via, -ae (f.)   14,86
    way

victōria, -ae (f.)   94
    victory

videō, -ēre, vīdī, vīsus   86
    to see

vīlis, -e (adv.)   48
    cheap, poor, base, vile

vinciō, -īre, vinxī, vinctus   109
    to bind

vincō, -ere, vīcī, victus   102,109
    to conquer

vir, virī (m.)   50
    man

virgō, -inis (f.)   50
    virgin, maiden

virtūs, -ūtis   54
    goodness, worth, value, power,
    virtue

vīs, vīs (f.) [plur: virēs, virium   31
    force, vigor, power, energy, virtue

vīsibilis, -e (adj.)   103
    visible

vīsiō, -ōnis (f.)   54,86
    vision

vīta, -ae (f.)   14
    life

vītō, -āre, -āvī, -ātus   90
    to escape, avoid

vīvificō, -āre, -āvī, -ātus   103
    to restore to life, quicken, vivify

vīvō, -ere, vīxī, vīctus   55,68,109
    to live

vīvus, -a, -um (adj.)   36
    alive, living

vocabulum, -ī (n.)   94
    designation, name; substantive; word

vocātīvus, -a, -um   90
    vocative

volō, -āre, -āvī, -ātus   90
    to fly

volō, velle, voluī
    to will, wish

voluntās, -ātis (f.)   104
    will, choice, desire, inclination

vōx, vōcis (f.)   78
    voice, sound

vulpēs, -is (m.)   90
    fox